Gopal Krishna Gokhale

Gopal Krishna Gokhale

Series Editor
Dr. M.H. Syed

Editor
Imran Ahmed **N.P. Sharma**

Himalaya Books Pvt. Ltd.
'Ramdoot', Dr. Bhalerao Marg, Girgaon, Mumbai - 400 004
Tel : (022) 23863863, Fax : (022) 23877178
Email : himpub@vsnl.com

Edition : 2017
Edition : 2025

Published by : H.B.P.L.
"Pooja Apartments", 4-B, Murari Lal Street, Ansari Road,
Darya Ganj, New Delhi-110 002
Phones : 23270392, 23278631
Fax : 011-23256286 Email : hphdel@vsnl.com

Sole Distributers : HIMALAYA PUBLISHING HOUSE PVT. LTD.

Branch Offices

Mumbai : "Ramdoot", Dr. Bhalerao Marg, Girgaon, Mumbai-400 004.
Phones : 23860170/23863863 Fax : 022-23877178
Email : himpub@vsnl.com
Website : www.himpub.com

Nagpur : Kundanlal Chandak Industrial Estate, Ghat Road, **Nagpur - 440 018.**
Phone: 2738731, 3296733 Telefax : 0712-2721215

Bengaluru : No. 16/1 (Old 12/1), 1st Floor, Next to Hotel Highlands, Madhava Nagar, Race Course Road, **Bengaluru - 560 001.**
Phone : 22281541, 22385461, Telefax: 080-22286611

Hyderabad : No. 3-4-184, Lingampally, Besides Raghavendra Swamy Matham, Kachiguda, **Hyderabad - 500 027.** Phone: 040-27560041, 27550139,
Mobile:- 09848130433 Telefax: 040-27560041

Chennai : No. 85/50, Bazullah Road, T. Nagar, **Chennai - 600 017.**
Phone: 044-28344020, 32463737, 42124860

Pune : No. 527, "Laksha" Apartment, First Floor, Mehunpura, Shaniwarpeth, (Near Prabhat Theatre), **Pune - 411 030.**
Phone: 020-24496323/24496333/32326733

Lucknow : Jai Baba Bhawan, Near Manas Complex, Church Road, Aliganj, **Lucknow - 226 024.** Phone: 0522-2339329, 9305302158, 9415349385

Ahmedabad : No. 114, "SHAIL", 1st Floor, Opp. Madhu Sudan House, C.G.Road, Navrang Pura, **Ahmedabad – 380 009.**
Phone: 079-26560126, Mobiles: 09327324149, 09314679413

Ernakulam : No. 39/104 A, Lakshmi Apartment, Karikkamuri Cross Rd., Ernakulam, **Cochin – 682011**, Kerala. Phone: 0484-2378012, 2378016,
Mob.: 09344199799

Bhubaneswar : 5 Station Square, **Bhubaneswar (Orissa) - 751 001.**
Mobile: 9861046007, E-mail:- orissa@himpub.com

Indore : Kesardeep Avenue Extension, 73, Narayan Bagh.Flat No. 302, IIIrd Floor, Near Humpty Dumpty School, Narayan Bagh, **Indore (M.P.) 452 007**
Mobile: 09301386468

Kolkata : 108/4, Beliaghata, Main Road, Near ID Hospital, Opp. SBI Bank **Kolkata - 700 010.** Mobile: 09910440956, E-mail:- nkmitra@himpub.com

Guwahati : House No. 15, Behind Prajjyotish College, Near Sharma Printing Press, P.O. Bharalumukh, Guwahati - 781009 (Assam
Mobile: 07439040301; 07439040302

Printed by : Infinity Imaging Systems, New Delhi.

Preface

Biography, is now a form of literature, very much in vogue. In fact, biography is a description or account of someone's life and the times, which is usually published in the form of a book. A biography is more than a mention of personal facts (life, education, work, relationships and death), it also portrays the subject's experience of events. Technically speaking, a work is biographical, if it covers, all of a person's life. Biography writing has a long history. A biography is real. Ancient Greeks developed the biographical tradition, which we have inherited, although until the 5th century AD, when the word 'biographia' first appeared, in Damascius' "Life of Isodorus," biographical pieces were called simply "lives". It is quite likely that the Greeks were drawing on a pre-existing eastern tradition. Certainly Herodotus' "Histories" contains more detailed biographical information on Persian kings and subjects. The earliest surviving pieces, which we would identify as biographical are Isocrates' "Life of Evagoras" and Xenophon's "Life of Agesilaos," both from the fifth century BC. "Parallel Lives" by Plutarch, a Greek writing under the Roman empire, is a series of short biographies of eminent men.

The Golden Age of English biography emerged in late eighteenth century, the century in which the terms "biography" and "autobiography" entered English lexicon. The classic works of the period were Samuel Johnson's "Critical Lives of the Poets" and James Boswell's "Massive Life of Johnson". Generally American biography followed English model. By World War I, cheap hardcover reprints had become popular. The decade of the 1920s witnessed a biographical 'boom'. Later, biographical writings developed a lot and today biographies are written and compiled in the finest form of the genre. In India too, biography, as a form of literature has been evolved, cultivated and polished over the years. Here is an effort to promote this tradition further.

This series of biographies of great men, great women and celebrities in all walks of life is an adventurous academic endeavour, in its own right. A team of researchers and compilers has worked for a good period of time to accomplish the project. For this purpose, hundreds of books by eminent authors and editors have been consulted and referred to. We have benefited from various works, liberally, in order to illustrate and enrich this effort of ours. Present book is devoted to the great personality of Gopal Krishna Gokhale.

One of the pioneers of Indian national movement, Gopal Krishna Gokhale was a senior leader of the Indian National Congress. Gokhale gave voice to the aspirations of millions of Indians, who were looking for freedom from the British rule. Gandhiji considered him as his political guru. Apart from being a political leader, Gopalkrishna Gokhale, was also a social reformer. He founded the "Servants of India Society", an organisation, dedicated to the cause of common people. Gopal Krishna Gokhale's contribution to the making of Indian nation is invaluable. Gokhale came in contact with Mahadev Govind Ranade, whom Gokhale called his guru. When Indian National Congress held its session in Pune in 1895, he was made the secretary of the Reception Committee. From this session, Gokhale became a prominent member of Indian National Congress. For a while Gokhale was also a member of the Bombay Legislative Council. Later, he became a Member of the Imperial Legislative Council.

This is a compact and comprehensive account of the above mentioned great life, which is bound to attract the attention of scholars, researchers, students and the general readers alike. Let's hope this humble effort would receive a warm welcome and due applause.

— ***Editors***

Contents

1

Journey of Life

Gokhale's ancestors had played an honourable part in the national history of this Maratha race. One of them had received the title of Raste — loyal — from the grandson of Shivaji, Prince Shahu, on account of his faithfulness in connection with certain financial responsibilities which had been entrusted to him. Other members of the family had held posts in the civil administration of the Maratha state under the Peshwas, who governed it during the eighteenth century.

They were Brahmins of the Brahmins, orthodox and scrupulous in their own religious observances, and yet accustomed to deal with men of many different races, castes and types, Above all, they possessed the instinct of responsible leadership, which became so marked a characteristic of the most famous of their race. They are also said to have been men of originality and initiative, and of a generosity which sometimes placed them in considerable financial difficulties.

Birth and Ancestry

Gopal Krishna Gokhale was born on May 9, 1866, at the little village of Katluk, in the Chiplun Taluk, Ratnagiri District, Bombay Presidency. He came of the sturdy Maratha race, which had never completely bowed before the Muslim conqueror, and which still preserved — as it does to the present day — vivid memories of the great period of Maratha revolt and independence under the national hero, Shivaji, and his successors.

The father of Gopal Krishna Gokhale was named Krishna Rao Gokhale. He was educated at Kolhapur, where, by a strange chance, he was a fellow-student of the great Ranade, who was later to become his son's guide, philosopher and friend. Krishna Rao Gokhale was compelled by poverty to give up his studies, and to take a poorly-paid post at Kagal, near Kolhapur, where his high-spirited nature is said to have brought him at first into conflict with petty-minded superiors, though afterwards it won for him respect and fair treatment.

Krishna Rao Gokhale was married to the daughter of Bhaskar Pant Oka, who was a leading member of a village-community in the Chiplun Taluk of the Ratnagiri District. Although this lady had received nothing of what is usually known as education, she was a great force in her son's life. She was deeply religious, with the acute sense of the horror of sin which is characteristic of the best Hinduism. She was also a typical Hindu woman in her single-hearted devotion to her husband and her children.

Early Education

For some ten years Gopal Krishna Gokhale lived the life of an Indian village boy, in close touch with the beauties and also the ferocities of Indian nature. He became acquainted at first hand, in his most impressionable years, with the hard lot of the Indian peasant. This early experience gave him throughout his career an invaluable sense of the fundamental realities which underlie all Indian political — as well as social and economic — questions, viz. the relation of the peasant to the government, to the landlord, and to the soil which he cultivates.

A large part of Gokhale's skill and wisdom, in regard especially to questions of finance and education, may be traced to the fact that he, unlike others, knew in his own person what the real India, the India of the villages, actually is and feels and thinks. However high he might rise, he was always at heart a man of the people, a member of an immemorial peasant community.

Secondary Education

When he was about ten years old, Gopal Krishna Gokhale was sent to Kolhapur for his secondary education, in company with his elder brother, Govind Rao. Three years later the boys' father died and their mother was left in very straitened circumstances, with four daughters to support, as well as her two sons. It became necessary for Govind Rao to give up his education, and to take his mother and sisters to a village in another district, where a small post had been found for him, through the kindness of an uncle, on a pay of Rs. 15 a month, or about five shillings a week. However, in spite of the miserable smallness of his pay, and the responsibilities which he had to bear, Govind Rao Gokhale, who was only 18 when the change took place, managed to pay for his younger brother's education.

He himself had been grievously disappointed at having to give up his studies; but he was determined that Gopal Rao should not do the same; and out of his Rs. 15 he sent monthly more than half for his brother's support. This fact is typical of the extraordinary solidarity of Hindu family-feeling. It also illustrates the value which is set upon education by the enlightened classes in India, and the sacrifices which they are prepared to make in order to obtain it.

There are a number of stories indicating the hard fight which young Gokhale had to make in order to get his education, even with this generous support from his brother. On some occasions he had even to forego one of his meals each day, in order to bring down his monthly bill in the hostel in which he lived. On other occasions he was compelled to economise by studying at night by the light of street lamps, in order to save oil. He was also obliged to do his own cooking for a time, in order to reduce his expenditure yet further, even though this involved the loss of much, valuable time from his studies. All this is typical of the desperate struggle which many Indian students — probably indeed a majority of them — have to go through in order to fit themselves for their work in the world. His experiences of the hardships of a poor student's lot may be held to be partly accountable for the great value which Gokhale always placed upon education, and for the gallant fight which he made for many years in order to place it freely within the reach of every Indian boy, however poor.

College Education

Gokhale passed the matriculation examination in 1881, and went straight on to college, studying first at the Rajaram College in Kolhapur, and later at the Decem College, Poona, and the Elphinstone College, Bombay. He was a quiet and industrious student; and both at this time and all through life showed himself to be possessed of an extraordinarily retentive memory. He is said to have learnt almost the whole of Scott's Rokeby by heart and to have been able at a moment's notice to give the exact context in which any difficult word is used in that book. Later on, when he became a teacher in Poona, it is said that he was in the habit of giving from memory to his class, as dictation-exercises, passages which he had casually read through in the morning paper before coming to school. It is also said that in the endeavour to train himself in the art of public speaking in English he learnt by heart Paradise Lost and large portions of the speeches of Burke and John Bright. The many hours which he spent in this toilsome exercise bore fruit later in the marvellous command which he possessed over the English language as a medium for clear and incisive reasoning.

Gokhale studied in the Elphinstone College at Bombay for his B.A. degree, specialising in mathematics. The teacher in this subject was Professor Hawthornthwaite, who was well known not only for his ability as an educationalist, but for the sympathetic interest which he took in his students. He is said to have held a high, opinion of the young Maratha Brahman, who however only took and second class in his final examination, which he passed when only just 18 years of age. During this later period of his education Gokhale was relieved, from the sense of crippling poverty which had hitherto pursued him and from the painful knowledge that his studies were imposing a cruel burden upon his brother; for he had been successful in winning a scholarship of Rs. 20 per month.

His Process of Self-training

After a short period of hesitation as to whether he should take up Law or Engineering, or go to England in order to fit himself to pass the competitive examinations for the Indian Civil Service, Gokhale finally decided to make education his life-work, and took an assistant mastership in the New English High School at Poona.

This was an institution which had been started five years before, in 1880, by a group of public-spirited Poona gentlemen, who were convinced that in this way they could render valuable service to their city and their country. Gokhale began work on the meagre salary of Rs. 35 per month. He found that he was faced by great difficulties in the task which he had undertaken; and it is characteristic of his thoroughness and diligence that at first he wrote out every day, and committed to memory, whatever he would have to say in the class in explanation of the English texts which he had to teach — for he began work as a teacher of English. He also learnt the texts themselves off by heart; and made a great impression upon his students by teaching Gray's Elegy without a book in his hand. Herein is disclosed the secret of much of his usefulness in later life — his immense capacity for taking pains for the sake of any cause to which he stood committed.

He still kept up his own studies in English, as a means of fitting himself to become a good public speaker. He used to ask one of his neighbours to examine him in the passages (especially from Burke's Reflections) which he learnt by heart, the arrangement being that Gokhale paid his friend one anna for every mistake which he made in his recitation. It is said that the bargain proved a bad one from the point of view of the neighbour, who would sit for hours waiting vainly for even one mistake. Another plan by which he trained himself at this time was that of resolving that he would commit a certain number of pages to memory every day and then fining himself if he failed to accomplish the right number.

The result of all this self-imposed labour was that Gokhale came to have a very remarkable power of eloquent and dignified speech in the English language, whilst his memory became trained as a magnificent tool for the retention of all manner of facts and figures, and therefore as an invaluable assistant to him in, his work as a statesman.

During this period of his life Gokhale was also running a coaching-establishment for students anxious to pass the Public Service Certificate Examination. In addition to this he was studying law, and kept his law terms by going from Poona to Bombay every weekend. In short, he was already showing that fierce intensity of energy which later: became such a prominent feature of his character, and finally wore him out.

Out of the small salary which he received for his services as a schoolmaster, Gokhale was by now sending home more than half, in an effect to pay back to his brother, Govind Rao, some of the debt which he owed to him for his education.

Deccan Education Society

In Poona at this time there were a number of influences tending to call a young man of character and intelligence to the service of his country rather than of himself. Foremost amongst these was the Deccan Education Society, which controlled the school in which Gokhale was teaching. Two of the members of this society, which had at that time only recently come into existence, were Tilak and Agarkar, the joint founders of the New English School. Gokhale was constantly in touch with these educationalists, both of whom had a very great influence over him, though in the case of Tilak this influence steadily decreased with the passage of the years, whilst in that of Agarkar it increased. It was largely owing to his deep respect for Agarkar that, after considerable hesitation, Gokhale finally resolved to join the Deccan Education Society. This was an act of great self-sacrifice for a young man in his position.

It entailed a willingness to be content for at least twenty years with the small sum of seventy-five rupees a month (£60 a year) as allowance. The decision to join the society was therefore equivalent to a renunciation of all ambitions for wealth and prosperity. It was the taking of a kind of monastic vow. The chief obstacle in the way of this decision was the opposition of Govind Rao Gokhale, who had himself sacrificed so much in order that his younger brother might have the opportunity of becoming a great man in the world. However, once his brother's consent had been gained, and the way thus opened before him for the great step, Gokhale embraced with joy the opportunity of becoming one of a band of men who were doing so much for their country, and were deservedly held in such high esteem.

He said to one of his fellow-students of law, 'You will roll in riches and drive in carriages, while I shall go on foot through life'; but he never seems to have regretted his decision; and the Deccan Education Society became for him a congenial training-ground, in which as one of a compact group of men earnestly seeking the highest .good of their country, he was able to fit himself for a wider service. Meanwhile Gokhale had been trying his hand at journalism, and in the year 1886 wrote many articles for the Mamtha. A year or two later, having been transferred from the teaching of English to the teaching of mathematics, he published a textbook of arithmetic, which ran into a number of editions and secured the warm approval of many distinguished educationalists.

Work in Fergusson College

In 1884, it had been decided by the Deccan Education Society that the New English School should be developed into a college; and the first classes of the now famous Fergusson College were consequently opened, early in 1885. Before long Gokhale was teaching English in the new institution. It is recorded that at first he found considerable difficulty in mastering the nautical phraseology of Southey's Nelson, which was one of the books he had to teach. With his usual thoroughness he was not content till he had taken several trips to Bombay, on purpose to study the appearance and construction of the ships in the harbour, and so to fit himself for explaining these difficult matters to his students. Gokhale remained in connection with the Fergusson College till 1904, although for the latter part of this period he was compelled frequently to be absent from Poona.

Besides mathematics arid English he taught at various times history and political economy, and was indeed playfully known as 'the professor-to-order'. He was willing enough to adopt, and to serve the college by teaching whatever subject in his repertoire was most required; for he held strongly the opinion that in the present condition of Indian education what is chiefly needed is not specialists who have restricted themselves to the life-long study of one subject only, but all-round men who are competent to lend a hand wherever help is most required. Indeed, Gokhale never even applied the title 'Professor' to himself.

Just as his English studies had exercised a great influence upon his ability to express himself with weight and eloquence as a public-speaker, so Gokhale's mathematical proclivities served to give him that comprehensive grasp of the mathematical aspects of statesmanship, which rendered possible his great budget speeches of later years. His exactness of mind, the manner in which he understood abstruse financial questions, and his power of producing matter of fascinating interest from repulsive masses of statistics, may all be traced to the fact that for so many years he had bent his best efforts to the mastering not only of English literature but of the dry bones of mathematics.

One of his most distinguished old student's records of Gokhale that as a teacher of English he was methodical in the extreme:

> "He never slurred over even the easiest passages, and took great pains in explaining all the allusions, and especially the historical references."

Another old student says, in connection with Gokhale's lectures on Burke:

> "Every thought of that famous political philosopher brought forth from his silver tongue a stream of illustrations chosen from the everyday life of a citizen, so that the dullest received a clear impression of the tenure of the book. To the more ambitious set of students were thrown occasional hints on higher studies in politics.... To have heard Gokhale lecturing on Burke's Reflections was to have drunk at the fountain-head of constitutionalism."

In spite of the multifarious activities in which he was engaged. Gokhale found time for various forms of recreation. As a boy he had been fond of cricket, and he had for long a passion for billiards. At one period he spent hours on this game every day; and he told one of his friends that when he sat out in the open on hot-weather evenings he would amuse himself by playing imaginary strokes on the stars. He was also keenly interested in chess, cards and other games, all of which he played with a characteristic intensity of concentration. The same friend, quoted above, says that on one occasion he played cards with Gokhale for fourteen hours out of the twenty-four.

Gokhale's passion for exactness was especially notable in connection with his style as a writer of English. The clearness and grace which mark his speeches are also to be seen in his letters; and it is said of him that when he had to write even the most trifling note, he would never write it hurriedly, but would always choose his words and frame his sentences very carefully, sometimes spending a lengthy period of feverish thought in search of the exact word which he required. He was extremely well-read in English literature, and his retentive memory enabled him to bring forward a wealth of quotations and illustrations with which to embellish any subject which might be under discussion, whether in the ordinary course of conversation, or in his public speeches.

In his speeches Gokhale showed a rare fluency and power of just expression, which is the more remarkable in view of the fact that he spoke generally with only a half-sheet of notepaper to guide him. His style of speaking was free from pomposity; and he impressed his hearers with the chastity of his thought. The musical clearness of his voice was also a great asset to him.

During his career as a teacher in the Fergusson College, Gokhale seems to have impressed his students more as a teacher of history than in any other capacity. But they felt that his chief interest in the subject lay in the lessons which his mind was continually gleaning from the past for the sake of the future of his country. He would often in his lectures stray away from the matter in hand in order to discuss pressing questions of current political interest. One of his students says:

> "In a course of lectures on English history he turned aside for a week to give us a resume of the history of Ireland since the Union. The course of Irish history he always regarded as somewhat similar to that of India, and he never lost an opportunity of impressing on the minds of his pupils the long course of steady work and disinterested sacrifice which the Irish leaders have shown during the whole century.
>
> National greatness, he felt, could not be achieved in any other way. He used to take in regularly the Dublin Freeman and the tri-weekly edition of the London Times, even in his early days, to keep himself well posted in English political thought. As regards his

> teaching proper he read almost all the available literature on any point before he entered the class, and for the whole hour the flow of his words never stopped.... He did not much care for the history of India, as he thought that more lessons can be learnt from the history of Europe, both ancient and modern, which presents a well-marked evolution of the democratic idea, than from any detailed account of the numerous dynasties of rulers that ruled in India — for this, he thought, was very nearly what the history of India practically amounts to."

He was also a skilful and inspiring teacher of economics, and on this subject he entertained for a time the idea of doing some original research work, probably in connection with bi-materialism, and of publishing the results. However in time he deliberately abandoned this idea, on the ground that his country needed his services in a broader field than that of the expert either in economics or in any other sphere of merely academic research.

Friendship with Mahadev Govind Ranade

It was at this period of his life that Gokhale came under the influence of Mahadev Govind Ranade, the man who more than any other, not even excepting G. G. Agarkar, was responsible for his development into a great servant of India. Ranade was at this period the most distinguished of all the citizens of Poona, indeed he was often called 'the uncrowned King of Poona'. He was a man of great personal dignity and force of character, which at the same time possessed a fund of sage political wisdom which made him an admirable guide for a young enthusiast of the type of Gokhale.

The cultural renaissance .which during the past few years had been making itself felt in Maharashtra, and which had borne fruit in various literary and educational undertakings, as well as in a very definite stirring of the public conscience with regard to questions of social reform, was centred around Ranade, who was also an enlightened leader and thinker in regard to political and economic questions, The first meeting between Gokhale and Ranade is said to have taken place under somewhat amusing circumstances. The New English School had on one occasion arranged a function in the Hirabagh at Poona, and had invited all the most distinguished gentlemen of the city to attend it. Gokhale was acting as doorkeeper, and had instructions to admit only those who could show tickets. Amongst others, Ranade had been invited, but when he arrived at the gate he found that he had forgotten to bring his ticket with him. Gokhale, who was not at that time acquainted with Ranade even by sight, refused to admit him. The situation was saved, however, by another gentleman who came up and, explaining matters to the conscientious doorkeeper ushered Ranade in with all honour. This same gentleman, Aba Saheb Sathe, was afterwards the means of arranging for an interview between Ranade and Gokhale, as a result of which the latter became in a short while the devoted disciple of the great reformer.

Ranade perceived the great possibilities latent in Gokhale, and set himself to develop them, by a hard and exacting process of training, so that they might be effectively realised for the benefit of India. Gokhale for his part began to entertain an unbounded affection and respect for his guru, in whose presence, it is said, and foe would never sit down. It would be hard to discover any side of Gokhale's public activity which was not profoundly affected by Ranade's influence. For fourteen years this relationship endured, until the death of Ranade, which took place in 1901. During the first part of this time, disciple and guru were in constant contact, and Gokhale received a rigorous training in that industrious accuracy which marked all Ranade's work, and which was the keynote of Gokhale's subsequent success as a statesman. Ranade sent him straight to original documents; made him work through masses of Blue Books; gave him petitions and memorials to draft which entailed long and laborious research; was unsparing in his demand for articles and memoranda on all manner of subjects of public interest, which could only be mastered by the hardest and most rigorous industry.

'Under instructions from Ranade, the disciple set to work with intense application. Many were the dreary hours spent in hunting up these materials; many were the nights when sleep was denied to the young man, because work had a stronger claim. Even fever was not admitted as an excuse. "Fevers would go away if medicine were taken," the exacting master would say, "but a

Wednesday lost could not be reclaimed.'" (Wednesday being the day when they usually met for their work).... Ranade never showered any praise on Gokhale in his presence, nor did he chide him if he could not approve of his productions. What he did not, like he recast without any fuss. But by degrees his confidence in the young man grew; and Gokhale was entrusted with the work of drafting weighty memorials to the Government, one of which he had to finish at one almost continuous sitting of twenty-two hours.

Secretary of the Sarvajanik Sabha

Ranade made Gokhale one of the secretaries of the Sarvajanik Sabha of Poona, which was at that time the chief political association in India. This society made it its aim carefully to consider every subject of public importance which arose, and to submit the views of the people to Government in the form of lengthy and weighty memoranda, to which Government was in the habit of giving very careful attention. For a number of years the work of drafting these memoranda fell almost entirely upon Gokhale, under the superintendence and oversight of Ranade. They are written in a concise and effective style, and in a spirit of constructive statesmanship which shows how rapidly the influence of Ranade was developing in Gokhale those qualities which were to make him in later years the great force he was for nation-building.

Increased Responsibilities During the years 1887-91, the Deccan Education Society passed through trying times, owing to differences of opinion which, had risen between G. G. Agarkar and B. G. Tilak, largely on questions of social reform, with regard to which Tilak adopted an unprogressive attitude. The situation was eventually relieved by the retirement from the society of Tilak, accompanied by Namjoshi. This for the time being greatly weakened the personnel of the college staff: for Tilak had been professor of mathematics and Namjoshi had performed the onerous task of the collection of funds.

It was really Gokhale who stepped into the place of both these gentlemen; for he took up the teaching of mathematics which had been in Tilak's hands, and he was also called upon by his colleagues to become successor to Namjoshi as organiser and collector of the college finances. In this way, although an immense new burden was laid upon Gokhale's shoulders, he rapidly became the chief representative of the society before the eyes of the outside public; and he gained invaluable experience both of the practical management of a great institution, and of the labours and anxieties involved in all public-spirited work. He became an expert judge of men, with a wide knowledge of the manner in which they may best be approached and dealt with in order that public ends may be rightly served. He became, in other words, a tactful and accomplished leader of Sarvajanik.

It was in this way that all through his life Gokhale's self-sacrificing readiness to undertake personal responsibility, often of a very arduous character, in connection with the causes in which he believed, became the means of fitting him for wider spheres of national usefulness. He never shirked a duty, or sought to avoid a responsibility however busily occupied every moment of his day might be; and from each new duty and responsibility thus undertaken, he gained some fresh equipment to become a great servant of India.

Secretary of the Deccan Education Society

The work of collecting funds for the Deccan Education Society, which Gokhale had undertaken, was no sinecure. The society had decided to erect a new building for its college. The old building in the city of Poona had to accommodate both the high school and the college classes, and was becoming impossibly overcrowded. Consequently, Gokhale set to work at the task of collecting the amount needed for the new building, devoting to this task his weekends and his vacations. It was work of the hardest and most unpleasant character, involving a great deal of travelling, many exasperating rebuffs, and not a few disheartening experiences in regard to promises never fulfilled.

However, through this work Gokhale made many friendships, and became one of the best known figures in Maharashtra. The contacts thus established were afterwards of material assistance in keeping him in touch with the movement of public opinion, especially in the country districts. As a result of his untiring devotion in the cause of his college the new buildings were opened in 1895, entirely free from debt. During this period, in addition to his work as one of its professors, and as its chief collector of funds, Gokhale was secretary of the Deccan Education Society. In this capacity he had much important correspondence to carry on with Government, and many problems to solve in connection with the personnel of the society's workers.

The Constitution of the society provided for a double system of control, partly through the board of life-members, and partly through the council of the society. This dual control did not always make for smooth working; and Gokhale as secretary had many knotty problems to solve. However, in time he became not merely the trusted representative of his colleagues before the outside world, and their spokesman and protagonist in all relations both with the general public and with Government, but their guide and helper in the difficult questions of personal relationship which arose within the society itself.

As a Journalist

Meanwhile, as secretary of the Sarvajanik Sabha, Gokhale was steadily accumulating political experience under the sure guidance of Ranade. The headquarters of the Sabha in Poona formed a meeting-place where citizens who were interested in public questions gathered every evening for informal discussions, which ranged over a great variety of subjects. In the same place a large amount; of study was carried on, in connection with the political history of the West and its possible bearing on the future of India, and also in connection with a great variety of economic and industrial questions.

Gokhale took his share in all these activities, and profited, greatly by them. He had also been made responsible for the editing of the quarterly magazine conducted by the Sabha, though, he had politely refused the honorarium of Rs. 40 a month which, had been offered him in connection with this editorship, as he felt that it was not right to receive pay for work of this character undertaken for the sake of his country. Meanwhile, constant articles from his pen were appearing in Agarkar's Anglo-Marathi weekly, the Sudharak. Indeed, the English part of this paper was mainly written by Gokhale, who in this way obtained an invaluable opportunity for analysing and clearly expressing the: mass of ideas regarding public questions which he was acquiring in connection with his studies under Ranade and his work for the Sarvajanik Sabha. Ranade always insisted that where his own and his lieutenants' opinions led them into conflict with the: opinions held by Government, criticism must be expressed in a moderate and constructive manner; and thus Gokhale was trained to be not simply a critic of existing systems and institutions, but an organiser of something better to take their place. It was this quality of constructiveness that made him a true nation-builder in his wider activities of later life.

As a Teacher

Through all these varied activities Gokhale's teaching-work in the Fergusson College went steadily forward. His students are said to have stood rather in awe of him, though he was careful to make himself perfectly accessible to them. One of them records of him:

> "He spoke freely to them, and encouraged them to tell him of the difficulties that were felt by the student world. Even in the dark days of rampant extremism, there were a perceptible number of young men who remained true to the principles of moderation, mainly through the influence that emanated from Gokhale....
>
> With several of the more promising students he came more intimately into contact, and gave them special personal help in their studies.... He was also always on the look out for promising young men to join the society as life-members, and several of us have received the first impulse towards life-membership of the society from him. Needless to say, there was no improper influencing on his part, beyond a frank discussion of all problems of the country; and the duty of spirited young men to do some public work without regard to self-interest was impressed upon them. No attempt was made to hustle them into taking the step of joining the society."

It is obvious how every element in Gokhale's environment during this early period of his manhood was converted into an opportunity for self-training in the service of his country. He was intensely eager to be of use, and his fiery energy led him to follow up one opening after another as these presented themselves before him. His character being what it was, full of self-sacrificing zeal, .and marked by an indefatigable spirit of industry, whatever he laid his hand to seemed to prosper; and as the causes he advocated went forward to success/he himself was moulded by them, and by the loyal service which he gave to them, into a man who was genuinely great, because his aims lay beyond himself, and because very faculty he possessed was subordinated to his high ideals.

Gokhale's Political Principles

In fact, Gokhale deliberately turned his back upon popularity. His opponents of the Tilak school had a great popular following which they attracted and retained by methods of which he did not approve. He might have fought them with their own weapons; but in this case he would have had to sacrifice his principles, and this was impossible for him.

Mainly on account of the methods of propaganda which were followed by Tilak, and which Gokhale and his followers have never cared to follow, Gokhale has never been a popular hero in Maharashtra. Of course he had always his band of faithful followers who remained attached to him through thick and thin, and whose attachment was a source of great comfort to him.... He hated shams of every kind, and this is why he spoke equally strongly on the defects of Lord Curzon's administration, or on the outrageous treatment of Indians in South Africa, and on the Indians attitude to the depressed classes in their own country.

One of Gokhale's main political principles — and one which brought him into acute disfavour with the 'extremists' — was his insistence on the necessity to India of the British connection. His aim was not an India independent of the British Empire, but Dominion Status within that Empire. This was the end for which he continually laboured. In the middle years of the nineteenth century, Dominion Self-government had been rapidly and generously extended to the English-speaking colonies of the

Empire. The time had now come, in his belief, for the beginnings of a similar movement in regard to the great Eastern dependency. In the nature of things it was an end to be attained by constitutional methods, by education of Indian opinion, by making the most of every avenue open to the expression of that opinion, by practical demonstration of the fact that Indians were capable of responsible government, and by the painstaking manipulation of all legitimate means by which pressure might be brought to bear, both upon the Indian and the English governments, for the liberalising of constitutional machinery in India.

This method of working demanded immense patience, and involved crushing disappointments. It involved a two-fold movement proceeding simultaneously — that of the extension of enlightenment and the development of character on the one hand, and that of constitutional advance on the other. Both were in the nature of the case slow processes. There was no swift and easy road to the millennium of independence. The boon must be deserved.

It is easy to see that such an outlook was not calculated to appeal to the ardent nationalists whose numbers were rapidly increasing all over India. Especially to the students, and above all, to the students in his own homeland of Maharashtra, it seemed (as it still seems) that Gokhale's method was insufferably tedious; that it involved an undignified dependence upon English clemency; that it was inconsistent with the dignity of a great people, whose traditions of victorious independence lay in the still recent past.

Yet Gokhale never abated his insistence upon these twin principles — that advance must be constitutional advance, deserved through the spread of enlightenment and education; and that the British connection was essential to the well-being of India.

Again, as has already been noticed, Gokhale insisted, in season and out of season, upon the necessity of the Hindus carrying the Muslims with them in their growing national consciousness and demand for freedom. Good feeling and cordial cooperation between the two communities was the only basis upon which a sound and united national life could be built up. This was bitter doctrine to the advanced political school, who 'played upon the imagination of the ignorant and superstitious, depicting the horrors of contamination with the Muslim, which the liberal-minded'.

In regard to his relations with the Government, Gokhale stood first for a careful and thorough use of all the constitutional machinery already available for bringing Indian opinion to bear upon Government policy. In the second place he kept a vigilant eye upon administrative detail, and was insistent upon the necessity for reform and redress, whether in a general financial policy, or in any matter of official high-handedness, as for instance with regard to the partition of Bengal.

The immense pains which he took in working up his facts and figures, and in substantiating his position in every possible way, especially with regard to his great Budget speeches, made him far more than a mere leader of opposition in the Legislature. Though he never held any responsible office as a legislator, he was known to be a genuinely constructive statesman, whose criticisms were to be welcomed in the same spirit in which they were offered, as an honest attempt to help the Government to discharge its obligations to India in the right manner.

Thus, when Gokhale pressed for constitutional reform, his opinions, and advice carried immense weight, above all in his insistence that, reform should be generously offered, rather than conceded under compulsion. His attitude may be indicated by a passage from one notable speech:

> The Government will no doubt put down — indeed it must put down — all disorder with a firm hand. But what the situation really requires is not the policeman's baton or the soldier's bayonet, but the statesman's insight, wisdom and courage. The people must be enabled to feel that their interests are, if not the only consideration, at any rate the main consideration, that weighs with Government, and this can only be brought about by a radical change in the spirit of the administration. Whatever reforms are taken in hand, let them be dealt with frankly and generously. And let not the words, "too late," be written on every one of them. For while the Government stands considering, hesitating, receding, debating within itself, to grant or not to grant, that

> is the question" — opportunities rush past it which can never be recalled. And the moving finger writes, and having writ, moves on.

These noble words were followed by the granting of the Morley-Minto reforms, which may be regarded as due in no small measure to Gokhale's influence and to the warnings which he had uttered. Still more were the Montagu-Gielmsford reforms, which came ten years later, a concession to his spirit of sane and liberal statesmanship, and a memorial to his constructive workmanship. He would not have approved of all aspects of those reforms. He would have considered them dangerously delayed; and he would have been outspoken in his denunciation of the tragic events of 1919 which reacted so disastrously upon the fashion in which the new Constitution was received in India. None the less those reforms in themselves, and above all when considered as an instalment of future self-government, are a real measure of the national usefulness of Gokhale's life-work.

Sir William Wedderburn wrote thus of Gokhale:

> "In no case did he fail to produce a profound and favourable impression by the accuracy of his information and the cogency of his arguments. At personal interviews he was equally successful. To the credit of British statesmen of all parties it must be recorded that they have all been willing to give a hearing to Gokhale, and it is no secret that, as Secretary of State for India, Lord Morley accorded to him prolonged interviews, at which he set forth fully the needs and aspirations of the Indian people. The information thus imparted influenced in no small degree the concessions granted in the Morley-Minto reforms."

These words serve to bring out one of the most important of Gokhale's principles in regard to his work for his country — that work must be done thoroughly. He gave unsparingly of his time and efforts to the investigation of the causes in which he was concerned, and to the working up of all available evidence regarding them. He was effectually aided in this task, on the one hand by his marvellous memory, and on the other by the rigorous training which he had received under Ranade during the period when, as secretary of the Poona Sarvajanik Sabha, he had been employed in working up cases to be presented to Government in regard to various public questions. But memory and training were only tools employed by the man's own personality — by his indomitable will, which refused no sacrifice of comfort or leisure for a cause he believed in, and by his character of thoroughness, of honesty, of persistent diligence.

Secretary of Congress

These then were the principles which Gokhale brought to his public work. The first important task laid upon him with regard to the organisation of public opinion was the secretaryship of the Bombay Provincial Conference, which he held in 1893 and 1894. He acquitted himself so well in regard to this arduous and thankless piece of work that he was given the honour of being made one of the secretaries of the National Congress, which was held at Poona in 1895. The arrangements for a Congress entail the finding, or building, of accommodation for many thousands of guests, the erection of an immense 'pandal' or temporary hall of assembly the settling of ten thousand details regarding the food, the drink, and the comfort generally of the delegates, and above all the collection of a very considerable amount of money, whereby all these various expenses may be met.

Gokhale brought to the task all his accustomed energy and capacity for detail; but he found himself hampered at every turn by the influence of the 'extremist' school which has been referred to above, and which at this period was showing not merely indifference but actual hostility to the Congress, mainly on the ground that the Congress had become identified with the cause of Social Reform, to which they were bitterly opposed. This hostility crystallised into a demand that the All India Social Reform Conference, which in recent years had been allowed to hold its sittings in the 'pandal' of the Congress, should be deprived of this privilege, and should be compelled to make arrangements for its accommodation elsewhere. Eventually, in spite of the fact that this pettifogging point of view was by no means generally entertained, it was decided by those responsible for the Congress that the concession should be made; and, in consequence, a very great deal of additional work was rendered necessary, as a separate place of assembly had to be erected for the use of the Social Reform Conference.

In other respects also the extremist party made Gokhale's work very difficult; for example, by their efforts to pack the Reception Committee. They are said even to have descended to threats of physical force. It actually became needful to begin the issue of a new journal, the Rashtra Sabha Samachar, in order to counteract the influence of the Kesari; and Gokhale was responsible for writing this.

The unpleasant experiences connected with his work as secretary of the Congress of 1895 were in the long run of much benefit to Gokhale, in training him in the management of men, and in the administration of a great political undertaking. They may also have had much to do with the development in him of that admirable faculty for differing from his opponents in a courteous and amiable manner which marked him in later life.

In 1896 the reactionaries succeeded in capturing the Sarvajanik Sabha; and a year later their methods brought them into conflict with Government, as a paid lecturer appointed by them had made some rash assertions, which were neither explained nor withdrawn. Consequently Government passed an order to the effect that the representations of the Sabha, which had been of such service in the past, could no longer be considered. Some time before this happened, however, Gokhale had resigned his secretaryship of the Sabha, since he found it impossible to work under the new conditions, and with the help and advice of Ranade had started, a new society, the Deccan Sabha, which continued the constructive type of work which has been carried on for so long by the Sarvajanik Sabha.

Welby Commission

It had been increasingly impressed during the past few years upon Gokhale's mind that the right programme of constitutional advance for India lay along the line of a progressive association of Indians in the control of the country's finances. He perceived how intimately in the history of England the development of democratic institutions had been connected with the enforcement of the people's claim to a voice in the disbursement of the taxes which they paid. He perceived also the immense force which had been given to the cause of American liberty by the appeal to the maxim, 'No taxation without representation', a maxim which was in itself a revival of an ancient constitutional principle of English history. These convictions led Gokhale to throw himself with increased energy into the study of the problems of Indian finance, from every possible point of view; and in cooperation with Rao Bahadur G. V. Joshi, who was an expert economist, he soon made the Deccan Sabha a notable instrument for the spreading of enlightened interest in financial affairs.

In his public speeches on the Congress platform and elsewhere Gokhale also gave abundant proof of his thorough-going grasp of Indian economic problems. In 1896, a Royal Commission was appointed, presided over by Lord Welby, in order to enquire into the financial relationships of India and England; and public bodies in India were invited to send their representatives to London in order to lay their views before the Commission, which did not itself visit India. The Deccan Sabha decided to accept this invitation; and as neither Ranade nor Joshi could themselves go to England, the task of laying the Sabha's views before the Welby Commission fell upon Gokhale, who was then only 31 years old.

He made the most of this opportunity, spending three months in a concentrated endeavour to make his evidence before the Commission as comprehensive and convincing as it could possibly be. When he felt himself prepared, Ranade put him through the most searching cross-examination, taking up the official point of view for this purpose, as the Commission itself was largely composed of redoubtable official experts. After a rigorous test Ranade pronounced himself satisfied with his pupil's equipment; and Gokhale embarked for England, in the company of (later Sir) E. Wacha, who was also to give evidence before the Commission, and to whom he soon became greatly attached.

Economic Problems

Gokhale duly appeared before the Commission, and was heard for two whole days. His evidence, which was delivered in a manner at once both cogent and profound, made his reputation as one of the foremost Indian economists and statesmen. His general attitude to the financial problems of his country may be summed up in the following sentence from his evidence:

> 'Whereas the capacity of the country to bear increased burdens is growing perceptibly less, our expenditure, under the existing conditions of administration, is rising higher and higher, necessitating a heavy incidence of taxation, exhausting all our fiscal reserves, and, what is still more alarming, thrusting on our hands expanding responsibilities.'

He was firmly convinced that the revenue of India, depending as it did very largely upon the land tax, was of a fundamentally inelastic character; and he also held that the salt tax, which formed the most important source of revenue next to the land tax, was not only incapable of being made to yield more revenue, but was the highest tax that has ever been imposed upon a prime necessity of life and called urgently for reduction.

He urged therefore that the expenditure of the Indian Government should be adjusted to the fact of this inelasticity of income — or at least to the fact that income could only be expected to expand with the normal growth of the population, and with definite improvement in Indian conditions of life. He pointed to the terrible famines which were experienced in India as proof of the fact that the country was incapable of bearing increased financial burdens, and indeed that the burdens already imposed upon her were too heavy for her strength.

He regarded the proceeds of the income tax and the salt tax as the only trustworthy indication of the real financial position of India, and maintained, both in 1897 and later, that neither of these was showing any decided increase, the second even failing to keep pace with the normal growth of population.

Hence, he concluded that both the upper and the middle classes, whose state of prosperity is shown by the proceeds of the income tax, and the masses of the population, whose position is indicated by the salt tax, were in anything but a satisfactory condition economically. Increase of revenue under land tax he refused to regard as indicative of increased prosperity, since the people were forced to pay the enhanced taxation under this head on pain of parting with their land. Increase under excise merely showed that drunkenness was more prevalent than formerly; and the increase under the heading of 'stamps' merely showed that the people were becoming more litigious.

It cannot be denied that the series of devastating famines which occurred in India at the end of the nineteenth century lent considerable weight to Gokhale's often repeated contention that the material condition of the masses of the Indian population was deteriorating, rather than improving. He was never tired of drawing attention to this phenomenon, 'the saddest in the whole range of the economic history of the world'. His position is thus summed up by one of his Indian biographers:

That a peasantry inferior to none in industry, frugality and patient suffering should, at the end of half a century of an uninterrupted peaceful rule, find itself in a worse plight than it has ever been in, was a painful fact demanding the earnest and immediate attention of Government, which could best be focused by having a formal investigation made, where the non-official student of the subject should be invited to cooperate with official representatives.

As time passed, and the period of famines was succeeded by one of increasing prosperity, Gokhale ceased to urge his thesis that the people of India were actually becoming poorer; but he never till the end of his life ceased to insist upon the necessity for rigorous economy, or to protest against any indication that the Government of India were tending to overlook the very narrow limits within which any projected attempt to increase the revenue must be confined, owing to the peculiar inelasticity of the sources of taxation.

Expenditure on Army

With regard to the details of his evidence before the Welby Commission, Gokhale drew especial attention to the expenditure on the Indian army, and in this connection made the following points: First, the percentage of revenue spent upon the Army was very high when considered in comparison with this percentage in the case of other countries, (given at that time as, India 35 per cent, Russia 21 per cent, France 19 per cent, Japan 16 per cent, Italy 13 per cent). Second, the proportion of British troops to Indian in

India (one to two) entailed an unnecessary burden upon the Indian taxpayer. Third, the army had been increased by 30,000 beyond the military needs of the country as laid down by the Army Commission of 1879, even though this Commission had taken into consideration the possibility of extensive operations with States lying beyond the North-West Frontier of India. Fourth, the Indian Army was kept practically on a war footing, and thus was enormously expensive. Most of the countries of the West had adopted short-service systems, which enabled them to have large numbers of trained men available at short notice, whilst keeping down the numbers and expense of their permanent military establishments. This system had been adopted by England herself a quarter of a century before; but its benefits had not been extended to India. Fifth, there had taken place a great increase in the numbers of officers employed in the Indian Army; but at the same time the field of employment for Indian officers had been contracted rather than extended.

Throughout his life Gokhale kept up this campaign against the excessive military expenditure incurred by the Government of India, and against its unwillingness to provide facilities for Indians to take up a career as officers in the army. His position was thus summed up by himself.

No pouring out of money like water on mere standing battalions can ever give India the military strength and preparedness which other civilized countries possess while the whole population is disarmed and the process of demilitarisation continues apace.... India is about the only country in the civilized world where the people are debarred from the privileges of citizen soldiership and from all voluntary participation in the responsibilities of national defence.... What I am anxious to see is the adoption of some plan whereby, while a position of greater self-respect is assigned to us in the work of national defence, the establishments necessary during peace and war times may be separated, and thus our finances may be freed from the intolerable pressure of an excessive and ever-growing military expenditure.

Gokhale's position as a life-long leader of opposition meant that, with regard to great issues on which he was permanently convinced of the wrongness of the policy adopted by the

Government of India — as for instance in this matter of military expenditure — he must continually, year after year, give voice to the same protests in a manner that should be both forcible and new. In this difficult task he succeeded to a very remarkable degree. He took infinite pains in adding new arguments and figures to the presentation of his case and in finding new angles and points of view from which to present it.

His attitude was fearlessly critical of what he believed to be a great injustice to his country; but he managed to express his convictions in a manner which was moderate in tone and constructive in spirit, and he always succeeded in stimulating attention and interest, even in regard to questions at which he had been hammering for many years. In this matter of Army expenditure his main thesis continued the same — that the crushing weight of the military budget should be reduced by bringing into existence some system of Reserves, through which it should no longer be needful to keep the Army permanently on what approximated to a war-footing; that public defence should be made a matter of national concern by making it possible for members of the educated classes of India to take up the career of army officers; and that England should bear a part of the heavy cost of the Indian Army, since that Army was largely employed for purposes which ought to be regarded as imperial rather than Indian.

Indianisation of Services

In his evidence before the Welby Commission, Gokhale laid emphasis upon another serious defect in the financial administration of his country, namely, the costliness of the great Indian Services. This also remained a matter upon which he continued till the end of his life to urge reform. Connected with this was the fact, upon which he laid great emphasis, that the proportion of Indians in the higher services was extremely small.

The financial loss entailed by this practical monopoly by Europeans of the higher branches of the Services in India is not represented by salaries only. There are, besides, heavy pension and furlough charges, more than 31 million sterling being paid to Europeans in England for the purpose in 1890. The excessive costliness of the foreign agency is not, however, its only evil.

There is a moral evil which, if anything, is even greater. A kind of dwarfing or stunting of the Indian race is going on under the present system. We must live all the days of our life in an atmosphere of inferiority, and the tallest of us must bend, in order that the exigencies of the existing system may be satisfied. The upward impulse, if I may use such an expression, which every schoolboy at Eton or Harrow may feel, that he may one day be a Gladstone, a Nelson, or a Wellington, and which may draw forth all the best efforts of which he is capable, is denied to us. The full height to which our manhood is capable of rising can never be reached by us under the present system. The moral elevation which every self-governing people feels cannot be felt by us. Our administrative and military talents must gradually disappear, owing to sheer disuse, till at last our lot, as hewers of wood and drawers of water in our own country, is stereotyped.

Gokhale proceeded then to show in the case of each service how extremely small a share Indians had been given to their country. It may seem of little advantage of an incident in the story of a long fight which has been won; but it must be remembered that here was an Indian who was unmistakably a born statesman bringing forward a thesis which was then almost new, at any rate in the august environment of a Royal Commission. In his fearless, but at the same time sane and reasonable statement of the Indian point of view regarding the Army, the Services, and other kindred subjects, Gokhale was striking the first great blow in a crusade which was to absorb his magnificent energies to the day of his death. The fact that, in this direction and that, the crusade has now been successful must lend the greater interest to this first major engagement.

On Education

In regard to Education, Gokhale also expressed to the Welby Commission a point of view which was to become characteristic of him in the future.

The meagreness of the Government assistance to public education in India is one of the gravest blots on the administration of Indian expenditure. No words can be too strong in condemning this neglect of what was solemnly accepted by the Court of Directors in 1854 as a sacred duty.

There are more than 537 thousand towns and villages in India, with a total population of about 230 millions, and yet there are less, than a 100 thousand public primary schools for them. The population of school-going age in India is about 35 millions, out of whom only about four millions, including those attending private or unaided schools, are under instruction, which means that out of every 100 children of school-going age; many growing up in darkness and ignorance, and consequent moral helplessness. Comment on these figures is really superfluous.

Gokhale's Attitude to the Problem of Unity

In later years, though his interests became more deeply engaged with national and imperial problems, Gokhale still continued to take the warmest interest in the well-being of the capital of Maharashtra. Many of his opponents were men whose Maratha patriotism was so intense as to blind them to the interest of India as a whole. But whilst Gokhale was a loyal Maratha, he showed an admirable wisdom and sanity in refusing to allow any sectional loyalty to interfere with his loyalty to India as a united nation. He could be enthusiastic for the well-being of Poona. He could serve, as he did for many years, as a member of her municipality, and as its president. He could risk his life to save her from plague. But for this local patriotism was always rightly blended with a wider national patriotism.

The most significant illustration of this quality of balanced loyalty, by which the claims of sectional interest were given full weight, but were never permitted to interfere with national well-being, may be found in Gokhale's attitude to the Muslim leadership. As has already been noticed, the extremist politicians, who were continually in bitter opposition to Gokhale, were the party of fanatical Maratha nationalism, and therefore the party of irreconcilable animosity against the Muslims. From time immemorial Maratha nationalism had been built up on conflict against this secular enemy of the race; and in the present also the smouldering fires could easily be kindled into violent conflagration. It was true that the interests of India as a whole demanded, from every point of view, unity of outlook and effective cooperation between Hindus and Muslims. But this consideration, which weighed so heavily with Gokhale, was beyond the restricted view of his opponents. Their slogan was, in effect, Maharashtra first; India if possible next; but the Muslims nowhere'. Gokhale clearly perceived the fatal dangers of such a position, and stood like a rock for his principle of friendly cooperation with the Muslims in the interests of India as a whole.

The effect of the two policies became evident at a later date. The spirit of extremism made it impossible, when constitutional reforms were introduced, to avoid the application of the fatal principle of communal electorates^ which perpetuated the division of the country into two opposing camps. The animosity between the communities being what it was, the election of Hindu representatives to the legislatures by Hindus alone, and that of Muslim representatives by Muslims alone, inevitably resulted in the choice of extreme Hindus on the one hand and of extreme Muslims on the other; and thus the divisions became more and more pronounced. The Hindu-Muslim Pact arranged by the Congress of 1916 proved only a temporary palliative; for the roots of animosity remained deeply implanted in the two communities, and the elections for the reformed councils provided from time to time, through their consecration of the communal principle, a means of automatically keeping resentment alive. As soon as the temporary fervour of the Non-cooperation Movement subsided, discussion and riot broke out with increased bitterness; and the problem of inter-communal conflict remains today the most baffling and disheartening obstacle in the pathway towards a free Indian nationhood.

Indeed the Pact of 1916 ultimately resulted in an aggravation of the prevailing animosity; for it introduced the principle of communal representation into the very heart of the national movement, and it bestowed upon the Muslims an inequitable over-representation which was bound ultimately to lead to resentment and increased friction.

Gokhale looked at the whole question from the point of view of a statesman and a constitutionalist. He saw no hope in a policy of separate electorates, which would merely perpetuate divisions, and would give every opportunity for their becoming bitterer. He believed that it was essential for the future well-being of India that there should be joint electorates. At the same time he perceived that communal cleavage being what it was (and still is), separate representation must somehow be secured for the Muslims; for otherwise their cooperation could never be gained in the coming democratic regime. He believed therefore that seats would have to be reserved for them in the legislatures of the future. How was this to be done without introducing the principle of communal electorates?

Gokhale's final solution to this problem may be roughly sketched as follows: There should be large constituencies, each returning several members, of whom one or more (according to the numerical proportions of the two communities in the area in question) must be Muslims. But the electorates must not be divided. The Hindus should vote for the Muslim representative or representatives, and the Muslims for the Hindu. In the case, for instance, of a constituency returning three members, of whom one was to be a Muslim indebted for this outline of Gokhale's final position regarding Unity to a gentleman who was for many years in close touch with Gokhale, each Hindu would have three votes, one of which must be given to a Muslim candidate: and so also with' the Muslim voters.

A system of communal representation secures, in practice, that the most anti-Hindu-Muslim and the most anti-Muslim-Hindus will be elected; but under the system just outlined the most pro-Hindu Muslims and the most pro-Muslim Hindus would be chosen. Thus, the communal animosity, which has become so markedly embittered in recent years would be decreased, instead of strengthened by the introduction of democratic institutions. There can he no question that Gokhale was right with regard to this contention.

It is becoming every day more evident that communal-hatred is the most serious of all obstacles to the development of a free Indian nationhood. It is the tragedy of the past twenty years of political evolution that Gokhale's advice regarding this supremely important issue has not been followed, and that the building up of representative organs of government has been permitted to proceed along the lines of communal cleavage. The setting right of this tragic mistake will be the most important task of those responsible for future constitutional advance in India.

General State of Affairs

Such was the fashion in which Gokhale began his career as the spokesman of his country's aspirations and resentments before her English rulers. He summed matters up as regards the general position of India in the following terms:

- *First* — the buffer of the Company's Government, which fairly protected Indian interests, is gone, and there is no effectual substitute.
- *Second* — we have no effectual constitutional safeguards against the misapplication of our revenues for extra-Indian requirements.
- *Third* — the control vested in the Council of the Secretary of State under the Statute of 1858, is rendered almost nugatory by the alteration of its status under recent Amending Acts.
- *Fourth* — the control of Parliament, as against the Secretary of State, has become entirely nominal, owing to the latter being a member of the Imperial Executive, with a standing majority behind him. The old periodical enquiry by Parliament and its jealous watchfulness are gone. In fact, we have at present all the disadvantages of Parliamentary Government without its advantages. In the case of all departments except the Indian, ex-ministers think it their duty, and also feel it to be their interest, to exercise the closest watch on the proceedings of their successors, with a view to passing the most adverse criticism that may be possible. In regard to India alone, ex-ministers vie with, and sometimes even go beyond, their successors in extolling all that exists and all that is done. The responsible opposition in this country thus abdicates its functions in the case of India only.
- *Fifth* — the Government of India, as at present constituted, cannot be much interested in economy. Almost all internal administration having been made over to Local Governments under the Decentralisation Scheme, questions of foreign policy/large public works, and military questions absorb almost the whole attention of the

Government of India. Further, the Finance Minister excepted, every other member of Council, including, since 1885, the Viceroy, has a direct interest in the increase of expenditure.

- *Sixth* — neither in England nor in India is there the salutary check of public opinion on the financial administration. Parliament is ill-informed and even indifferent. And the supreme and local Legislative Councils are simply powerless to control expenditure, since the Budgets have not to be passed, and no resolutions in reference to them can be measure.

Remedies

To these defects in the existing condition of this Gokhale proposed the following remedies:

- *First* — that the budget should be voted in the Supreme Legislative Council, in which an official should be retained.
- *Second* — that a committee of England to which non-official might have the right of appeal; toe duty of reporting to Parliament from time to time on matters of Indian finance should be assigned to this committee; it should take cognizance of all appeals addressed to it as above, and should exercise general control over the administration of Indian expenditure.
- *Third* — that Section 55 of the Act of 1858 should be amended. This section, as it stands at present, enacts that except for preventing or repelling actual invasions of Her Majesty's Indian possessions, or under other sudden and urgent necessity, the revenues of India shall not, without the consent of both Houses of Parliament, be applicable to defray the expenses of any military operation carried on beyond the external possessions of such frontiers by Her Majesty's forces charged upon such revenues. He urged that this section should be so amended as to provide that, "except in cases of actual or threatened invasion, the revenues of India shall not be used for military operations beyond the natural frontiers of India (these frontiers being once for all defined), unless, at any rate, a part of such expenditure is put on the English estimates.

- *Fourth* — That the Legislative Councils of Madras, Bombay, Bengal, the North West Provinces (i.e. the United Provinces), the Punjab and Burma should return one member each to the Imperial Parliament. "Six men in a House of 670 would introduce no disturbing factor, while the House will be in a position to ascertain Indian public opinion on the various questions coming up before it in a constitutional manner." He pointed out that the small French and Portuguese settlements in India already enjoyed a similar privilege.
- *Fifth* — that special knowledge of finance be regarded as a necessary qualification of the Viceroy. "It would be a great advantage if the Viceroy, instead of being his own Minister for Foreign Affairs, were to be his own Finance Minister. At any rate the immediate connection with the Foreign Department should cease, the department being placed like other departments in charge of a separate member of the Executive Council."

A study of Gokhale's evidence before the Welby Commission will show a very remarkable power of analysis and criticism with regard to the existing system of affairs. His concrete proposals, which have just been considered, give ample evidence of the powers which were developing in him, and which were to bear such ample fruit later in his life.

Life in England

The experience of life in England was one of considerable strangeness from many points of view to the young Brahmin, who was orthodox in regard to the food he ate and the clothes he wore. One of his fellow-witnesses before the Commission, who was brought into very close contact with him at the time, speaks thus of him:

> 'He was exceedingly shy. That shyness was greatly enhanced by reason of finding himself in strange company. To him it was wholly a new experience to live in an English house with English ladies and gentlemen and Parsees. He was a Hindu, and though

> on board the mail steamer he had seen something of cosmopolitan life and mixed with passengers of different races and creeds, he could not have realised till he had come to live with us what was domestic life in an English suburb.'

Moreover, on his way across France, Gokhale had the misfortune to suffer an accident, which had the effect of injuring his heart. His condition became serious; but on account of his shyness and strangeness he did not for some time let anyone know that anything was wrong. Finally, however, Wacha found out about his suffering, and a doctor was consulted, who took a very serious view of Gokhale's condition, declaring indeed that unless steps were promptly taken, death would result:

> 'Mrs. Congrave, a highly polished lady residing in that house, volunteered to work as Gokhale's nurse. No sister could have nursed better; and none could have kept Gokhale so cheerful and bright all through that serious illness.'

Plague in India

During the time when he was absent in England on his work in connection with Welby Commission, Gokhale's fellow-countrymen were becoming acquainted for the first time with that terrible scourge which has done so much damage in India ever since, bubonic plague. At first the nature of this disease and the right measures to adopt for combating it were very imperfectly understood; and when the plague reached Poona certain courses of action were initiated by the D. E. Wacha authorities which led to great popular discontent.

Stringent regulations were put into force with regard to segregation, disinfection of houses, compulsory inspection of infected localities, and so forth. Moreover the very serious mistake was made of entrusting the enforcement of these new (and from the Indian point of view revolutionary and oppressive) measures to British troops, who, however well-meaning, could not be expected to understand popular prejudices and to deal with them in a tactful and sympathetic manner.

The consequence was that a loud outcry arose in Poona regarding the behaviour of the British soldiers, especially of those whose duties made it needful for them to intrude into the home-life of the people. A large number of correspondents from India, many of them gentlemen 'in a very respectable and responsible position in life, pleaders, professors and journalists', began to write to Gokhale whilst he was still in England giving him lurid details of the horrors which were happening in the city which he loved so well, and accusing the Government of Bombay of gross mismanagement in having made arrangements under which such occurrences were possible.

Gokhale unfortunately took the matter up without waiting for further proof of the reports which he had been receiving. As a result of the popular resentment in Poona two European officials had been shot on their way back from the Birthday celebrations at Government House. The news caused a great sensation in England, and certain English newspapers urged very drastic action in response to the murders. In an endeavour to counteract such proposals Gokhale made public use of the reports which he had received concerning the behaviour of the British troops which had led indirectly to the murders. The Government of Bombay took the matter up, and instituted an enquiry, which did not substantiate the accusation which Gokhale's friends had made. Thereupon Gokhale's agitation at home was stigmatised as malicious and false.

Apology Incident

This was the atmosphere in which the young statesman, who had deserved so well of his country by his work before the Commission, returned to India. At Aden he was met by letters from some of the friends in Poona who had given him the false information, beseeching him not to reveal their identity to the Government. Gokhale had already decided to bear the whole responsibility for the affair. When he reached Poona he found himself unable to obtain the support of witnesses to the statements which he had made on his friends' authority in England. These friends, 'with the exception', K. Natarajan tells us, of Pandita Ramabai, failed him in what he called 'his dark hour of trial'. Consequently he decided that the only honourable thing which he could do under the circumstances was to submit a full and unconditional apology to Government. In this decision Ranade and other friends upon whom he relied strongly supported him.

The apology created a tremendous sensation in India. It greatly increased the respect in which Gokhale was held by those whose respect was really worth having. In reputable and responsible quarters he came to be regarded as a man who put truth and honour above expediency or popularity; and who was therefore to be relied upon in the future. The moral courage which the apology had demanded was appreciated at its right worth.

On the other hand, however, the 'extremist' section of Indian opinion greeted the incident with a chorus of execration and insult. Gokhale was taunted with having betrayed the national cause, with having trickled to the foreign oppressor. His honourable straightforwardness was interpreted as despicable and time-serving cowardice. So fierce was the feeling aroused against him, in spite of his great services to the national cause in connection with the Welby Commission, that it appeared that his public career inevitably was at an end. There could be no future for one who had incurred, however honourably, such universal detestation amongst the rank and file of his fellow-countrymen.

Gokhale felt his position exceedingly keenly. His nature was a very sensitive one; and criticism, especially harsh and unjust criticism, always caused him great agony of mind. One of his friends has said of him:

> 'An adverse remark, casually made, was sufficient to upset his mind and to deprive him of sleep for the whole night'.

Yet he refused to give way before the storm which had broken, upon him. To one who reproached him, though in a friendly-manner, on account, of the ampleness of the apology, and the humiliation which (in the speaker's opinion) it had brought upon the country, he replied, with sorrow and dejection, but at the same time with a staunch determination:

> 'You can scarcely have an idea how, sorry I feel to hear from you that my conduct has brought no little

> humiliation on my country. I accept that as your frank and honest opinion, and I take it for what it is worth. But I tell you that you will, I hope, live to see of a day when I shall cover my country with glory by way of compensation for the wrong which I am alleged to have done to her; and then critics of your type, who are now running me to death, will be converted into my admirers.'

As one of Gokhale's Indian biographers has observed:

> Thoughtful people will agree that under the circumstances he was fully justified both in giving the apology, and that the step he took was the noblest action of his life. Years hence, when the political questions of these days are forgotten or finally disposed of, this sacrifice of his position and prestige in the eyes of his countrymen, and his risking a complete voluntary eclipse as a public man, will be counted as his greatest title to the-respect of posterity.

The Effect of the Apology Incident upon Gokhale

The incident had a decided effect upon Gokhale's character. On the one hand he became more than ever careless of popularity. He learnt to judge questions on their merits, and to take action accordingly, irrespective of what public opinion might or might not say. He became more self-reliant, perhaps more reserved. On the other hand he learned to test his evidence more thoroughly before committing himself. He became more cautious and prudent.

The apology incident raised him both with the Government and his own self. To the former his views thereafter were bound to be peculiarly deserving of consideration as proceeding from a man who understood his business and his honour no less. To his own self this incident imparted the strength to stand alone against the world; If only he had the support of his own convictions.

One who knew Gokhale very well, and was in the closest touch with him for a number of years, has told the present writer that the meticulous sense of honour which Gokhale showed in this affair was characteristic of him in many different relationships.

Both in public speeches and in the articles which he wrote for the press, he was always extremely careful to give credit to his opponents for the best possible intentions, and to represent their point of view, not in the worst light possible, but in the best. If in his personal relationships with other men he ever felt that he had acted wrongly, he would take especial pains afterwards to set things right. On one occasion he had been somewhat short-tempered with his private secretary in connection with some business connected with the Press managed by the Servants of India Society. Very late that same night, when the person in question was asleep in his room, Gokhale came to his door and with unaffected humility asked his pardon for his rudeness to him earlier in the day.

Election to the Imperial Legislative Council

A fairly in 1902 ill-health led (afterwards Sir) Pherozeshah Mehta to resign his seat on the Imperial Legislative Council. This seat, which was filled by election from among the non-official members of the Bombay Legislative Council, was conferred upon Gokhale by a unanimous vote; and thus at the early age he entered upon his career as the chief representative of his country in the central organ of Government.

From that time till his death, a period of thirteen years, he worked incessantly in this capacity of imperial legislator at his task of expressing and rendering operative the viewpoint of enlightened, Indian opinion. Under the constitutional arrangements then in existence touch of his criticism of things as they were, and much also of his constructive suggestion for the future; had to be packed into the speeches delivered from year to year on the imperial Indian budget; and in consequence it will be found that a study of these speeches constitutes the best method of discovering what the mind of Gokhale really was regarding major national issues, and how he proposed to improve the existing condition of things In his country.

Budget Speeches

These annual budget speeches came to be more and more important for the country as a whole; for the spirit in which they were delivered, and the constructive suggestions for the future with which they abounded; made them an invaluable Indication of the way in which the Indian Government must move, if in a time of growing extremism it was to retain the goodwill and cooperation of the responsible sections of Indian opinion.

Gokhale was to the last the most brilliant member of the Imperial Legislative Council, and was popularly called - the Leader of the Indian Opposition, though he himself did not consider that his duty was merely to oppose Government, but that it was to put before Government the Indian point of view on every question. His annual budget speech was a treat to which everybody, both friend and opponent, looked forward, the one with delight, and the other with fear.

An answer had to be given to his arguments, and it is not everybody who could do it at a moment's notice, if at all. On one occasion Lord Kitchener privately asked him the points on which he wished to touch so far as military expenditure was concerned; and out of consideration for the great soldier, who was no debater, Gokhale did not emphasise certain points as much as he would have liked to. His budget speeches always bore their fruit in the succeeding years' budgets. He was always on the side of retrenchment, and did not want Government to take more from the tax-payers than was absolutely necessary.

This is the opinion of one who has since risen to high office as a legislator and administrator, concerning the significance of Gokhale's budget speeches.

Another well-known representative of responsible Indian opinion speaks as follows:

> Gokhale's entrance into the Viceroy's Council opens a new chapter of usefulness in his life, and some of his greatest triumphs were achieved there. His first budget speech delivered there, on the 26th March, 1902, came as a revelation to everyone in the country, official and non-official alike. Nothing like it has ever been known before in the history of Indian political life. Since then he has delivered twelve Budget speeches, and they have been looked forward to

> annually. As far back as 1904, during his very early years in the Viceroy's Council, Brodrick, then Secretary of State, wrote to the Governor General in Council to give effect as far as possible to Gokhale's suggestions in forming the estimates for the following year; and the Budget of 1905-06 was in a real sense his triumph. Even the foremost of his political opponents, Lord Curzon, was led to say, "God has endowed him with extraordinary abilities, and he has freely placed them at the disposal of his country," and counted it a pleasure to cross swords with him as a foreman worthy of his steel.... Lord Minto, having heard the Budget speech of 1906, perhaps the greatest of all those great speeches, said that even in England there were very few men oil the front benches capable of such an effort. Sir Edward Baker said that he could wish for nothing better than that Gokhale should succeed him as finance member. Sir Guy Fleetwood Wilson spoke of the Budget debates in the Viceroy's Council, in the absence of Gokhale, as the play of Hamlet with Hamlet left out. Sir James Meston compared him to the great Gladstone in possessing the rare and happy knack of making facts and figures live and speak with a deep human voice. The Right Hon. E. S. Montagu.... writing about Gokhale says, His grasp of things, both in essentials and in details, was not the least valuable of the assets that he brought to the service of his country. It is not too much to say that his annual contribution to the debate on the Budget proposals in India was one of the outstanding features of the proceedings of the Viceroy's Council, and was eagerly awaited, even by those who could not see eye to eye with him in his criticisms.

These opinions are here quoted in order that, at the outset of a consideration of the work done by Gokhale as a member of the Central Legislature of India, it may be realised how profoundly that work impressed both his fellow-countrymen and English statesmen who came into contact with him. The fact that he was always in opposition, and therefore had no opportunity to put his principles into practical demonstration through actual legislation, may make his manifold activities during the next thirteen years appear unfruitful.

As a matter of fact, however, those activities had a decisive effect upon the future of his country, not only through the financial reforms introduced as a result of his annual budget speeches, and not only through the influence which he exercised upon the constitutional changes connected with the names of Lord Minto and Lord Morley, but even more through the demonstration which they afforded, spread over so many years, of the fact that, given democratic conditions of government in India, a type of Indian statesman will emerge who is admirably equipped to utilise those institutions, in a spirit of constructiveness and of moderation/for the well-being of his country.

Later Years and Demise

Gokhale continued to be politically active through the last years of his life. This included extensive travelling abroad. In addition to his 1908 trip to England, he also visited South Africa in 1912, where Mahatma Gandhi was working to improve conditions for the Indian minority living there. Meanwhile, he continued to be involved in the Servants of India Society, the Congress, and the Legislative Council while constantly advocating the advancement of Indian education. All these stresses took their toll, however, Gokhale died on Feb 19, 1915 at forty nine years of age.

2

National Leader in the Making

A meeting was called at Poona, in order to give evidence of the fact that public opinion supported Lord Reay, who was a very popular governor, in his refusal to go back upon his word: and also in order to deprecate any interference with the matter from England, as there had been signs that such was contemplated. The ablest speech prepared for the meeting was that of Gopal Krishna Gokhale, who was then a young man of 22. It was taken as read at the meeting itself; but (in accordance with what apparently became Gokhale's practice on all important occasions) it had been written out in full, and was handed to the reporters of the Times of India and the Bombay Gazette, which newspapers gave it very warm praise for its force and clearness. The affair served to bring Gokhale into public notice, with the result that in the next year (1889) he was asked to be one of the speakers at the Indian National Congress.

First Public Speech

Gokhale's first public speech was never actually delivered, though it brought him considerable credit. A large meeting of the citizens of Poona had been convened in order to support the action of Lord Reay in regard to a notorious case of official bribery. Lord Reay, the then Governor of the Bombay Presidency, had given an undertaking in connection with this case that any subordinate officials who gave evidence which might be incriminating to themselves should be given an amnesty from any legal penalties to which they might thus lay themselves open. The evidence given under this guarantee was, however, so damaging, and revealed a corruption so widespread, that an agitation was raised in certain quarters that some of the guilty parties who came under the amnesty should be forced to retire from public service.

Work in Indian National Congress

The Congress, which had been founded a few years previously in order to supply a means for the voicing of Indian aspirations after constitutional advance, was at this time a strictly decorous body of moderate reformers; but its deliberations were already beginning to have a definite significance for the awakening nationhood of the country; and it was a great honour for a young man of 23 to be asked to take part in them, even though at first the part assigned to him was a very minor one. However, in the Congress of 1890 he had a much more important function to fulfil, as he was asked to support the resolution on the Reduction of the Salt Duty. His speech on that occasion was the first blow struck in a long crusade, which only ended with the triumph of 1906 when the tax was reduced to a minimum figure.

From this time forward Gokhale was one of the most important personalities of the Indian National Congress, In 1892, at Allahabad, he took up the cudgels on behalf of another cause which remained a heartfelt concern with him throughout the rest of his life, namely the Indianisation of the public services. He was now rapidly becoming known throughout India as one who brought to the national cause not merely immense powers of industry and of detailed application, but a deep moral enthusiasm, which can best perhaps be compared to that which had distinguished John Bright, the groat tribune of the common people of England. Gokhale was not a mere machine for the digestion of statistics and the manipulation of Blue Books; but he was one who saw the issues of national emancipation in terms of right and wrong, and who possessed the capacity for imparting to his fellow-countrymen his own ardent moral convictions on all such issues.

Capacity for Hero-worship

Ranade One of the great forces in Gokhale's life at this time was his capacity for hero-worship. His relations with Ranade have already been noticed. Those relations were to continue to exercise a great influence upon the younger man till Ranade's death, and were to leave a permanent impression upon Gokhale's character. In this connection it will be of advantage to quote some memorable words spoken by Gokhale on a later occasion about his friend:

> The younger men who came in personal contact with him felt as in my presence, not only uttering "nothing base", but afraid even of making unworthy thoughts while in his company. The only other man who has exercised a similar influence on me in my experience is Dadabhai Naoroji. Among Ranade's great qualities one of the most prominent was his utter, absolute unselfishness. As I have already told you, he was incessantly several fields, but never did he seek the least recognition, getting, or not getting, credit for this or that. Indeed nothing pleased him more than to do his work — not only political, but almost of every kind — from behind somebody else. His great anxiety was to get more and more men to be interested in and associated with the work. I do not think anybody ever heard Ranade say, "I did this, I did that." It was as though the first person singular did not exist in his vocabulary. The felinity with which he sought to discipline himself almost to the last days of his life was another of his great qualities. By nature he was very sensitive, feeling keenly injustice or meanness in any shape or form; but his constant effort to discipline himself enabled him to preserve his calmness even under the most trying circumstances. The normal state of his mind was indeed one of quiet cheerfulness, arising from a consciousness of work well done, and from humble faith in the purpose of Providence. But even when he was seriously displeased with anything,

or disappointed with anyone, or suffered inwardly owing to other causes, no one who did not know him intimately could detect any trace of that suffering on his face. And never did any one — not even those who stood nearest to him — hear him utter a word of complaint against those who might have done him personal injury. He insisted on having all attacks on him in newspapers carefully read out to him. He was constantly before the public in one capacity or another, and his views, therefore, came in for a good deal of criticism — friendly and unfriendly almost from day to day. The appreciative notices that appeared he did not always read through. I know — because I sometimes had to read the papers to him—he never read them himself, his sight being defective. But all unfriendly criticism he made a point of hearing. He wanted to know if there was any idea therein that he could accept. And in any case, even if there was pain in hearing all that was said, that pain itself had its disciplinary value.

One more great quality of his I would like to mention, and that was his readiness to help all who sought his help — and especially those who were weak and oppressed. He was accessible to all, even the humblest, at all hours of the day. No one ever wrote to him without receiving a reply. He listened patiently to everyone, whether he was able to help or not. This indeed was to him a part of his practical religion. After, the Amraoti Congress of 1897, when we were returning to this part of the country, he and I were, for one night, the only occupants of our carriage. At about 4 a.m. I was suddenly roused by some singing in the carriage and on opening my eyes I saw Ranade sitting up and singing two verses of Tukaram again and again, and striking his hands together by way of accompaniment. . . . The verses were these: "He who be friends the weary and the persecuted — he is a true

> saint, and God Himself is to be found there"; and, "Be you humble and seek the favour of saints. If you want to meet God, this is an easy way."
>
> As I sat listening to these verses, I could not help realising how constant was Ranade's endeavour to live up to this teaching, and how simple and yet how glorious was the rule of life that it inculcated. It was a rich moment in my own life. The scene indeed will never fade from my memory.

A man's true nature is to be known from his enthusiasms. The ideals are the real man. In his unbounded love and reverence for his guru, as shown in these quotations, we see into the soul of Gokhale far more clearly than is possible through the reading of any number of speeches delivered by him. He was a man into whose life had come a great personal influence of goodness, self-sacrifice and devotion, a man who had seen and valued aright the worth of these things, and a man who was determined to live his own in accordance with the ideal thus set before him.

Dadabhai Naoroji

Ranade's personal influence was by far the most important single element which went to the making of Gokhale; but he had other heroes upon whom he tried to model his own character. Chief amongst these was Dadabhai Naoroji, who as member for Central Finsbury in the British House of Commons did a great work in bringing the needs of India before the English people. When Gokhale was 27 years of age a great demonstration was organised at Poona in honour of Naoroji, who was then in India, and was to preside at the National Congress. Gokhale threw himself heart and soul into the work of preparing for this function, and was so eager to be of service to the great man that, as a sort of unofficial aide-de-camp, he drove to the meeting on the coach-box of the carriage in which Naoroji rode. Many years afterwards, on the occasion of the celebration of Dadabhai Naoroji's eighty-first birthday, Gokhale spoke of him as follows:

> How is it that Dadabhai Naoroji has in the course of time attained in the hearts of millions of his

countrymen, without distinction of race or creed, a place which rulers of men might envy, and which in its character is more like the influence which great teachers of humanity have exercised on those whose thoughts and hopes and lives they have lifted to a higher plane? To us he is not merely a great political leader — the foremost of our time, and for the last half century. It is because he embodies in his personal all that is high and noble in our land, and stands as the sacred representative of our national aspirations for the future, that our deepest devotion is given to him. He had attained this position before many of us were born, and few are those among us whose earliest awakening to the claims of nationality has not been influenced by his teaching and his example. Eighty years ago, when Dadabhai Naoroji first saw the light of day, if any one had ventured to predict that he would one day stand forth as the most trusted spokesman of a united India, such a man would have been set down as a dreamer of wild dreams. In 1825 the power of the Marathas had just been overthrown; and though the first generation of British administrators, foremost among whom will always stand the honoured name of Elphinstone, had taken in hand the work of consolidation in a spirit of wise and liberal statesmanship, the people on this side were naturally sullen and discontented, and not without a vague expectation that their own Government would return some day. Western education had then hardly begun — the Charter Act of 1833 was still some way off — and the idea of the different parts of this great country drawing together in a common feeling and a common aspiration could have been no more realised even mentally than is the idea of a united Asia realised by us today.

'I think it is to the infinite honour of British rule and the wise and large-hearted policy followed in the administration of the country — especially in matters

> of education — that what was then almost difficult to conceive has now already become a fact and a reality. And to Dadabhai Naoroji and the earliest band of Indian reformers that worked with him belongs the credit of understanding aright the true meaning of the new order of things and the possibilities that it implied for their countrymen, and of throwing themselves heart and soul into the work of realising those possibilities in practice. Since then one generation of workers has entirely disappeared from the scene, and of the next only a few are left — may they long remain with us!—to guide us. But Dadabhai Naoroji has all through remained in the forefront of the movement, and neither age nor disappointment has chilled his ardour, nor has absence diminished his hold on his countrymen....'

It is noteworthy, with regard to both the addresses quoted above on Gokhale's heroes, that when, at the prime of his powers, the great statesman looked back upon the influences which had made him, he chose out for especial mention qualities which may be spoken of as spiritual rather than mental.

It was not so much their ability as statesmen, administrators or politicians which had appealed to him, as the fact that they were marked by a type of character which he describes as 'saintly' — that in contact with their spirit he had come to acquire a higher ideal of what human nature might mean in 'purity, simplicity, gentleness, self-denial.' In the midst of all his intense political activity, and equipped as he was with a keen practical intellect, and with a magnificent capacity for hard, slogging, detailed work, there was always a deeper side to Gokhale's personality, a life of the spirit which comes to the fore on occasions such as those instanced above, where he is speaking out from his heart the meaning to him of the great men whom he looked upon as his guides and preceptors.

G. G. Agarkar

Another great formative influence in Gokhale's life was his association with Agarkar. This gentleman was not only a distinguished educationalist, but was also a social reformer of deep convictions, and a journalist who exercised a great deal of influence in the Maratha country. In this capacity he had first written for the Kesari of which journal he had been the main editor; but the increasing influence of B. G. Tilak upon the Kesari; and his opposition to many of Agarkar's views with regard to social reform, finally led the latter to start the Sudharak, and to retire from his connection with the Kesari. In the control of the Sudharak he and Gokhale became very closely associated, Gokhale writing the English portion of the paper, whilst Agarkar took the major part, which was in Marathi.

Gokhale's articles generally dealt with political questions, whilst those written by Agarkar were mainly concerned with social reform, on which subject he wrote with extraordinary force and cogency. Occasionally, however, Gokhale wrote the Marathi portion the both spoke and wrote his mother-tongue excellently), whilst Agarkar wrote the English articles. The Sudharak had at first a hard struggle to pay its way; for in those days social reform was anything but a popular cause. Later, however, it did much better. Gokhale's connection with the paper lasted for some four years; and there can be no doubt that his close association with a man of the fearless outspokenness, and the contempt for popular prejudices which marked Agarkar, had a great influence upon the development of his character.

Social Reforms

Gokhale himself did not feel able for a long time to take any leading part in connection with the movement for social reform. In his own life there had been a tragedy. Shortly after his father's death and when still a young lad, he had been married, by his uncle's instrumentality, to a girl who was afterwards found to be suffering from an incurable disease, and who could not be his real wife. His relatives pressed him to take a second wife; and after much hesitation, he consented to do so.

Though he had obtained the permission of his first wife to this step, and though, it was taken at a time in his life when he had apparently not begun to consider the rights and wrongs of such questions, he felt for long afterwards that this episode precluded him from taking the leaden movements for social reform. There came a time, however, when in spite of the consciousness of having thus committed, as one of his Indian biographers remarks, 'a sin against society', he felt himself impelled to speak" out strongly with regard to the treatment of the depressed classes amongst his fellow-countrymen: and to point out the inconsistency of the persistence of such treatment in view of the resentment felt throughout India towards the similar treatment of Indians in South Africa. On one occasion he gave great offence to orthodox Hindus by partaking of refreshments at the headquarters of a Poona Mission, but he paid no attention to the agitation which was raised at the time, or to the social penalties which were threatened against him.

Moreover, he was always a staunch supporter, by sympathy and personal counsel and influence, of anyone who felt called upon to take a decided stand against reactionary opinions or customs.

Relations with B. G. Tilak

It was largely with regard to questions of social reform that the famous estrangement developed between Gokhale and his notable contemporary and rival in the affections of the Maratha people, B. G. Tilak. Tilak was the older man; and Gokhale used to say that his original decision to join the Deccan Education Society and to devote his life to the service of his country had been due to his admiration for Tilak rather than to his admiration for Agarkar, though later he was destined to come into such close and cordial relationships with the latter. Tilak was a man of great personal force of character; but he was a very hard man to work with as a colleague, and his views steadily developed in a direction contrary to those of Gokhale and Agarkar, especially in regard to questions of political agitation and of social reform.

After Agarkar withdrew from the Kesari and founded the Sudharak, there were frequent 'battles royal' between the two Maratha leaders in the columns of their respective journals; and matters became very strained in the Deccan Education Society, and in the counsels of the Fergusson College. It was a great relief to the other members of the society when, in 1890, as has already been recorded, Tilak decided to break his connection with it, taking with him Namjoshi. After his resignation, Tilak began rapidly to gravitate towards the orthodox side of things. This greatly increased his popularity; for orthodoxy in regard to questions of social reform was still very definitely the popular point of view. The public of Poona had distinctly sided with Tilak over the question of his resignation from the society; and he soon began to exercise an increasingly significant influence in regard to political affairs. His attitude became one of intransigent opposition to Government; and later, as is well-known, he coquetted with doctrines of physical force in a manner which led eventually to his imprisonment.

The contrast between these two leaders, Gokhale and Tilak, became more and more emphasised as the years went by. Gokhale believed in social reform, and in constitutional methods for the winning of a better and freer future for his country. Tilak became more and more orthodox and extreme. In consequence Tilak was always, at any rate amongst his Maratha fellow-countrymen, the more popular figure. So in fact he remains today; but, none the less, the .methods of Gokhale are the methods in accordance with which the new India is being created before our eyes.

In consequence of his popularity with the rank and file of the Hindu citizens of Poona it was generally true that on those not-infrequent occasions when a direct issue was joined between Gokhale and Tilak, the latter won what appeared to be a victory. He succeeded in capturing the Sarvajanik Sabha, by adroit manipulation of its elections. He made great capital out of Gokhale's apology to Government in connection with the affair of the Poona murders. He became the leader of a party in the Congress which it was increasingly difficult for Gokhale to control; and right at the end of Gokhale's life, after Tilak's return from jail, he was responsible for the so-called 'compromise controversy' which may be said to have broken Gokhale's heart.

In various other relations the divergence of spirit and policy between the two leaders was made more and more definitely apparent as the years went by. Perhaps it could scarcely have been otherwise. A man of strong views who essays to lead a people still largely uneducated along the paths both of social reform and of well-consolidated constitutional advance, is bound to find that he rouses opposition on the part of those who prefer methods less radical as regards Social questions, and more precipitate in the field of politics. It was Gokhale's misfortune that the protagonist of this inevitable reaction was one of his own old friends and colleagues, and a man for whom he had himself entertained in early days a deep personal admiration.

Hindu-Muslim Relationship

In no connection was the difference between these two great Marathas more marked than with regard to the perennial problem of Hindu-Muslim relationships. Tilak being both an orthodox Hindu and a strong Maratha nationalist, became inevitably more and more definitely an anti-Muslim. The Maratha State had been up, in the seventeenth century, on a strong anti-Muslim nationalism. In the course of constant wars, Shivaji, the founder of that State, had proved more and more conclusive his own and his people's right to repudiate all Muslim pretensions to overlordship. During the eighteenth century the Maratha armies had gone out eastward, northward and southward, to the conquest of the Muslim power.

They had shattered the great Mughal Empire into pieces, and had ruled its former provinces. There had sprung up amongst them a fierce contempt for the Muslim system of religion and conduct. For a couple of generations after the British conquest, this spirit had lain dormant; but with the Maratha renaissance which came in the last two decades of the nineteenth century, it began to reawaken. The focus of danger was the celebration of the great Muhammadan festival of the Muharram, in which an imposing procession took place through the streets of Poona. In the old days the Hindus had freely joined in the celebration of Muharram; but the rising tide of Maratha nationality made the orthodox Hindu party more and more restive at such fraternisation, and more and more insistent in their opposition to the slaughter of the cow — the Hindu sacred animal — by Muslims.

Tilak became the protagonist of this new anti-Muslim sentiment, and began to organise and develop the worship of the Hindu god, Ganpati, in opposition to the Muharram celebrations, exhorting the Hindus to take no share in these, but to concentrate oil, a revived worship of Ganpati. This advice was eagerly listened to, especially by the orthodox upper classes; and it soon became apparent that the movement had in it the seeds of a dangerous estrangement between the Muslim and Hindu communities. Men of the type of Gokhale, who thought for India as a whole, and knew that the most pressing of all her problems was that of a permanent and solid reconciliation between the two communities, beheld Tilak's activities in this respect with the greatest concern.

Gokhale was always insistent upon the necessity for bringing about a good understanding between Hindus and Muslims, of creating and fostering opportunities for their friendly cooperation, instead of emphasising their differences. He strongly opposed all attempts to create a Hindu class-consciousness in opposition to Islam. The gulf was already wide enough. The memories of ancient conflicts must be allowed to die. Every agency must be encouraged which enabled Hindus and Muslims to work together harmoniously for the good of India as a whole.

Here again Gokhale was taking the unpopular side, and of necessity found himself more and more definitely estranged from his old colleague.

If Ranade, Naoroji and Agarkar acted as great positive influences In Gokhale's development (and to these must be added another famous name, that of Sir Pherozeshah Mehta, the Parsee leader for whom Gokhale always entertained a profound admiration, and with whom he declared he would rather stand alone than be in agreement with the rest of the world) Tilak formed an almost equally decisive influence of a negative significance. The two men seemed to be driven asunder by a disruptive force. Increasing extremism on the part of Tilak led to a deeper realisation of the meaning and value of constitutionalism on the part of Gokhale. As Tilak's orthodoxy grew more narrow, so Gokhale perceived more clearly the necessity for basing India's welfare upon a genuine and widespread development of liberal-mindedness, enlightenment and sterling character.

As Tilak found himself emphasising more and more the ideal of Maratha nationality, founded upon a revival of opposition to Islam, Gokhale found himself compelled more and more energetically to plead for a comprehensiveness of spirit which should be willing to sink all communal differences on behalf of Indian nationality. As Tilak centred his orthodoxy of Hindu belief, and his revival of the Maratha spirit, around a new symbolism, in the worship of the image of Ganpati, Gokhale was more and more effectually impressed with the need for dispensing: with such symbolism, and for making the Congress — and later the new Councils of the Minto-Morley reforms — the real focus of Indian nationality.

Finally, as Tilak's popularity grew amongst the rank and file of a people still largely uneducated, Gokhale perceived ever more clearly the emptiness of mere popularity -- which he was too great a man ever to covet for its own sake — and the supreme necessity of a widespread system of popular education.

3

Legislator in Bombay

Famine Problems

Those years were a period of famine, and of consequent financial depression; and Gokhale made many suggestions in the Legislative Council with regard to methods by which the famine administration of Government might be improved, and the difficulties consequent upon famine in the general work of Government overcome. In fact, Gokhale's work as a legislator begins from the early months of 1899, when he was elected as representative of the Municipalities of the Central Division of the Bombay Presidency to the Bombay Legislative Council. He remained a member of this body, for some two years, during which his ability made a marked impression in Western India.

He had himself had experience of village life, and he regarded himself as custodian of the rights of the peasants, and as champion of their cause in the terrible trial through which they were passing. He criticised the existing system of relief, on the ground that labour was too greatly concentrated on large relief works. Such large works give a great opportunity for the outbreak of epidemic diseases. They also require that the destitute people shall travel over large distances in order to reach the centre of relief; and, amongst the ignorant and unprogressive classes who suffer first from a famine, the consequent home-sickness, leading to frequent absence from work, is a serious obstacle to the effectiveness of the relief. He also maintained that the Famine Code, for all its wisdom and beneficence, was too rigidly administered. There was a tendency to exact compliance with standards of work which were often beyond the capacity of the enfeebled workers; and, if the standards were not complied with, petty officials were apt to resort to fining, and to other disciplinary measures, which seriously interfered with the popularity and effectiveness of the relief given.

He also maintained that the Bombay Government had been too niggardly with regard to the giving of gratuitous relief, and in this respect had lagged seriously behind other provincial Governments. Gokhale never ceased to take a deep interest in famine-relief; and to the end of his life he continued the champion of the voiceless multitudes who are the chief sufferers from famines. Except perhaps with regard to his plea for enhanced liberality in the bestowing of gratuitous relief, in respect to which the evils of pauperisation are now felt to be more serious than he recognised, his main contentions have become axioms of famine-policy. Relief-works should be small and scattered, rather than large and concentrated. They should be so placed as to enable as large a proportion of workers as possible to return to their own homes every evening.

There should be a wise measure of elasticity and leniency in regard to the exacting of given standards of work; and harsh disciplining of the workers should be sedulously avoided, as liable to lead to desertions and consequently to enhanced destitution.

Furthermore the spirit in which famine is now fought — a spirit which makes the organisation and carrying through of a great famine-campaign in India one of the most beneficent activities ever engaged in by any government — may in no small degree be traced to Gokhale's persistent advocacy of the principle that the fearful tragedy of a famine should be regarded and dealt with as a great human problem, rather than as a matter merely of demonstrative machinery and technique. Here, as in many other relations, Gokhale's strong sense of human values made his work for his country a genuine labour of love.

Land Alienation Bill

Closely connected with the question of famine in the mind of Gokhale was the question of the land-revenue. Here again a highly complicated and technical economic problem became for him a matter of intense human interest; for he knew from his own experience what is meant in a village home by such stark facts as agricultural indebtedness and the incidence of the land-tax. During the time when he was a member of the Bombay Legislative Council a Land Alienation Bill was brought by Government before that Council. The purpose of the Bill was thoroughly sound — to provide the beginnings of a solution for the very serious problem constituted by the hopeless indebtedness of a large proportion of the peasantry who had fallen completely under the power of the village moneylenders.

It was believed by Government that one of the chief reasons for this indebtedness was the power possessed by the peasants to mortgage their lands — often on exceedingly unfavourable terms. The result of their possession of this power was that the land was rapidly passing out of the hands of the peasants into those of the money-lenders, and that the peasants were tending to become mere tenants on an extremely insecure tenure of the lands which had been their ancestors' and their own. In a great number of cases, indeed, the position of the peasants was worse even than this; for their indebtedness was so great that they had fallen into the position of land-serfs, working upon fields which had been their own, for a miserable allowance of food, barely sufficient to keep body and soul together, this being all that the money-lenders, who took all the rest of the produce of the land in payment of their debts, would allow to them.

Government proposed to render this miserable subjection of the peasantry impossible, by restricting the power of the owner of land to mortgage his land and by allowing him to borrow only on the security of the year's crop. All lands which had been forfeited to Government on account of the inability of the holder to pay his land tax, and all waste lands in future to be brought under cultivation, whether through the progress of irrigation or in other ways, were to be granted by Government on a new kind of inalienable tenure, which, it was believed, would greatly strengthen the position of the peasantry against the money-lenders.

The problems which the Land Alienation Bill were intended to solve had become more than usually pressing, owing to a succession of famine years; and the position of the peasants in Western India was indubitably very bad. Furthermore, anyone opposing the Bill laid himself open at once to the odious suggestion that he was an agent of the money-lenders, endeavouring to secure them in a position from which they were able to enslave the peasantry. The Government case was made out with great force and ability.

The member of the Bombay Government who introduced the Bill in the Council had argued powerfully for the Government view that it was the existing fixity of tenure, and the power of transfer, which had reduced large numbers of the land-owning peasantry to the position first of rack-rented tenants and then almost to that of serfs. The Survey and Settlement Commissioner, with a wide-reaching knowledge of the conditions under which the peasants were living, and a genuine desire to improve their lot, had expressed his emphatic opinion that the only way of doing so was to restrict their powers of alienating their land.

None the less there was great public indignation against the Bill. A large number of petitions protesting that it was grossly unjust to the peasantry were sent in from political bodies such as the Bombay Presidency Association, the Sarvajanik Sabha and the Deccan Sabha. Meetings were held in the rural districts all over the Presidency and resolutions against the Bill were passed and forwarded to Government.

Gokhale's Opposition to the Bill

In this agitation Gokhale took a very prominent part. He realised as thoroughly as anyone the miserable condition of the peasants under existing circumstances. But he maintained that to seek to improve that condition by lessening the peasants' rights over their ancestral fields was not only morally unjustifiable, but was a gross betrayal of their true interests. The problem of agricultural indebtedness could only be solved by genuinely constructive statesmanship. The peasants must not be deprived of their rights in this way, but must be set in a position which would make it possible for them to stand on their own feet and to defend their rights for themselves, because they were economically independent.

The effect of the proposed Bill would indeed be a disastrous weakening of the peasantry, instead of a strengthening, since it would enable the Government to confiscate land on account of non-payment of revenue for only one year. There would thus come about a wholesale process of nationalisation of the land, under which Government would be able to become the proprietor for a small fraction of the market value of the land.

His Speech

> Some passages from Gokhale's speech delivered on August 23, 1901, at a meeting of the Bombay Legislative Council, Poona will serve to indicate the grounds upon which he based his opposition to the Bill:
>
> The only party whose position is improved by the Bill are the Government themselves; I do not mean to say that the framers of the Bill have this object in view. But that cannot alter the fact that this will be the result of the proposed legislation. In the first place... the Bill constitutes an emphatic assertion of the principle of State-landlordism, and this is bound to have far-reaching consequences. The Bill means a nationalisation of forfeited lands, which alters completely the character of the land-tenure in the Presidency....
>
> The wide discretionary powers which Government proposes to take under the Bill will enable them whenever they like — though this is not desired at present — to grant short leases or take land for public purposes without any compensation, or allot it to whomsoever they please. This is a real danger, because the tendency of revenue officers generally is to put the widest possible interpretation on the powers of Government, for the purpose of enhancing the Government revenue in every possible way.

Does anyone imagine that a measure of such far-reaching tendencies would have been introduced in England and rushed through Parliament with so much precipitation in spite of the unanimous protests of the people? And I submit that the deliberation which becomes in England a duty of Government, owing to the power of the electors should also be recognised by the British Government in India as a duty under a sense of self-restraint. What is the position here today? We, the elected members of this Council, are absolutely unanimous in resisting this Bill, and though our voting power is not large enough under the Constitution of this Council to prevent the passing of any measure which Government are deter mined to carry, we represent, when we are unanimous, a more force which it is not wise to ignore. For better or worse you have introduced the elective element into your Councils, and according to your own English ideas, you must now accept us as speaking not for ourselves individually, but in the name of those who have sent us here. And if a standing majority has been secured to Government under the Constitution, its real purpose, I take it, is not to enable Government to ride roughshod over our unanimous expression of opinion, but to prevent the non-official members from combining and overthrowing anything that Government may have done. This, I submit is the only true interpretation of the present Constitution of this Council.

Nothing can fill us with greater sadness than this spectacle of Government trying to any a measure in such haste and without proper deliberation — a measure that is bitterly resented by the agriculturalists, that has roused the apprehensions of the money-lenders, and that is condemned by the educated classes with one voice and in no uncertain terms. Is it fair; is it wise that Government should reduce us, the elected members, to a position of such utter

> helplessness that our united appeal should not secure even a brief postponement for a measure of such great importance?

His Rebuttal of the Accusation of Supporting the Money-lenders

The same speech delivered by Gokhale on this occasion, against the Land Alienation Bill of the Bombay Government, contained another notable passage, which throws light on the manner in which Gokhale felt himself called to be the defender of the common people, and shows how bitterly he had felt the accusation that his opposition to the Bill had been prompted merely by a narrow-minded and corrupt support of the money-lenders:

> I have with regret seen it suggested by some of the official supporters of the measure that the educated classes are not really in touch with, and do not understand, the true wishes and feelings of the great body of agriculturalists in this matter, and that their opinion on this Bill is not entitled to any weight. Such a suggestion, I submit with due deference, is inaccurate as a statement of fact and questionable in point of taste. How would these gentlemen like it, if we turned round and said, what do these Collectors and Assistant Collectors really understand of the true feelings of villagers? When they happen to go to a village, in the course of their official duties, what actually takes place is this: They pitch their tent at some distance from the place, unless there is a traveller's bungalow anywhere near, make a few enquiries of the village or taluka officials that are always in attendance, and visit, perhaps, a few spots in the neighbourhood. Their knowledge of the vernaculars no more qualifies them to enter into a free conversation with the villagers than does the English of Macaulay and Johnson, which we study, enable us to understand without difficulty the vigorous language of a British or Irish soldier. Meanwhile, it is the interest of the village officials that as few complaints should reach these officers as

possible and that they should go away well pleased; and the termination of the visit of inspection is regarded with feelings of genuine relief. I think such a way of putting the matter has in it just that amount of truth which makes the whole description look plausible. But I feel bound to say that it is grossly unfair to a large number of very deserving and very conscientious officers of Government. The truth is that the English officials in this country understand the ryot (the peasant) from one standpoint, and we understand him from another, and between the two our knowledge of him is certainly not the less deep or instinctive or accurate.

Then again it has been-stated that only the money-lenders and their champions are opposing this Bill, and to our great regret and astonishment we find the Secretary of State for India declaring in Parliament that it is all a money-lending agitation. Now all I can say in this matter is that there cannot be a more complete or a more grievous misapprehension of the true facts of the situation; and the circumstance that the Secretary of State should have lent the weight of his authority to this misapprehension shows to my mind how entirely out of touch those who are responsible for advising him are with the real sentiments of the agricultural population. The agitation against the Bill is emphatically not a money-lending agitation.

We are not money-lenders ourselves, and there is no earthly reason why we should champion the interests of the money-lender more than those of the ryot, even if the instinctive sympathy which all human beings feel for the weaker party in any struggle were to be withheld by us from the poor ryot. And speaking for myself, . . . I will say this: that it was my privilege to receive my lessons in Indian Economics and Indian Finance at the feet of the late Justice Ranade, who was

> always a friend of the poor ryot, and who, it is well known, greatly interested himself in the passing and the subsequent successful administration of the Deccan Agriculturalists Relief Act. It is not therefore possible, unless I am prepared to play false to the teachings of my departed master, that in any agrarian discussion I should range myself against the interest of the ryot, or be swayed by a special feeling of partiality for the money-lender. No, my Lord, it is because I believe, and very firmly believe, that this Bill will prove disastrous to the best interest of the agriculturalists, and not because it is likely to do any harm to the money-lender — which I do not think it really will, that I deem it to be my duty to resist the passing of this measure to the utmost of my power. . If it is true, as I have heard it alleged, that the agriculturalists themselves do not dislike this Bill, may I ask how it is that, while the petitions against the Bill have poured in upon the Council in a manner perfectly unprecedented—and many of them are signed by large numbers of agriculturalists — there is not a single petition from any agriculturalist in favour of the Bill.

This extract demonstrates Gokhale's outstanding faculty and shows how ready he was. He qualifies his assertion regarding the aloofness of the Government officials from the common people, by acknowledging that there were honourable exceptions. He repels the cruel suggestion, which had been made in the highest quarters, that the opposition to the Bill was support corruptly given to the money-lending interest, not with the passionate resentment which such a suggestion deserved, but with a courteous and restrained logic.

Constructive Suggestions

Gokhale's criticism of the Government proposals was not a merely negative one. He believed that the Bill constituted a measure of robbery directed at the most dearly-held privilege of the agriculturalist — namely, his unfettered rights over his land — but he knew that its motive was sound; for he had first-hand knowledge of the appalling evils of agricultural indebtedness. He fully realised that every effort must be made to free the ryot from the clutches of the money-lenders; but he was convinced that a better method of achieving this end could be found than that of depriving the peasant of his rights over his own property. Consequently he suggested that the problem should be tackled by the starting of agricultural banks, from which the peasants would be able to obtain loans on easy terms, without the danger of falling into hopeless and permanent indebtedness:

> 'What the ryot needs is money, or what is nearly the same thing, cheap money. And if you do not reduce what he pays at present to the money-lenders, or do not advance anything from the coffers of Government to help him, how can you give any relief to the ryot? It is, I submit, not possible to improve the position of the agriculturalist by a mere manipulation of the legislative machine.'

Thus, began Gokhale's campaign for the improvement of the condition of the peasants by means of Cooperative Credit Societies, through which the existing burden of indebtedness might be taken over, the peasants freed from the money-lenders, and facilities be afforded for their obtaining cheap money when necessary for future needs. The position of the Indian agriculturalist was to be improved, not by a limitation of his rights but by a beneficent and constructive policy on the part of Government, which should relieve him of his burdens, and teach him through cooperative effort to avoid such burdens in the future, whilst placing within his reach that essential factor to his success — cheap money whereby he could tide over hard times.

The Land Alienation Bill was finally passed through the Bombay Legislative Council by the use of the official majority, and in face of the practically unanimous opposition of the elected members. As a protest against this procedure the elected members marched out of the Council Hall. The Act however was not largely applied, whilst the wide extension of cooperative credit societies, and their great success in the Bombay Presidency, has established the correctness of the point of view taken by Gokhale.

District Municipal Act

Only one other considerable measure came before the Bombay Legislative Council during the time when Gokhale was a member of it. This was a Bill to amend the District Municipal Act, dealing with the Constitution of municipalities, their functions, their conduct of business, the control of their accounts, and so forth. Gokhale was a member of the Poona Municipality for a number of years, and at a later period became President in which capacity he did admirable work, introducing improved methods of business procedure into the municipal meetings, and in various ways making the work of the municipality more efficient and expeditious. He took great interest in the District Municipal Act, and was an active member of the Select Committee appointed in connection with it.

The mover of the Bill referred appreciatively to his services in this connection. In one respect, however, Gokhale's apprehension was aroused by the Bill. He proposed an amendment to delete from it the words or by sections of the Bill in regard to municipal elections; and he spoke as follows against any introduction of the principle of sectional representation into municipal politics:

> We value local self-government not only for the fact that local work thereby is better done, but also for the fact that it teaches men of different castes and creeds, which have long been kept more or less apart, to work together for a common purpose. There are, in all conscience, causes for differences enough among, the different sections in this land, and I submit that the Legislature should do the best interest of the country without the very strongest reasons, give any statutory recognition to these differences. There is nothing m the nature of local government which implies any conflict between the interests of one section and another.

This utterance is notable as Gokhale's earliest enunciation as a legislator of the principle to which he afterwards attached so great importance, that the introduction of democratic institutions into India should be rigorously safeguarded from any tendency to sanction, or to accentuate communal differences.

Temperance

Gokhale was also able to assist the cause of temperance during his time in the Bombay Legislative Council, by urging not only that Government should raise the price of intoxicants, but also that they should reduce the facilities for obtaining them.

He believed' on principle in total Prohibition, but until a policy of Prohibition became possible, he held that it was the duty of the authorities, in view of the ravages wrought by the drink-habit, especially amongst the poorer classes of the population, to make drink not only more expensive but also more hard to obtain.

Spirit of Work

Throughout this period of his life Gokhale was continuously engaged in the investigation of this aspect or that of the work of administration and legislation.

He made very full use of the right of iterations accorded to members of the Council; but he made his criticisms in a courteous and friendly spirit, which went far to secure adequate consideration by Government of the points which he raised.

He proved many times over that he was not a destructive opponent of everything which Government might do, just because it was done by Government, but that his chief aim and desire was that the lot of his fellow-countrymen might be improved through the constructive cooperation of officials and non-officials in the cause of the people as a whole.

Death of Ranade

In the midst of these activities, many of which entailed prolonged and painstaking research into various aspects of the administration, Gokhale suffered a great personal grief in the loss of his friend and guide, Justice Ranade.

The relationship between these two men had been for some: fifteen years a very close one; and the younger man felt that he owed his ideals and inspiration almost entirely to the elder, for whom he had a profound admiration and love. He wrote as follows to one of his own brilliant juniors concerning his loss:

> Since I wrote to you last, my great master, Ranade, has passed away. What his death means to me is more than I can tell you. I feel as though a sudden darkness has fallen upon my life, and the best part of the satisfaction of doing public work is, for the present at any rate, gone. Of course I recognise that it is my duty, as it is that of so many others, to struggle on, faintly it may be, but ever in faith and hope — trying in our own feeble manner to uphold the banner unfurled by him, cherishing with love and reverence the ideals to which he gave his matchless life. But it is a dreary task; and I do not know if men like myself will be enabled to accomplish even a small portion of it. However, the attempt must be made, and there happily the responsibility of us human beings ends.

One of the Indian biographers of Gokhale, himself a brilliant educationalist, writes thus of the relationship which had existed between Gokhale and Ranade and which had borne such remarkable fruit in the training of the younger man for the service for his country:

> 'The story of this friendship is one of the most beautiful romances in modern Indian history. For years they were engaged together in the close study of the progress and destiny of nations, the inner meaning of public events, the far-off results of action, the discipline of failure, service and sacrifice, and the infinite play of human motive and passion, not only in profound treatises of political philosophy, but also in the ephemeral effusions of the daily press, and in ponderous government publications. Surely there is no fairer sight on earth than the close communion of two such kindred spirits and it has brought untold blessing in its train on us all.'

About the same time Gokhale lost his second wife. He did not marry again, his two daughters being entrusted to the care of some relatives for their upbringing.

Leaving Fergusson College

The new type of work which he was thus taking up, necessitating prolonged and frequent absences from Poona, made it no longer possible for Gokhale to continue his work as a professor in the Fergusson College. He had served for eighteen years in the Deccan Education Society, and during most of that time had undertaken, and successfully carried through, extremely onerous duties in connection with the raising of financial support for the society, most of his holidays being employed in this manner. His college lectures, especially during the latter part of his service, had been 'nothing short of weighty statements on all political, historical and economic questions and he had come to exercise a very remarkable influence upon his students.

The wrench which he felt on giving up this familiar form of life, and the doubts which assailed him on launching out into the career of a political leader, pure and simple, are finely expressed in the reply which he gave to a farewell address presented to him by the students of his college.

In reading this speech, it must be remembered that Gokhale was retiring from a post which brought him in the sure, if not princely, income of Rs. 75 pm, and that in the future he and his family would have to depend upon a pension of Rs. 30 pm (about £25 per annum); and this after eighteen years of exhausting work, in the course of which many lakhs of rupees had passed through his hands. He was compelled, moreover, at the same time to relinquish the small additional income which he had been able to make as an examiner in the Bombay University.

His Farewell Address to the College

He took the opportunity, when replying to the farewell address presented to him on retiring from the college, to review his past experience and to disclose a few of the hopes that drew him on to further service of his country.

Gokhale had become a Fellow of Bombay University in 1895, and for one year had also been a member of its Syndicate. Amongst many other, activities in connection with the university, he had been largely responsible for the drafting of new courses in history and economics, and for the inclusion of political science in the B.A. course. He had also strongly advocated the retention of history as a compulsory subject in the B.A. course, as he was convinced of its usefulness as a means of training in citizenship.

Some of these revealing passages may firstly be reproduced here:

> Hope and faith, and seek only the satisfaction which comes of all disinterested exertions. This is not the place where I may speak of my future hopes or lines of work. But one thing I know, and it is this: Whether I am permitted to press onwards and prove of some little use to the public in another capacity, or whether I have to return a weather-beaten, tempest-tossed, shipwrecked mariner, my thoughts, as you have said in your address, will constantly be with this institution and on the other hand, I shall always be sure of a warm and hospitable welcome within these walls whenever I choose to come-here.
>
> And now, before concluding, I wish to say one thing to the students of this college.... The principal moral interest of this institution is in the fact that it represents an idea and embodies an ideal. The idea is that Indians of the present day can bind themselves together, and putting aside all thoughts of worldly interests, work for a secular purpose with the zeal and enthusiasm which we generally find in the sphere of religion alone. The ideal is the ideal of self-help, that we may learn slowly but steadily to rely less and less upon others, however willing to bear our burdens, and more and more upon ourselves. I trust that you, the students of this college, will keep this character of this institution steadily before your eyes — that your devotion to it, your enthusiasm for it, will be commensurate with the nobility and importance of its work, that even when you feel disposed to criticise it, you will speak of it with that loving solicitude with which you mention a parent's fault, and that you will

> always do what lies in your power to further its interest and enlarge the sphere of its usefulness and influence.
> This farewell address to his old college is an excellent example of Gokhale's oratory. In it are combined the clarity and eloquence of expression, and the restrained expression of deep emotion, which are characteristic of all his best public speaking. The tone of loyal affection for his old college, which runs through the whole, gives us the man himself on the strongest and most typical side of his character — his capacity for losing himself in a great cause.

This same instrument of Gokhale's oratory was now to be employed with decisive effect in the counsels of the Central Government.

4

An Illustrious Career

The development of modern Indian political thought is closely linked with the development of the Indian national movement. During the course of the national movement two distinct streams of thought appeared within the Indian National Congress prior to the emergence of Gandhi as a prominent political figure. These two streams of thought are popularly known as the Moderate and the Extremist school. The early phase of Indian national movement was dominated by the moderate thinkers such as Justice M. G. Ranade, D. E. Wacha, Pherozeshah Mehta and Dadabhai Nauroji who laid down the foundations of liberal political thinking in India. Gopal Krishna Gokhale was one of the leading moderate thinkers of his time.

Among all the liberal political thinkers of pre-independent India, Gokhale enjoys a unique position both as a man of liberal ideas and as a practitioner of liberal faith. The political ideas of Gokhale in the light of the liberal tradition of political thinking that characterised the early phase of the Indian national movement. The development of Gokhale's political career and the formative intellectual influences that shaped his political thinking. His political thought with respect to his responses to British rule in India, his ideology of liberalism, his views about 'ends and means' in politics, his Political Programme and his economic and social ideas, all reflects his dimensions of personality.

The moderate thinkers stood for a liberal political outlook and advocated an all-round but gradual social progress. They significantly differed from the extremist thinkers like Tilak, Aurobindo Ghosh, B. C. Pal and others with respect to their understanding of the British rule in India, their perception of the social reality in India, their ideas regarding the social and political goals and the means to realise them.

Broadly speaking, the moderates appreciated and welcomed British rule in India and believed that it will set in the process of modernisation of Indian society. They insisted more on social and economic reforms as they sincerely felt that mere political independence would mean nothing without attaining the minimum level of social and economic progress. Gokhale was a major liberal thinker after M. G. Ranade, who had contributed greatly to the liberal way of politics. As an ideal disciple of M. G. Ranade and the revered 'Political Guru' of Mahatma Gandhi, Gokhale provided a major intellectual link between Ranade and Gandhi.

Development of Gokhale's Political Career

In order to understand Gokhale's political thought it would be essential to first see the manner in which Gokhale's political career developed. It would be quite clear that his political activities are intimately linked with his beliefs and various influences that guided him.

Biographical Sketch

Gopal Krishna Gokhale was born in a middle class Chitpavan Brahmin family at Kotluk — a small village in Ratnagiri district on May 9, 1866. His father Krishnarao was employed first as a clerk but later on rose to the position of police sub-inspector. He died when Gopal Rao was hardly thirteen years old, leaving two sons and four daughters behind. Govind Rao, the elder brother of Gopal Rao shouldered the responsibility of the family.

Gopal Rao took his primary education at Kagal near Kolhapur and completed his matriculation in the year 1881. He had his higher education in three different colleges, viz. the Rajaram College at Kolhapur, the Deccan College at Pune and the

Eliphinston College at Bombay from where he completed his graduation in 1884. At one time he thought of becoming an engineer but ultimately decided to devote himself to the cause of education.

In Pune a band of patriotic young men had already started a secondary school, called The New English School, under the inspiration of a veteran nationalist Vishnushastri Chiplunkar. Gopal Rao accepted the job of a teacher in the New English School. His sincerity impressed the proprietors of the Deccan Education Society, and they made him a life-member of the Society. Soon Gopal Rao was promoted to the post of lecturer in Fergusson College — a college run by the Deccan Education Society itself, and since then he devoted almost eighteen years of his life to the teaching career.

During his teaching career he was introduced to M. G. Ranade and since then he volunteered his talents and services to the cause of public life under the able guidance of Ranade. He became the Secretary of the Sarvajanik Sabha — a public body that was chiefly activated by M. G. Ranade to articulate the interests of the common people. The Sabha had its influential quarterly and Gopal Rao worked as an editor of the quarterly. For some years he also wrote in the English Section of the journal 'Sudharak' started by Gopal Ganesh Agarkar, a veteran social reformer in nineteenth century Maharashtra.

In the year 1889 Gopal Rao attended the session of the Indian National Congress for the first time and since then he was a regular speaker at its meetings.

In 1896 when Tilak and his associates captured the Sarvajanik Sabha Ranade and his followers including Gokhale dissociated themselves from the Sabha and founded a new association called the Deccan Sabha. Gokhale took keen interest in the activities of the Sabha. On behalf of the Sabha he was sent to England to give evidence before the Welby Commission which was appointed by the Government to suggest ways of more equitable distribution of expenses of the administration between the British and the Indian Government. This was his first trip to England. His excellent performance raised a lot of expectations.

In 1899 he was elected to the Bombay Legislative Council. In 1902 he retired from the Fergusson College and devoted the remaining thirteen years of his life entirely to political work. During this period he was elected, term after term, to the Imperial Legislative Council where he made a mark as an eminent Parliamentarian. His budget-speeches, in particular, have become classics as they contained so much constructive but at the same time fearless criticism of the Government's fiscal policies.

At the instance of Mahatma Gandhi, Gokhale also took keen interest in the affairs of the Indians in South Africa. In 1910 and 1912 he moved resolutions in the Imperial Legislative Council for relief to Indian indentured labour in Natal. He went to South Africa at Gandhi's invitation in 1912 and played a significant role in tackling the problems of Indians settled there. In 1913 he raised funds for helping the South African Satyagraha Movement. Gokhale's strenuous routine ultimately caused his untimely death in Feb. 1915.

Formative Influences

Political thought and ideas do not evolve in a vacuum. They emerge in a particular social atmosphere. A thinker is a product of his times. Gokhale was no exception. His ideas and thinking were influenced mainly by the leading personalities of his time and the events he encountered.

As a product of the British educational system Gokhale was bound to acquire a modern outlook towards life which characterised the English educated elite of his time. During his student days he learnt by heart Beaten's 'Public Speaker', repeated passages from Bacon's 'Essays' and The Advancement of Learning', mastered Fawcett's 'Political Economy' and memorised Burke's Reflections on the French Revolution. All this had a far reaching effect on the development of his political ideas.

The liberal philosophy of John Stuart Mill made a profound impression on him and he was particularly inspired by Mill's political doctrines. As a student of history, Gokhale was particularly impressed by the Irish Home Rule Movement. The coherence, dynamism and democratic evolution of European history, considerably influenced his thinking and led him to believe that there is much to learn from the West.

Among the Indian personalities it was M. G. Ranade who influenced Gokhale to a great extent. Gokhale always took pride in being a follower of Ranade. He was particularly impressed by the social and economic ideas of Ranade. While Gokhale had a deep respect for the sacrifice made by nationalist leaders like Tilak and others he was not much attracted by their nationalist ideology and this made him move closer to the moderate thinkers like D. E. Wacha and Pherozeshah Mehta, who exercised considerable influence on him in matters of party organisation and technique.

Contemporary liberal politicians in England such as Morley and others also had a considerable influence on Gokhale's political career. Gokhale always looked to Gladstone and Morley with a reverential attitude and believed that they would apply just Principles to the governance of India. Gokhale's political thinking essentially represented the liberal ethos of his time and it was that liberalism which shaped his social and political ideas.

Sources of Gokhale's Political Thought

Gokhale was not a political thinker in the strict sense of the term. He did not produce any political treatise like that of Hobbes or Locke. Neither did he write a political commentary like Tilak's 'Geeta Rahasya' or Gandhi's 'Hind-Swarajya' which could be referred to in order to explain his political tenets. But we do have a number of articles written by him on various occasions that reflect his political thinking. Likewise the several speeches he made on important socio-economic issues and his correspondence with his contemporaries, now available in the form of collected works, enable us to explore his political ideas. There are some excellent biographies and scholarly works on Gokhale that also constitute an important source for the study of his political thought. Thus, with the help of all these sources it is possible for us to delineate the political thinking of Gokhale.

Gokhale's Political Ideology

Gokhale's political thought revolves more around the socio-political issues of his times rather than any basic political concept like that of the state or nation or sovereignty. Hence, in order to understand his political doctrines we have to refer to the basic political issues of his time and way he responded to these. Now the issues being many in number and complex in nature, the ideas that emerged as responses to these issues reflect the rich diversity of Gokhale's political thinking. In this lesson, however, we shall concern ourselves mainly with discussing Gokhale's political thought under three major headings, viz. Gokhale's responses to British rule in India. His liberalism and the political programme that he devised and worked for.

Responses to British Rule in India

Like most of the liberal Indian thinkers of his time Gokhale appreciated and welcomed the British rule in India. His appreciation of the British rule and particularly his insistence on the continuation of the British rule in India were based on two premises. In the first instance, like all the moderates, Gokhale was convinced that it was because of British rule that the process of modernisation of the Indian society had set in. The British upheld the concept of equality before law, they introduced the principle of representative government (on however limited a scale it might be) they guaranteed the freedom of speech and press.

All these things were certainly new. It was again the British who set in the process of political integration in India. There was much for Indians, to learn from the British and hence, Gokhale pleaded that we should bear with them for some time and make progress in the field of industry, commerce, education and politics. Gokhale was convinced that if British rule continued for some time, India would be modernised completely and eventually join the community of nations like any other independent state in Europe.

Gokhale believed that in keeping with their liberal traditions, the British would fulfil their pledges and bestow on India self-government once Indians qualified themselves for the same. This concept of 'England's pledges to India' was built upon the declarations of Thomas Munro, Macaulay, Henri Lawrence and above all Queen Victoria's Proclamation. In spite of the fact that from the end of Ripon's viceroyalty in 1884 to the August-Declaration of 1917 successive Viceroys and Secretaries of India emphatically repudiated the feasibility of introducing English political institutions to India, Gokhale still believed that by appealing to the British sense of liberalism, by convincing them of India's genuine capabilities the British would ultimately be convinced and would introduce to India western political institutions. It was this faith in British liberalism that made Gokhale plead for the continuance of the British rule in India.

His justification for the continuance of the British rule in India did not mean that he was totally satisfied with the British administration in India. For instance, he was a bitter critic of the high handedness of the Curzonian administration. He also argued on many occasions that the British raj was more raj and less British in the sense that it was reluctant to introduce English parliamentary institutions to India, yet he believed that British rule was destined to accomplish its providential mission in India.

Gokhale sincerely felt that the history of India had nothing to offer so far as the development of democratic political institutions was concerned. In a paper read before the Universal Races Congress, London, July, 1911, Gokhale admitted, "India did not develop the national idea of political freedom as developed in the west." He was convinced that the social and political institutions of the country must be reformed in the image of the west.

To him the European history presented a well-marked evolution of the democratic idea and was therefore useful in shaping our ideas of liberty and democracy.

The British connection would definitely serve this purpose and hence he welcomed the British rule in India. In one of his letters to his friend Gokhale wrote: "You must all realise that whatever be the shortcomings of bureaucracy... however the insolence of individual Englishman, they alone stand today in the country for order; and without continued order no real progress is possible for our people." Thus, to Gokhale British rule in India stood for social order which was the pre-condition of progress and hence he justified the continuance of British rule in India.

Liberalism

As noted at the outset Gokhale was essentially a liberal thinker. But his liberalism was slightly different from the classical liberalism that existed in the eighteenth and nineteenth century Europe. In order to understand the distinct character of Gokhale's liberalism it is essential to get ourselves acquainted with the liberal ideology in general.

Liberalism as an ideology may be defined as an idea committed to individual freedom, as a method and policy in government, as an organising principle in society, and a way of life for the individual and community. Liberty is the core doctrine of liberalism and it stands against coercive interference of any kind in any walk of life. In the *social sphere* liberalism stands for secularism. It advocates man's freedom from the shackles of religious orthodoxy and believes in freedom of conscience.

In the sphere of economy it appreciates the ideal of free trade coupled with internal freedom of production and external freedom of exportation. It stands for free competition implying no curb on import and export of goods. For this reason it stands for the exploitation of natural resources and distribution of economic dividends at the hands of the individuals. In the *sphere of politics* liberalism and instead of restricting the role of the state in economic life of the nation, he wanted the state to play a positive role in promoting industrial development and trade.

As a liberal Gokhale cherished the ideal of individual liberty. But to him, liberty did not imply the total absence of restraint; on the contrary, he felt that individual liberty could be usefully allowed only when the individuals behave with a sense of self-restraint and self organisation. He knew that the ideal of liberty could not be realised unless the citizens are guaranteed certain rights to freedom. To him the right of free expression and the freedom of press were essential to realise the ideal of individual liberty. He, therefore, opposed the Official Secret Bill in 1904 on the grounds that it was proposed to arm the government with a greater power to control the press.

Gokhale also favoured the right to private property and the freedom of contract. Commenting on the Land Revenue Code Amendment Bill Gokhale said that the ordinary citizen is as tenaciously attached to his proprietary rights over his holdings... that there is nothing he will not do if it is in his power to ward off what he regards as a direct or indirect attack on these rights.

And it is not difficult to understand that a proposal to take away from his power of alienating, when necessary, his holding should appear to him to be a most serious encroachment on his rights. Thus, Gokhale defended the right to private property, individual liberty and freedom of contract which essentially constituted the core of liberal doctrine.

In order to maintain individual liberty and essential civil rights, Gokhale proposed the establishment of representative institutions in the country. According to him the first prerequisite for the improvement of relations between Britain and India was an unequivocal declaration in England to put her resolve to help forward the growth 01 representative institutions in India and a determination to stand by this policy. However, Gokhale did not demand universal franchise. He proposed property qualification for enfranchisement. For example, for the village Panchayat elections Gokhale wanted that only such persons should be enfranchised who paid a minimum land revenue.

Gokhale also preferred the representation of interests along with the representation of people in the legislature. In his last testament and will be suggested that the Legislative Council in each province should constitute of 75 to 100 members. Taking Bombay as an illustration he pleaded for one seat each in the legislature for the Karachi Chamber, the Ahmedabad Mill Owners and the Deccan Sardars. He also suggested the principle of special representation for the religious minority. Recognising the communal differences between the Hindus and the Muslims, Gokhale pleaded for separate representation of the Muslims. Thus, as a liberal, Gokhale on the one hand defended the concept of individual liberty and on the other hand supported the establishment of representative institution in a limited sense.

Gokhale's ideas regarding the role of state remarkably differed from that of classical liberalism. Classical liberalism pleads for a laissez-faire state. The only functions that classical liberalism grants to the state are police functions. They believe that a government which governs the least is the best. But Gokhale, following the footsteps of Justice M. G. Ranade pleaded for state-intervention to regulate the economic and social life of the country. Here Gokhale differed remarkably from J. S. Mill. Gokhale wanted the

Government to intervene in the economic life for the sake of industrial development and agricultural prosperity. He wanted the government to intervene not only in the processes of distribution but also in the process of production. According to Gokhale the purpose of government was to further the moral and material interests of the people. In order to realise this purpose the government cannot remain unconcerned towards the unnatural restrictions in the path of development.

According to Gokhale the government should remove these 'unnatural restrictions' and accelerate the pace of development. Gokhale said: "Indians needed a government which subordinates all other considerations to the welfare of the Indian people, which presents the indignities offered to Indians abroad as though they were offered to Englishmen and, which endeavours by all means in its power to further the moral and material interests of the people in and outside India." Thus, to Gokhale the state should not be a 'police state' only, but it should embark upon welfare activities and intervene in the economic life of the country whenever necessary. We can conclude that Gokhale's liberalism was no doubt inspired by the liberalism of Mill but it significantly differed from the classical liberalism in two respects. On the one hand it did not advocate the extreme individualism, emphasising the negative meaning of liberty and on the other hand it pleaded for necessary state intervention in the economic and social life of the country.

Political Goals and Programme

Gokhale's understanding of the British rule in India was one of the factors that determined his political goals and programmes. As noted earlier Gokhale sincerely believed that India's connections with the British were going to help her in many ways in the long run and hence any idea of severing these connections was always repugnant to his mind. The political goal which he put forward, therefore, was that of self-government for India. The earlier Congress leaders were satisfied with the idea of the 'good government' which meant an efficient and enlightened government. But Gokhale, like Dadabhai Naoroji, gradually realised that no good government was ever possible without having self-government.' Moreover, he felt that the British had given good government in the sense that they had established law and order in the society but then the time had come to associate the Indians with the work of government and this was possible only if the British granted self-government to India. In his Presidential address to the Banaras Congress (1905) Gokhale said, "Now the Congress wants that all this should change and that India should be governed, first and foremost, in the interests of the Indians themselves. This result will be achieved only in proportion as we obtain more and more voice in the government of our country."

Thus, instead of insisting only on 'good government' Gokhale went a step further and demanded self-government for India. But what did self-government mean? Gokhale's idea of self-government was different from that of the extremist thinkers like Aurobindo or Bipin Chandra Pal. By self-government he never meant complete independence for India. He wanted self-government only within the limits of the British Empire. In other words, he wanted that kind of a rule which existed in the self-governing colonies of the British Empire. The extremists like Aurobindo wanted complete independence for India, having no connection with Britain. Gokhale did not go to that extent while demanding self-government.

Neither did he prefer the term 'Swaraj' for self-government, as Tilak did. Tilak's concept of Swaraj had wider implications and it ultimately aimed at the attainment of complete independence. Gokhale in no way hinted at complete independence. Again, for Tilak, Swaraj was the birth right of the people for which no specific conditions were required. Gokhale on the other hand thought that people should qualify themselves to be worthy of running the representative institutions. He thought it reasonable that the sense of responsibility required for the "proper exercise of the political institutions of the west can be acquired by an eastern people through practical training and experiment only," Gokhale sincerely believed that this 'practical training and experiment' on the part of the Indians would be better achieved if India maintained the British connection.

Having fixed the goal of 'self-government' Gokhale designed a political programme and devised appropriate methods to implement it. His political programme envisaged several reforms. These reforms could be grouped under four heads.

- Those which aimed at securing a larger share of the people in the administration and control of their affairs; these included a reform of the Legislative Council, the appointment of Indians to the Secretary of State's Council and the Executive Councils in India, and a steady substitution of the Indian for the European agency in the public service of the country.
- Those which sought to improve the methods of administration, such as the separation of judicial from executive functions, police reforms and similar proposals.
- Those which proposed a readjustment of financial arrangements with the object of securing a reduction of burdens of the taxpayers and a more efficient application of the available resources. Under this head came reduction of military charges, the moderating of land assessments, etc.
- Those which urged the adoption of measures calculated to improve the condition of the masses. These included a vigorous extension of primary education, facilities for industrial and technical instruction, grants for improved sanitation and a real attempt to deal with the alarming indebtedness of the peasantry. Gokhale believed that if the Indians concentrated all their energies on some such programme they might, within a reasonable time see results which would not be altogether disappointing. In his Presidential address at the Banaras Congress (1905) Gokhale expressed his hope that for the first time since the Congress movement began the Radical and Liberal party in England would come into real power and a strong current had already set in England against that narrow and aggressive imperialism. It was this hope that motivated Gokhale to go for a programme which he had proposed on the Congress platform.

The methods Gokhale advocated to realise his political goal and programme were essentially constitutional. To him constitutional agitation was the only way to realise our political aspirations. To Gokhale constitutional agitation meant primarily prayers and petitions. However, Gokhale did not rule out passive resistance as an act of last resort. At a meeting held in the Town

Hall at Bombay on Sept.; 9, 1909 Gokhale said: "...in the circumstances of the Transvaal, passive resistance such as that organised by Gandhi is not only legitimate, but is a duty resting on all self-respecting persons.

What is this passive resistance? Passive Resistance to an unjust law or an oppressive measure and a refusal to acquiesce in that law or measure and a readiness to suffer penalty instead which may be prescribed as an alternative. If we strongly and conscientiously feel the grave injustice of a law and there is no way to obtain redress, I think, refusal to acquiesce in, taking the consequence of such refusal is the only course left to those who place conscience and self-respect above their material and immediate interests."

However, Gokhale's passive resistance differed from that of the extremists. While the extremist leaders like Aurobindo or Tilak pleaded for passive resistance as a measure of attack, Gokhale pleaded for it as a measure of defence. Further, Gokhale's ideas of passive resistance categorically excluded rebellion or aiding or abetting a foreign invasion. The extremists, on the other hand, did not rule out the possibility of rebellion or violence. Lastly, Gokhale advocated passive resistance only as the last resort to be taken when all other methods of redress had failed and here too, the passive resistance movement must be moral, spiritual and carried on without any vindictiveness.

We can, therefore, say that theoretically Gokhale believed in passive resistance but he did not advocate that measure in India as he sincerely felt that a 'thousandth part of the possibilities of constitutional agitation had not been exhausted in India's struggle for self-government.' He also felt that the methods of passive resistance could not possibly be used in India since there was not enough popular feeling. Hence, Gokhale opposed Tilak's political methods. Moderation was the watchward of Gokhale's politics and he never deviated from it.

In contrast to the extremist leaders Gokhale relied more on the constitutional methods than on mass-agitation, more on enlightening the British public opinion on Indian issues than on pressurising them with the threat of organised mass-movements. This, again, speaks of his liberal faith.

Economic and Social Views

As noted earlier Gokhale's economic and social ideas constitute a part of his political thinking. He was not an economist in the strict sense of the term. Neither was he a social thinker with deep sociological insight. However, as a leader of the Congress and as a member of the legislature Gokhale had to ponder over many socio-economic issues of the time which, in turn, gave birth to his economic and social ideas. These ideas reflected his way of thinking which considerably influenced the process of social change of his time.

As far as his economic ideas are concerned Gokhale owes much to Justice M. G. Ranade and Prof. List, a German economist. Both Ranade and List differed from the classical economists such as Adam Smith and Ricardo. Ranade argued that 'Political Economy being a Hypothetical Science, its propositions are not based upon axiomatic truths like those of Euclid and do not absolutely and universally hold good, like the latter, true in all times.' Therefore, if a particular economic policy was suited to England it was not necessarily valid for India as well.

It was on this ground that Ranade opposed the policy of free trade in India as advocated by the classical English economists. Ranade argued that it was not the policy of free trade but that of protection which India needed. Ranade noticed that in Germany it was because of state initiative that the country was able to transform itself into a first rate modern power, and hence he pleaded that the state should take initiative in accelerating the process of industrialisation. Like Prof. List, Ranade thought that the trade policy of the country is integrated with its general economic policy and therefore he felt that 'the government should guarantee or subsidise private efforts till private enterprise could support itself... should advance loans to private capitalist at low interest and help them in the choice of places and the selection of the form of investment.' According to Ranade, the grave problem before India was that of poverty and it could not be removed until the process of industrialisation set in. The policy of free trade, open competition, as followed by the British administrators were not conducive to the growth of industrialisation in India and hence Ranade advocated state intervention in the economic life of the Country.

Gokhale made a careful study of Indian finance from 1874 to 1909 dividing this period into four phases comparing the growth in expenditure with the growth of revenue. The results are given in the table below:

Average annual increase in Revenue and Expenditure

Period	*Increase in Revenue*	*Increase in Expenditure*
1874-1884	1.25%	0.67%
1884-1894	1.5%	1.5%
1894-1901	1.5%	1.5%
1901-1909	2.5%	5.0%

On the basis of his study Gokhale concluded that the growth in expenditure tended to more than the growth in revenue, whereas in fact it was essential to keep the two in balance. Moreover, there was no point in having a surplus budget while the budget of the common man failed to balance itself. During a period of budgetary surplus, Gokhale recommended that the state adopt the following measures:

- a reduction in state demand on land by 25 to 30 per cent,
- the creation of a fund of million sterling to rescue the Indian agriculturists from the load of debt,
- the activisation of cooperative credit societies through establishing agricultural banks on Egyptian model,
- the promotion of industrial and technical education and the sanctioning of the increased expenditure for this purposes,
- free and compulsory primary education,
- improvement of the finances of the local bodies.

It is evident from the above proposals suggested by Gokhale that he was of the opinion that it was of no use to have surplus budget when the budget of the common man failed to balance itself. If there was to be a surplus budget the surplus must be devoted to the work of promoting development functions of the state.

Gokhale was also aware of the state of the agricultural life in India. He saw that the agricultural industry in India was in a serious depression and the crop yield per acre was low. In such circumstances he resented the increase in the land revenue demanded by the state. He made it clear that he regarded land revenue and the indirect taxes as together placing an unbearable burden on the poor. He wanted the state to give importance to irrigation and scientific agriculture as measures for agricultural prosperity. He disapproved the excise duty on cotton textiles which in his opinion was imposed to counter balance the duties on imports. Gokhale thought that such a duty further burdened the poor.

Following the German economist Prof. List, Gokhale pleaded protection for the new industries in India on the ground that she was an industrially backward country. Gokhale observed; "...he (List) says that when a country is industrially backward... comes into vortex of universal competition — competition with countries which use steam and machinery in their production — the first effect is to sweep of local industries and the country is thrust back on agriculture for some time. But then, he says, comes in the duty of the state. When such a situation is reached, the state should step forward and by a judicious system of protection it should foster such industries as are capable of being fostered so that the country may once again enter on its industrial path with the aid of the latest appliances and ultimately stand successfully the competition of the whole world. India should follow this advice of List.' In short, Gokhale stood for the industrial development, advocated state-initiative to further the process of industrialisation, demanded protection for infant industries and thus paved the way for capitalist development.

Gokhale did not stop at merely criticising the fiscal policy of the government but also advocated the cause of Swadeshi. However, he did not identify Swadeshi "with boycott. To him the Swadeshi movement was both a patriotic and an economic movement. So far as its patriotic aspect was concerned it meant devotion to motherland but the movement on its materia) side was economic. It ensured a ready consumption of such articles as were produced in the country and furnished a perpetual stimulus to production by keeping up the demand for indigenous things. To Gokhale the question of production was a question of capital, enterprise and skill and whoever could help in one of those fields could be called a worker in the Swadeshi cause. Gokhale did not mind even to seek governmental cooperation in the cause of Swadesh. Through the Swadesh movement Gokhale sought to lay the foundations of indigenous capitalism.

In the sphere of social reforms Gokhale sided with Ranade. Like Ranade, Gokhale also believed that social reforms must go along with political reforms. As early as in 1890 Ranade had advocated certain reforms, viz. (i) not more than a year's income should be expended on the marriage ceremonies of son or daughter; (ii) that the boys should not be married before the ages 16, 18 or 20 and the girls before the ages of 10, 12 and 14; (iii) Polygamy should be prohibited; (iv) no one should marry after the age of 60; (v) that efforts should be made to promote female education. By and large Ranade believed that all these reforms should be introduced gradually, and the state might be utilised to bring about social change through legislative procedure whenever it was absolutely necessary. But on an average, Ranade believed, that 'popular initiation' rather than 'imposed laws' would be helpful in reforming the society. However, it must be noted here that Ranade was not totally against the state intervening to promote social reforms as Tilak was. Gokhale followed Ranade in this respect. He was of the opinion that the state must help the progressive elements in the society. He thus supported the motion on the Civil Marriage Bill. With the support of an influential and enlightened minority Gokhale wanted the state to proceed with measures of social change.

Gokhale suggested free and compulsory elementary education. The elementary education meant something more than a mere capacity to read and write. It meant the greater moral and economic efficiency of the individual — and hence he strove hard to insist on compulsory free education. He also suggested prohibition of liquor and other measures of public health so as to remove hindrances and hardships from the path of the development of individual personality.

It could be easily noticed from the reforms suggested by Gokhale that his programme of social reforms reflects his liberal faith. Liberalism attaches greater importance to individual dignity.

This dignity cannot, however, be restored unless the person is educated and enlightened. It is for this purpose that the liberal ideology advocates the all-round development of the individual personality. Gokhale as a convinced liberal attached utmost importance to this aspect of human life, viz., the development of personality. Caste barriers, racialism, communal disharmony, ignorance, religious fanaticism, subjugation of women, were all hindrances in the path of the development of individual personality and hence had to be removed immediately. Thus, Gokhale's social reformism was also the child of his liberal outlook. His ideas of spiritualisation of politics presupposed the moral purification of the individual along with that of his or her enlightenment which is implicit in his general programme of social reforms.

Summary

Gokhale was a moderate and liberal political thinker. His political ideas were largely influenced by the liberal thinker like Bentham, Mill and Ranade. So far as his political tenets were concerned he believed that:

- political progress of India must be based on law and order,
- his political goal was that of the colonial self-government,
- to him the constitutional agitation was the only means to attain the desired end.

He was a liberal thinker but differed from the classical liberal thinkers in certain respects, particularly with their ideas regarding the role of the state and their insistence on laissez-faire policies. In contrast with the classical liberal thinkers Gokhale advocated a positive role for the state in developing and modernising society.

Gokhale was an ardent social reformer. He favoured legislation in order to bring about certain social changes. His attitude towards social reform was essentially humanitarian and liberal. Religion as a particular sect or faith did not count much in his thinking although he insisted on the spiritualisation of politics. This morality was again based on secular considerations and did not refer to any religious dogma. As such he proved to be a precursor of Mahatma Gandhi in this respect. Gokhale was not a mass leader unlike Tilak and Gandhi. On the contrary, he was of the opinion that the enlightened, educated people, few in number should guide the society and lead the masses in a proper way. Hence, he exerted more to enlighten the educated classes on major socio-economic issues rather than to organise masses for political action. He believed in persuasion rather than confrontation.

In short, in the field of politics Gokhale laid the foundations of constitutionalism. In the field of economics he encouraged the process of capitalist development and in the field of social reforms he tried hard to enhance the dignity of the individual irrespective of his taste, race, religion, language and class. He was thus a moderniser of Indian society in every sense of the term.

Elementary Education Bill

Early in 1911 Gokhale introduced his Elementary Education Bill into the Imperial Council. It was a cautious measure, of a merely permissive character and depending very largely upon local enthusiasm for the cause of education. In spite of strenuous efforts which he made in its behalf, including long tours through the country in order to educate public opinion, the Bill failed. Government professed them unable to find the money, and there was an unfortunate and short-sighted opposition to details of the measure from some of the non-official members in the Council.

Gokhale's last speech on the Bill concluded as follows — in words which are perhaps the noblest of all his public utterances:

> I know that my Bill will be thrown out before the day closes. I make no complaint. I shall not even be depressed. I know too well the story of the preliminary efforts that were required even in England, before the Act of 1870 was passed, either to complain or to feel depressed. Moreover, I have always felt and often said that we of the present generation in India can only hope to serve our country by our failures. The men and women who will be privileged to serve her by their successes will come later. We must be content to accept cheerfully the place that has been allotted to us in our onward march. This Bill, thrown out today, will come back again and again, till on the

> stepping-stones of its dead selves a measure ultimately rises which will spread the light of knowledge throughout the land. It may be that this anticipation will not come true. It may be that our efforts may not conduce even indirectly to the promotion of the great cause which we all have at heart, and that they may turn out after all to be nothing better than the mere ploughing of the sands of the seashore. But, My Lord, whatever fate awaits our labours one thing is clear. We shall be entitled to feel that we have done our duty and, where the call of duty is clear, it is better even to labour and fail than not to labour at all.

His Bill was thrown out, as he anticipated. He was the first-great Indian to place in the forefront of his policy for his people's, rebirth the necessity for the education of the common people; and in the words of Sir Valentine Chirol, he 'extracted nothing; from official wisdom or parsimony but a frigid non-possumus'.

Police Administration

During the Council session of 1912 Gokhale made two important speeches, on matters concerning which be felt very deeply. The first was on the question of Police Administration and contained references to what he, like many other Indian public men, had to endure in this connection. He had suffered much from the stupid suspicions harboured by the police in regard to his political activities. Ranade before his day had to submit to have his letters opened; he himself was well aware how all his movements were shadowed. What he and others had to bear in this connection the following passages relate:

> As a matter of fact I must say I have been receiving such attentions for a very long time, but I have always taken it as (all) in the day's work; and I am free to recognise that the Government may think it necessary to keep in touch with all who are engaged in such work. What we are entitled to expect, however, is that the men who are employed in this duty shall do their work in a less clumsy and offensive manner than that

in which they do it at present. I will give the Council an illustration from my personal knowledge. I belong to a society of young men — I mean the other members are young men, though I am myself getting on in years — which has been brought into existence to supply a long-felt want, namely, that of young men trained in the study of public questions and engaged in public work in various fields as whole time workers. Now we may be right or we may be wrong in our view of things, in our estimate of the requirements of the situation. We have made up our minds to serve our country according to our lights, and we are prepared to accept the full consequences of our choice. And if the Criminal Investigation Department of the Government wishes to keep in touch with our movements, let it do so by all means; but we are certainly entitled, as peaceful citizens of this country, to expect that we should not be subjected to undue annoyance.

Some time ago one of the members of our society went to the United Provinces to take part in the Famine Relief operations. He did such excellent work there in that connection that Sir John Hewett thought it necessary to recognise the work in his Famine Report; and yet this gentleman was subjected to such open and continuous annoyance by the men of the Criminal Investigation Department that ultimately he had to complain publicly of it in the papers. He was not only openly accompanied by these men wherever he went, but one of them began to go the length of insisting on sitting on the coach-box of hackney carriages engaged by him for going about.

All this is really most grossly offensive — to put it no stronger than that. I do not say that they should not watch our movements, if they want to do so, though I strongly feel that it is .most foolish that Government should thus let loose a number of unscrupulous men, such as most of the Criminal Investigation Department men are, on innocent people. But, in any case, it is necessary that all this shadowing should be done in a less offensive and less clumsy manner.

The reports submitted by these men are secret. Nobody knows what is contained in these reports and everybody's good name is at the mercy of these people. I know of a report which was once submitted against me, and for which there was absolutely no foundation. I came to know about it simply through the courtesy of the Political Secretary to the Bombay Government, who happened to entertain a kindly feeling for me. I had made a speech at a mofussil place in the Bombay Presidency. Some time after I happened to meet this officer at a party, and he asked me to go and see him the next day in his office. He then asked me what things I had been saying, and he put the report into my hands. I was amazed to read it. I told him that I had never said any of the things attributed to me. He laughed and said of course he knew that I could not have said such things and he never took the report seriously.

This officer discredited the report because he knew me personally. But for one man whom these officers know personally there are ten, a hundred, a thousand men whom they do not know, and against whom reports are daily submitted — reports on which officials very often act. It is therefore necessary that an enquiry should now be ordered into the operations of this Criminal Investigation Department. The fact is this: A number of uneducated and in many cases unscrupulous men have been engaged for this work. The work is necessarily regarded as disreputable, and is looked down upon in every society. A man who goes about it surreptitiously and tries to find out behind the backs of people something about them must necessarily suffer from that disadvantage. Therefore, you cannot get good men for the work,

> and I recognise that constitutes a serious difficulty; but some way must be found out of it, for great irritation and bitterness is being caused in the minds of thousands of innocent people by the dangerous and unscrupulous activity of the Criminal Investigation Department men.
>
> Therefore, an enquiry must now immediately be undertaken into the whole of this business — into how these men are appointed, what their qualifications are, how they perform their duties, what supervision there is on them, and what, reliance is placed on their reports. The very fact that things are settling down again makes such an enquiry all the more necessary. For these men have to justify their existence, and therefore in the absence of anything really worth reporting they are sure to make up things which do not exist and report them to the Government.
>
> It was in this courageous and outspoken way that Gokhale drew attention to a grievance, which has done more than anything else to alienate from Government the mind of modern educated India. The present writer can bear personal witness that, amongst Government officials, Gokhale himself, as Sir Valentine Chirol says, 'was generally regarded as a mere disaffected agitator, only the more dangerous, because of his admittedly greater ability'.

Indentured Labour

In the same year, 1912, Gokhale made a noteworthy speech in defence of the Indentured Indian labourers in distant countries, on whose behalf his influence was destined to tell so decisively, and in whose ultimate liberation from a form of slavery he had so great and honourable a share.

> I do not think it necessary to describe to this Council at any length what this system really is. Its principal features may roughly be stated to be six in number.

Under this system, those who are recruited bind themselves, first, to go to a distant and unknown land, the language, usages and customs of which they do not know, and where they have no friends or relatives. Secondly, they bind themselves to work there for any employer to whom, they may be allotted, whom they do not know and who does not know them, and in whose choice they have no voice. Thirdly, they bind themselves to live there on the estate of the employer, they must not go anywhere without a special permit, and must do whatever tasks are assigned to them, no matter how irksome those tasks may be. Fourthly, the binding is for a certain fixed period, usually five years, during which time they cannot voluntarily withdraw from their contract and have no means of escaping from its hardships, however intolerable. Fifthly, they bind themselves to work during the period for a fixed wage, which invariably is lower, and in some cases very much lower, than the-wage paid to free labour around them. And sixthly and lastly, and this to my mind is the worst feature of the system, they are placed under a special law, never explained to them before they left the country, which is in a language which they do not understand, and which imposes on them a criminal liability for the most trivial breaches of the contract, in place of the civil ability which usually attaches to such breaches. Thus, they are liable under the law to imprisonment with hard labour, which may extend to two and in some cases to three months, not only for fraud, not only for deception, but for negligence, for carelessness, and — will the Council believe it? — for even an impertinent word or gesture to the manager or his overseers.

These are the principal features of the system, and when it is remembered that the victims of the system — I can call them by no other name — are generally simple, ignorant, illiterate, resourceless people belonging to the poorest classes of this country, and that they are induced to enter—or it would be more correct to say, are entrapped into entering — into these agreements by the unscrupulous representations of wily, professional recruiters, who are paid so much a head for the labour they supply, and whose interest in them ceases the moment they are handed over to the emigration agents, no fair-minded man will, I think, hesitate to say that the system is a monstrous system, iniquitous in itself, based on fraud, and maintained by force; nor will he, I think, demur to the statement that a system so wholly opposed to modern sentiments of justice and humanity is a grave blot on the civilization of any country that tolerates it.

The Objections to the Indenture System

The principal objections to the system are roughly five. The first is naturally its utter inequity. Sir, whatever view one may take of the agreements into which these poor people are made to centre under the system, to dignify them by the name of "fair contract" is to misuse the English language. For the stream is poisoned at its very source. It is significant that nobody has a good word to say for the professional recruiters who entrap and entice away these poor people. The recruiters are admittedly men who are generally ignorant and unscrupulous, and who, with the exception of perhaps a very few, have never been to the Colonies for which they recruit, and who, being paid so much per head, try by hook or by crook to get into their meshes as many persons as they can. The Government of India stands aside on the plea that it is a fair contract between the emigrant and his future employer. How can a contract be called a fair contract, the two parties to which are most unequally matched? How can it be a fair contract when one party to it is absolutely in a state of ignorance and helplessness, and the other party — the powerful party — takes care that it shall not know how much it is undertaking to abide by? Take, for instance, the penal nature of the contract. The terms that are explained to the emigrants, when they enter into indenture, never include a statement of the penal nature of the law under which they have to live. Here in Volume III of the Sanderson Committee's report the Council will find the agreements for the different Colonies reproduced. There is not a word here about the penal liabilities thrown on the poor creatures by the special laws under which they must live in the several Colonies. If this single fact is explained to them before they agree to emigrate, namely, that they will be placed in the Colonies not under the ordinary Civil law for the enforcement of the contract, but under a special penal law rendering them liable to imprisonment with hard labour even for trivial faults, I should like to see how many even of such ignorant, resourceless people agree to go to these distant places.

I say, therefore, that the stream is poisoned at the source; that it is not a fair contract: that it is a contract between two parties that are absolutely unequally matched, a contract vitiated by the fact that most important facts in connection with it are kept from the knowledge of one party.

Lack of Efficient Safeguards

The apologists of the system, however, urge that there are safeguards provided to prevent hardship and injustice to the emigrants when they go to their respective colonies. Two such safeguards are specially mentioned. One is that in every colony there is an officer, known as the Protector of Immigrants, especially to look after the interests of indentured immigrants. And, secondly, there are the magistrates to give the protection of the law to the immigrants against any cruelty that may be practised on them by their employers.

These safeguards look all right on paper; in actual practice, however, both are found to be more or less illusory. These men — the protectors and the magistrates — are officers of the Colonial Governments. They belong to the same class to which the planters belong. They are generally one in sympathy and in interests with the planters; and it is not in ordinary human nature that they should care to displease those with whom they have to live, with whom they have to mix socially — and all this for granting protection to poor, ignorant people from a distant land, in whom their interest is purely official.

The Suffering under the System

My third objection to this system is the vast and terrible amount of suffering that it has caused during the 75 years that it has been in existence. It is difficult to speak in terms of due restraint on this point. Even the hardest heart must melt to think of this phase of the question. I will not speak now of the imprisonments with hard labour endured for trivial faults; I will not speak of the personal violence which in some cases has been proved and in very many cases could not be proved, though alleged. I will not speak of the bitterness engendered in the minds of thousands when they realised that they had been deceived, that they had been entrapped, and that there was no escape for them. I will not speak of the homesick feeling, destroying their interest in life. These are all serious matters that could be charged against the system. But more serious even than these is the heavy mortality that has prevailed in the past in all Colonies under the system, a mortality which has been examined from time to time by Commissions of Enquiry, and which has been established beyond doubt — a mortality for which indentured emigration was prohibited to the Federated Malay States only last year, and which even today is admitted to exist in certain districts of Assam amongst the statute labourers.

Then the numerous suicides which have resulted from this system — poor innocent people preferring death by their own hands to life under it — are a ghastly feature of the system. All this constitutes a sum total of human misery which is appalling to contemplate, and which will be a standing witness against the system for all time. It is true that things are somewhat better now; but they cannot be very much better under a system which has inherent characteristics such as those that I have described. Moreover, as Lord Curzon said in this Council in 1901, even if such cases have occurred only in a few instances, the very fact that such cases can occur under the system constitutes a severe condemnation of the system.

My fourth objection to the system is the frightful immorality that is inseparable from it. This is a fact which has been admitted by everybody, among others by the Government of India and by the Sanderson Committee. The committees, who deal with all other phases of the indenture question, carefully avoid making any recommendation as to how the frightful immorality involved in the system may be remedied. Under the law, every hundred male indentured labourers must be accompanied by 40 females. Now very few respectable women can be got to go these long distances. Our men themselves do not really care to .go, much less do the women. The statutory number, therefore, is made up by the recruiters, as admitted by the Government of India in one of their despatches to the Secretary of State, by including in it women of admittedly loose morals, with results in the Colonies which one had better leave to the imagination of the Council.

A National Degradation

My last objection to the system is that it is degrading to the people of India from a national point of view. I do not think I need really say much on this aspect of the question. Wherever the system exists, there the Indians are only known as coolies, no matter what their position may be. Now, Sir, there are disabilities enough in all conscience attaching to our position in this country. And, I ask, why must this additional brand be put upon our brow before the rest of the civilized world? I am sure, if only the Government will exercise a little imagination, and realise our feeling in the matter, it will see the necessity of abolishing the system as soon as possible.

The Responsibility of Government

This is a question which really throws a great responsibility upon the Government. I am aware that the Government of India has from time to time taken up the position that they maintain an attitude of neutrality in this matter, that they do not themselves encourage indentured emigration, but that if people choose to accept certain terms and go, it is not for them to interfere. I would only ask the Council to contrast this attitude with the attitude which the Government has adopted in regard to the peasantry of the country, in legislating on lines to which I have already referred. I do not think that the Government can absolve themselves from their responsibility in this matter. In the first place, the recruiters are granted licenses to recruit by District Magistrates. That, in itself, imposes a responsibility upon the Government, because by granting licenses to these persons the Government make themselves to a certain extent responsible for the representations by which these men secure recruits. Then, the magistrates before whom the poor emigrants are taken and made to enter into agreements are the servants of Government. The third and last point is that, though the fact about the penal nature of the contract has been carefully kept out of all agreements all these years, the Government has so far taken no steps whatever to remedy this.

If you are prepared to abolish the penal nature of the contract under which these labourers have to work, the rest would be comparatively a very simple question, and I shall not press this "motion to a division; but, as I understand it, the penal provisions are the very essence of the system; without them the system cannot be worked. If penal liability is thus indispensable I ask why the Government has not taken steps all these years to see to it that this nature of the contract is explained to the emigrants before they enter into their agreements. Sir, this is really a most serious question for, whatever the Government may say, as a matter of fact everybody in the country believes that without the countenance of Government the system could not have gone on so long.

India is the only country which supplies indentured labour at the present moment. Why should India be marked out for this degradation? The conscience of our people, unfortunately asleep too long, is now waking up to the enormity of this question; and I have no doubt that it will not rest till it has asserted itself. And I ask the Government not to make the mistake of ignoring a sentiment that is dear to us, namely the sentiment of our self-respect. We have no doubt plenty of differences between the Government and the people in regard to the internal administration of this country; but those are matters which stand on a different footing. Outside the country, the Government of India must stand up for us on every occasion, must stand up for our dignity, for our honour, for our national pride. If they will not do this, to whom else can we turn?

I feel that though this system has been allowed to exist so long, yet its days are really numbered. It will soon cease in Assam, and then it cannot last very much longer in the case of the Colonies. And I am confident that a people who have spent millions upon millions in emancipating slaves, will not long permit their own fellow-subjects to be condemned to a life which, if not one of actual slavery, is at any rate not far removed from it.

> The Government, it is clear, are not going to accept this Resolution: that being so, the Resolution is bound to be thrown out. But that will not be the end of the matter. This motion, the Council may rest assured, will be brought forward again and again, till we carry it to a successful issue. It affects our national self-respect and therefore the sooner the Government recognises the necessity of accepting it, the better it will be for all parties.

Work for Indians in South Africa

This great speech on behalf of a voiceless multitude of his exiled fellow-countrymen places Gokhale in the ranks of that noble fellowship of the enemies of slavery, which includes the names of Wilberforce, of Clarkson, and of Garrison. Gokhale's sympathy did not stop at words. Although his health; was at the time very unsatisfactory, he sailed for South Africa in 1912 — at the invitation of M. K. Gandhi, and with the sanction and encouragement of the Colonial Office and the Indian Government — in order to seek some means of redressing the grievances of Indians, indentured and otherwise, in that country.

The reception accorded to him was excellent, and he succeeded in securing from the. South African authorities promise of better treatment for Indians in a variety of particulars. After his return to India, however, further difficulties arose, which led to the famous passive resistance campaign organised by Gandhi. Gokhale was immensely interested in this movement, and undertook a very strenuous campaign of public meetings up and down India in order to raise funds, and to educate public opinion in its support. The present writer will never forget the power and eloquence with which the great patriot addressed one of these meetings at Delhi, where he was in the audience.

The Public Services Commission

The strain of this campaign was however very severe, and it was incurred at a time when Gokhale's energies were also heavily engaged in the work of the Public Services Commission, of which he had been made a member. This Commission had been appointed to consider the claims of Indians to higher and more extensive employment in the public service connected with, the civil administration of the country. At the time when the appointment of the Commission had first been mooted, Gokhale had propounded four tests by which it might be estimated whether or no the Government of India was genuinely progressive, namely, first the attention paid to the moral and material improvement of the people; second, the pains taken to foster the development of local self-government; third, the degree to which the principle of representative government was in force In the legislatures; and fourth, the extent to which Indians were admitted into the ranks of the public service. He saw considerable signs of advance in regard to the first three of these four standards, but very little in regard to the fourth.

The work of the Public Services Commission proved to be very arduous, and his strength was failing. He did not live to see the completion of its task. Gokhale complained of the deep-seated prejudices with which the official witnesses were filled; the evidence given by such witnesses was little but a continuous cry of Indian incapacity. He told his friends at the Servants of India Society that he never had to undergo such severe mental strain as during this period. Six hours a day were spent in the hearing of evidence in public, and many hours had also to be spent on the studying of written statements. The strain was more than his weakened physique could stand. His already overworked system had combated with an enormous amount of public work of a very anxious character; and the South African affair was drawing his heart's best blood. For this fresh duty he practically worked through all the twenty-four hours of the day. Even dinner and recreation hour was given to some discussion or other in relation to this great question. He was always a light sleeper; and the anxiety and mental strain deprived him even of the little sleep he was accustomed to enjoy. Often in the dead of night he was heard pacing up and down his room, with half articulate utterances, showing his deeply absorbed state of mind.

The Indian Cause in South Africa

His doctors, both in India and in Europe, gave him clear warning of what would follow if he did not relax the strain... But he felt the issues involved in the work of the Public Services Commission to be worth every sacrifice he could make; and he never ceased his crusade on behalf of his suffering fellow-countrymen in South Africa, and in the other Colonies where the system of indenture was in vogue. In this great cause his efforts were ably seconded by C. F. Andrews, and he had the good fortune to find a sympathetic helper and adviser in the person of Lord Hardinge with the result that not long after Gokhale's death the evil system which had perpetuated for so long the spirit of slavery was brought to an end. In spite of the yeoman service done in the cause by other leaders, this triumph must primarily be regarded as won by Gokhale himself. How much these various cares oppressed him and how deeply he felt in regard to them is indicated by a letter written from England in May, 1913.

> The pressure of work and engagements has much increased during the last fortnight; and the ear-specialist whom I said this morning expressed his serious disappointment that it should be so. My ear has now improved a good deal — about half the normal hearing has returned; but he thinks that further improvement is possible, only I must have no work or engagements of any kind for about six months more. This is, as you will see, an impossible condition, and I must do the best I can in the circumstances. Already the prospect of a renewal of the South African struggle is hanging over my head like a sword. For if our countrymen find it necessary to resume passive resistance, I must return to India in time for the September Session of the Council, and raise a debate at Shimla on the whole question. And then we must do what we can to organise assistance for the cause throughout the country. This is extremely unfortunate from the standpoint of my health; for I don't quite know how far I shall be able to bear that strain in my present state. However I feel there is no choice in the matter, and I must take what comes.
>
> I have sent a long telegram to Polak this week, in which I have suggested to him that he should come

here as soon as passive resistance is resumed, and that after reorganising the London Committee (which is moribund at present) he and I should go together to India at the end of August. If he is by my side in India, the strain on me will be far less. I saw Lord Ampthill last Tuesday, and we have arranged to raise a debate in the House of Lords on the question at an early date. Our difficulty just now is that we are not yet in possession of all the amendments which have been accepted in the Union Parliament. We hope to get that information tomorrow.

Endeavouring Method of Education

By about the end of the first quarter of the 19th century, Elphinstone recognised that the more endeavouring method of winning loyally over the people was through education to which he thought to give greater attention. He put it that, "unless some exertion is made by the Government, the country will certainly be in a worse slate under our rule that it was under the Peshwas. I do not confine this observation to what is called learning, which in its present form, must unavoidably fall off under us but the humbler acts of reading and writing." In spite of this statement in 1824 the Bombay Education Society established at Bombay the English School, subsequently named Elphinstone High School. Two years later twenty-four primary schools were opened by the Society, and in 1827 a subscription was raised in Bombay to found Elphinstone College.

In the early and mid-Victorian periods England followed the policy of Liberal Statemenship just as much towards India as towards any other colony. This was embodied in the Charter of 1833 and Queen's Proclamation of 1858.

With the supremacy of Macaulay over the Orientalists in 1834 (which came as a result of Charter of 1833) there was an official commitment of British India to Western learning. As a result thereof the social revolution, on which a meagre attention was so far paid entered into a new and accelerated phase. Some organisations dealing with the social change in India were established for purposes like abolition of caste, idolatry and permitting widow remarriage. Under pseudonym of *Lokahitwadi* (adviser of what is good for the people). Sardar Gopal Han Deshmukh (1833-97) published "One Hundred Letters" advocating general reform among Indians along Western line. In one of these letters Deshmukh argued that the English had been sent by God to awaken Hindus of such terrible customs, as Sati, infanticide and Jagannath Slaughter.

One representative of Maharashtra population was a noble (Sardar) but a *shudra* gardener. Jcotiba Govind Phule (1827-90). Having acquired English education, even though Phule never entered into any prestigious high position in the hierarchy of British Administration, he believed British Rule was meant for all types of social reform. Champion of 'Untouchables' and leader of Non-Brahmins, Mahatma Phule as he came to be called, concluded that British had conquered India "to liberate the disabled *Shudras* from the slavery of the crafty Aryas". In the footsteps of Sardar Deshmukh and Mahatma Phule there were many who believed that through the British education social reform of orthodox Hindu society was possible but unlike the above they thought such social reforms were not the end in themselves. Rather they were necessary prerequisites for political change which might one day make British Rule unnecessary. There were many who held this opinion, of whom from our view point. Justice Mahadev Govind Ranade and Gopal Krishna Gokhale were most popular.

If on the one hand there were those who thought that the British were God-sent opportunity for the good of the country there were, on the other hand, those who developed a hatred for the British. One such example was that of a Brahmin youth. Vasudev Balwant Phadke (1845-1883). He tried to revolt against the British Empire nearly twenty years after the Mutiny. An insight into working of Phadke's mind could be found by his autobiography and diary captured by the British. He wrote: "My mind turned against the English, and I wished to ruin them. From morning to night, bathing, eating, sleeping. I was brooding over this, and I could get no proper rest. At mid-night I used to get up and think how this ruin might be done until I was as one mad." Phadke learnt riding and the shooting at the target He collected swords, spears, gun powder, lead and chain armours. He managed to raise an army and supported it by organising raids on Banias and other rich men in the village of Maharashtra. For these raids he formed a gang of lower caste tribe which was scattered around Poona and Satarah Districts, and whose people were strong and hardy. Unfortunately for Phadke, these men of low caste tribe were most interested in looting the Banias and other rich people and cutting out ears; and seemed less interested in the destruction of British Rule. The frustrated Phadke was being followed by the British armed forces and the poor man had to Hod refuge in a temple. He knew me success did not come in a big way to him in this world; and prayed for an opportunity in the country in the next.

The robberies committed by the gang of Phadke created not an insignificant terror in the Deccan already in the grip of famine. The Anglo-Afghan war had already created a feeling of incase in the mind of Higher British Authority. Phadke's revolt created a lot of problems for them at, least they thought so.

Lord Cranbrook, Secretary of State, for India wrote to the Viceroy, Lord Lytton on 31 March 1879: "... Sir R. Temple (Governor of Bombay) speaks of some disloyalty at Poona, but I hope it is nothing serious... It must be expected that with such a number of newspapers and rumours our difficulties in Africa and Afghanistan will be exaggerated ..may indicate a shaken allegiance.... Are there any extraneous agencies at work to affect the minds of the natives adversely?"

On July 21, 1879 Phadke was arrested and sentenced in 'Yervada' jail Poona and then deported to a den after being sentenced to life. In the den be made an unsuccessful attempt to escape but failed and died in 1883. The man wax an extraordinary character. He worked relatively as an unknown person serving as an accountant in the military depot. On account of refusal by the higher authorities in his military accounts office to grant leave of absence to sec his dying mother he nursed hatred towards British. He was a lonely man, always restless. He was able to raise up an army to revolt against British Empire. His mistake was to use the technique which could have been useful a hundred years ago. In any case he created a disturbance and terror in the minds of British. He showed an amazing courage and stamina against very heavy odds. This means that he had a Maratha pride the characteristic of the upper strata of the society. The fact that he was given a rousing reception at the Poona Railway Station when he was being taken from there to be transported to Aden was more than sufficient to alarm the authorities. The Governor of Maharashtra, Sir Richard Temple wrote to the Viceroy, Lord Curzon regarding the fear that he envisaged from *Chitpavans,* on 3 July, 1879; "But nothing that we do now, by way of education, emolument, or advancement in the public service at all satisfied the Chitpavans. They will never be satisfied till they regain their ascendancy as they had it during last century ...They esteem it their character on high to rule over the minds of the Hindus... Their past to them — their glorious past survives in their minds...' Again on 9th July, 1879 he wrote: "....barely sixty years have elapsed since the Chitpavans ceased to be rulers — the memory of all this is suit to this day comparatively freak in the minds of the Natives, fresher far than the memory of most of the great political events of Indian History."

"Now the Chitpavan tribe still exists in vigour and prosperity. They are inspired with nation sentiment and with an ambition bounded only with the bounds of India itself....". This shows that Temple's expression of the fear was deep in his heart His terror on account of Phadke's rebellion made him think that such rebels were real enemies of the "Raj".

English Education in Maharashtra

As a matter of fact the real challenge to the British came not from rebellion likc Phadkc's bat from those who got education in the schools and collegcs which wcrc foundcd by the British Government to educate the people on the basis of Western learning. The two prominent leaders were Bal Gangadhar Tilak and Gopal Krishna Gokhale about whom the present text is concerned. It is a strange fact — one may call it irony — that English education which was started in Maharashtra by Elphinstone and his successors to detach the people from the older order became the cause of challenge to the British instead of being their allies.

Mount Stuart Elphinstone who worked as Commissioner of Deccan, Governor of Bombay and the British Resident at Poona, was a very capable administrator who did not lack in foresight. He had closely observed the temporal and the moral authority which Brahmins in general and Chitpavan Brahmins in particular possessed. Elphinstone on the basis of vast experience as an administrator in Deccan could foresee that it was difficult to envisage that such a community could easily be loyal to the Raj. In 1819 he wrote: "I consider the Hindu religion to be one great cause of the people of this country being so far behind Europeans in laws and morals and I should be very glad to see that obstacle to their improvement removed." He would have liked that the Chitpavans and whole of Hindu community should be shed away from ancient beliefs, rituals, traditions and bigotry.

But he was fully conscious of the fact that to participate action on these lines was full of danger. And therefore he tried to bring about transition from the old to the new in as palatable manner as possible. He guaranteed the *Inams* and advances that were already in existence. He did not confiscate the temple lands and in fact continued to pay cash to temples and even to the individual Brahmans as was already in practice. He did not similarly discontinue the annual *Dakshina* festival in which the Brahmins used to assemble in Poona every year to pats a test in Hindu philosophy and rituals and receive cash awards from the State.

Privileged Status to Brahmins

One can see that the maintenance of *Dakshina* was a sort of approval to the privileged status of the Brahmins, and the opening of Poona Hindu College in 1821 was a step further in this direction. The main objective of this College was to educate young Brahmins in several branches of science and knowledge. Apart from some professorship in the *Vedas,* the College had chairs in *Advaita* (Philosophy), *Sastras* (Religion), *Viyakaran* (Grammar), *Niyaya* (Logic), *Vydic* (Medicinal).' That a separate college was to be set up to cater to the needs of teaching research in Hindu religion and classical learning seemed incredible to the critics of Elphinstone. Elphinstone on his part would not controvert with his critics: but he considered his plan as a transitional measure to be replaced by Western learning. He believed that eventually the *Dakshina* might be converted into scholarships for the students of schools and colleges set up on the Western model.

The next quarter of a century proved that after all Elphinstone was right in his way of thinking and doing. The *Dakshina* and the Hindu College went through the changes as anticipated by him. In September, 1849, the Bombay Government received a representation from a number of liberal Brahmins protesting against the old orthodoxy. The representation said, "...the old illiberal and barbarous prejudice of confining learning to the Brahmin caste and locking it up in stores which the great mass of the people will never be able or hope to open.. What the nation most wants is useful arts, science and morals and they should find there not certainly in the dead Sanskrit, but in the animated English literature."

In the Hindu College there were successive changes of the syllabi and curricula so much so that the Chairs in Sanskrit were replaced by English. Mathematics and Sciences. Forty-three years after it was found that the Hindu College was renamed as Deccan College: and became an institution meant for the dissemination of knowledge on the Western pattern. The *Dakshina* funds were transferred to Bombay Government for creation of scholarships and fellowships for learning on Western line. It was a unique change which could be brought about only through the wisdom and foresight of a man like Elphinstone in a palatable manner from old order to the new one.

Gokhale and Gandhi

Polak, however, who was closely associated with Gandhi in this cause of the Indians in South Africa, went to prison and long with his leader instead of coming to India as Gokhale desired.

When the Conflict Came to an End with the Gandhi

Smuts agreement in 1914 Gokhale was in India once more. He was able to receive Gandhi at the Servants of India Home on his return in triumph, and to show his unflagging interest in the cause of his oppressed countrymen. But his strength was visibly ebbing. Did he realise that this was the man who more than any other individual was to take his place in the national struggle? We have seen how greatly Gandhi honoured Gokhale. What Gokhale thought of his younger contemporary he has left on record:

> In all my life I have known only two men who have affected me spiritually in the manner that Gandhi does — our great patriarch, Dadabhai Naoroji, and my late master, Ranade, men before whom not only are we-ashamed of doing anything unworthy but in whose presence our very minds are afraid of thinking anything that is unworthy.
>
> Natarajan has described a scene when, during the last weeks of his life, Gokhale took him and another leading Indian into his confidence, in regard to difficulties that had arisen between the Viceroy, Lord Hardinge, and Gandhi as to the Indian cause in South Africa. The Viceroy, while strongly upholding that cause, was at variance with Gandhi, as to the right course to pursue; and Gokhale had the task of bringing about agreement.
>
> 'Gokhale', Natarajan relates, was much distressed. We could see that the difficulty of mediating between these two personages was severely straining his fast failing health.

Gokhale and Tilak

Nearly forty years before the birth of Bal Gangadhar Tilak and fifty years before that of Gopal Krishna Gokhale the Maratha confederacy had been overthrown and territory had come under the control of East India Company. Shivaji, indeed, was the great warrior, but his successors, Peshwas made themselves in power in land, but could not effectively control it. No wonder that the Maratha chiefs were defeated one by one; and the East India Company emerged to be the supreme political power in the Indian subcontinent.

After Shivaji and Peshwas, who commanded power over Poona, the *de facto* heads of the confederacy were the exalted Chitpavan Brahmins to which community both Tilak and Gokhale belonged. Both of them inherited proud even though tragic consciousness of belonging to the community which directed the destiny of Maratha powers when it was at its glory and also when it faced its essential downfall.

The origin of Chitpavan is still a mystery; but the most plausible meaning that the scholars believed in was that they were pure of mind. They were among unique princely class, who assumed temporal as well as spiritual power over their people. Mount Stuart Elphinstone, the British Resident of Peshwa's court at Poona who played a key administrative position, at once realised that it was easy enough to deal with Peshwas but much more difficult to deal with the large ruling caste of *Chitpavan* to which Peshwas belonged. The *Chitpavans* had monopolised the best land and the most fertile area of the State. Since they were also the hereditary' religious heads of their community they were bound to dominate the political, religious, economic and social life of Maharashtra.

Difference in the Philosophies of Tilak and Gokhale

We believe that for understanding the socio-politico programmes of reconstruction of Bal Gangadhar Tilak and Gopal Krishna Gokhale it is necessary that we first understand their different philosophies of life and the institutional patterns they were born in and brought up.

Philosophy of Life

For Tilak the philosophy of life was in a general way based on *Hindu Dharma* and for Gokhale on the accelerated development of the West and its impact on equality and liberty of the people, and faith in the Charter of 1833 and Queen Victoria's Proclamation of 1858 in regard to the British policies to be pursued in India during the colonial period, ruled first by the East India Company and after so-called Mutiny by his/her Majesty and the British Parliament respectively.

The philosophy of life *of Hindu Dharma* by which Tilak was greatly influenced was the interpretation of reality, and meaning and purpose of life. Between the three and five thousands years ago the *Rishis* (Saints) taught their disciples the basic ideas of *Hindu Dharma*. They left plenty of literature which may be treated as inspired by them through the messengers of Almighty or their own wisdom and knowledge (according to one's belief), which. contains profound knowledge and wisdom in the form of hyms of the *Rigveda, Samhitas* (Chapters of *Vedas*), the *Brahmanas,* i.e. religious documents after *Vedas* and *Upanishads* containing the elaboration of *Vedas* and the *History of Epics,* i.e. *Ramayana and Mahabharata.* These documents contained the Indian philosophy of life, morality and polity. Upon them the *Bharat dharma,* i.e., (way of life in India) was founded.

The saints believed that the imperfect and changing universe could not be the ultimate reality and the truth. They believed in the Perfect, Formless, the Permanent and Changeless in God — in *Brahma,* is Real and the True. This cannot be easily understood by the mind of the human being; and yet it is a pan of the human being itself. *Brahma* was considered to be the Creator, the Real, the True and the Absolute. *Brahma,* it may be added was the originator of universe and gave the universe ultimate meaning. Some schools of thinking which follow *Bharat Dharma* declined that the *Vedas* were divinely revealed and perhaps believed in the theory of outstressing of human mind and soul. They believed the supreme Absolute be known through experience and can be interpreted as universally, spiritually integrated and purposeful.

The universe is purposeful in the sense that the *Brahma* is inherent within its creations and they are capable of evolving self-consciousness and self-realisation. They evolved from the lower form to the higher form which is an evolutionary process and culminated in the Purpose of Creation. Self-conscious is the one who attained the highest stage in the evolutionary process and is potentially capable of understanding the Reality and also penetrating in True Nature, the *Atman,* the true Nature of man. Man himself is not God, and yet he is capable to be potentially one with God. The man is free to realise his true Nature or remain completely ignorant.

The moral purpose of creation. Saints said, was *Moksha,* i.e., fulfilment of liberation from the apparent Nature to the real Nature. This might be called the reabsorbation in *Brahma.* The apparent conflict and diversity are harmonised and integrated in the grand scheme of *Dharma.* It is not necessary for the man, according to the high principles of Hindu religion, to be confused, live in conflict and misunderstanding because there is no chaos in the Real Nature of the Universe. The classical Indian Philosophy of the right ordering of the thing in the society depending upon the integrated principles of *Dharma* is the inner law of each individual;

and if the human being so wishes, it can manifest itself into the social order of the meaningful. *Dharma* is a dynamic law which always remain dynamic. The real purpose of life is to realise that through this dynamism a man can live the life, the ideal of which is harmonious and purposeful living. Everyone potentially has the capability of achieving this ideal of *Dharma,* but he will have to have a conscious decision-making and free choice. Since the soul is the pan of God, it would experience a number of births depending upon the vices and virtue, i.e. *Karma,* of the human being until it becomes one with God. This may be called the *Moksha.*

The past actions of human beings are reflected in the present and the present ones in those of the future. *Karma* in itself neither rewards nor punishes, but each man is his own judge: and he can evolve a life which leads him from lower ordering to the higher ordering till he achieves the True Nature. If he does not work in a purposeful, peaceful cosmos he can also be at a distance from has true nature.

Higher Order of Cosmos for Man

The Rishis realised the higher order of cosmos for man. They thought that a man can attain *Moksha* directly by renunciation of the world. This, however, can be achieved only by a very few saintly people. So far as ordinary people are concerned they should not interfere with the process of birth and rebirth. Rather they should try to free themselves from the levels of *Karma* by performing selfless and desireless action to attain self consciousness and be one with *Brahma,* Such people should remember the advice of Lord Krishna when he said in the *Bhagavad Gita* "Man winneth not freedom from action by abstaining, from activity; nor by renunciation does he rise to perfection. Nor can anyone, even for an instant, remain really actionless: for helplessly is everyone driven to action by the qualities born of nature."

This shows that other worldliness may appear to be a part and parcel of *sanniyasin,* but all men even the Sanniyasin must be prepared to do the selfless services and devote themselves to morally responsible action to be one with God. The Gita, the sacred of the texts, teaches the lesson of *Swadharama* that is one's own religion, thereby meaning Hindu religion, Man is free to action; but his actions may be responsible or irresponsible; and thereby they may lead to cosmos or chaos. Thus, the potential of cosmos or chaos exists in the world, Freedom become beneficial and beneficent only because of an individual leading an orderly life by his *Swadharama.* That is the classical ideal of Hindu philosophy of life which meant not the law-less freedom but rather the lawful freedom, i.e. self-rule or *Swaraj.* Swaraj is manifested by a man living in accordance with *Swadharama.*

With a view to elaborating how the individuals should live in their *Swadharma,* the Rishis did not neglect the fact that most of the individuals work for wealth and power for the sake of enjoyment. They did not deny them their efforts; the only things they suggested was that they should acquire wealth and power through lawful means and the enjoyment of their lives should be regulated to *Dharma.* In this way their efforts would lead to their salvation.

Goals of Life

The four goals of the lives of the individuals were described as *Dharma, Artha, Karma* and *Moksha. Dharma,* i.e. lawful lives would be the basis of the next goal of *Artha,* i.e. the power and wealth; and of *Karma,* the fulfilment of their desire. These stages, if properly pursued would result in *Moksha.* This shows that the spiritual ends of lives of individuals are dominated by the worldly ends. They do not deny the worldly ends of the individuals; rather they give them their fullest meaning. All worldly ends, it is to be noted according to the Hindu religion art governed by the lawful power of *Dharma.* Thus, each individual leading this life in consonance with *Swadharma* leads to the utmost gain from this ordering of life. This would prepare every individual for the Real World. There is an intimate relationship between the spiritual good and the social good, the latter leading to former.

The lawful activities and duties of the human being would not only be socially valuable but also result in spiritual good. Therefore, the individuals have not been asked to renounce the fruits of their activities; they would also be dedicated to the spiritual end of life; The renunciation of worldly pleasures only means the renunciation of selfish, immoral and anti-social actions. This is in the real sense of the terra the message of the *Bhagavad Gita* — the lesson of *Swadharma.*

In regards to the individual relationship with society, each individual is supposed to possess life-situation in the communal life. The Cosmic harmony is manifested following the code and conduct of *Dharma.*

Social Harmony

This social harmony is manifested by *Swadharama.* If an individual behaves with others according to the peaceful code of conduct then social justice is assured. Social justice exists because it is based on spiritual justice and for no other cause; and therefore an individual must act according to the high ideal of spiritual justice to maintain social justice in the society. The just and harmonious society is peaceful, cooperative and there is no place for antagonism and base mentality and bitter feelings against others. This shows that the cooperative spirit is a part and parcel of society where social obligations are set at a high order. Every individual is to live and act according to his Inner Nature, i.e. *Swadharama.* If a socially just society co-exists with spiritually just society each individual moves to the fulfilment of the purpose of full life.

As a matter of fact in the society people have diversity rather than uniformity in the nature. Therefore, the Rishis have thought the individuals harmonise each one of them with the social order. The concept of *Swadharma* does recognise this diversity of individuals. In spite of this recognition each individual is supposed to have equal position provided that he carries on his duties assigned to him to the best of his abilities. The purpose of life, however, is realised through the perfection of one's role within the harmonious, social order. The main focus of attention is on the social cooperation in accordance with the life situation of each individual. No one should interfere or criticise others; rather he should do his duty in the best possible manner. Better think of yourself and the duty assigned to you rather than of others.

If everyone performs his duties whether in a high or a low position, to the best of his abilities he is a great person whatever his status of life might be. This type of society is harmonious, full of love and affection rather than of conflict and hatred. Each individual's happiness lies in doing his own duty without any malice towards others. Thus, each individual would have a sense of belonging to the community and the society. This is the only way in which social harmony is achieved amongst the greatest diversity. This leads not only to the happiness of each individual but also to the achievement of purpose of society which is to be one with God.

The *Bhagavad Gita* leaches this lesson when it says "Belter one's own dharma though the destitute of merit, than the *dharma* of another well discharged. Better death in the discharge of one's own *dharma,* the *dharma* of another is fraught with danger."

The Rishis have Laid down the four stages of each individual's Life characterised to duties of each. This is found in *Ashrama Dharma.* They proceed to describe the four stages of life *(Ashramas)* well recognising that an individual is supposed to perform a particular type of duty, again with the best of his capability in each one of them. The first stage of life is that of the *Brahmcharya,* the student life when he has to learn at die feet of his guru, to live a life of celebrity, serve his parents and teachers and build up his health through exercises of *Yoga.*

The second stage is that of *Grahsta,* the stage in which the person will marry, produce children and have a family; he would have to work and earn his livelihood and accumulate wealth and power, perform religious duties and fully participate in the activities of the world. The third stage is that of *Vanaprastha,* a retired person from the active life after having seen his grand child to do the honorary public service, teach, learn intensively the sciences and eventually mature to the finest in search of peace through meditation. The fourth is that of *Sanyasi,* when a man completely abandons worldly concerns and devotes himself completely to meditation with a view to realising the Ultimate Reality.

This shows that out of the four stages of life, the first three are concerned with worldly activities, have a socially conscious mind and a moral and upright conduct of life while living in the society itself. It is only in the last stage that a man has to renounce the worldly activities and the social life. If the whole span of life is supposed to be a hundred years than each stage would have a period of twenty-five years. It is to be added that in the Hindu religion living in the society with a socially conscious purpose is so important that Manu has devoted six of his twelve books of jurisprudence on the exposition of these rules of life in the society.

If a man wants to understand Reality and Purpose of life he has to pass through all the stages with full consciousness that three out of four are concerned with the worldly affairs in which the social harmony is to be achieved even when there is a great diversity. This is why the Hindu religion is generally understood by one phrase only. "The way of life". The most eminent scholar of Hindu philosophy. Sarvapalli Radhakrishnan has aptly said 'The *ashramadharam*... attempts to fill the whole of life with the power of spirit."

Unfortunately in the Hindu religion the system of *Varna* later on degraded itself into the rigid Caste structure. Varna described the social obligation of each individual according to his occupation and position in the social system. There were four Vamas: the *Brahmin,* the *Kshatri,* the *Vaisha* and the *Shudra.* In the early days of the rise of Hindu culture there was not a strong jacket division between four castes. It was natural that in a dynamic society it is always possible for a person belonging to one Varna to enter into another Varna. For instance, there are two prominent examples in the Hindu religion (when it was a dynamic Varna) when it so happened. Parshuram was Brahman by *Varna* because he was born of a Brahman father and Brahman mother.

Later on he became a Kshatriya and fought in War and killed other Kshatris. Similarly Vishwamitra was a Kshatriya by Varna but because of personal efforts he became a Brahmin. Later on when the Hindu society became a closed and defensive one, the Varna was attributed to the *Karma* during the period of one's own life and his activity after the birth into the another life gave him the position of Varna which determined his caste. Some scholars believe that Varna of each individual is determined not only by the Karma of previous life but that of present life as well.

The rigid caste structure became hereditary in the sense that the children of an individual in one caste remain in the same caste in which his parents were. As a matter of fact Varna was never thought to be determined in this way. The degeneration in the society resulted in the heredity of caste structure. The duty of the Brahmin was to study and disseminate the knowledge of the *Vedas* and *Vedanta,* investigate and further add to the knowledge in science and philosophy, and advise others in matter of Dharma.

The Brahmin was supposed to live the life of austerity, humbly and with the greatest simplicity and devote his whole time not only to learning and dissemination of knowledge but also to perform religious rights for himself and others: the Kshatriya's life is supposed to be devoted to protection of the society and state, fight, rule, and to wield power for the advancement of social purpose and purpose of life.

The Vaishaya was to have perfection in Art and Craft: accumulate wealth for manufacturing of goods for the purpose of trading and to follow the vocation of agriculture. The Shudras were supposed to perform the manual and residual services to the people of other *Varnas.*

Defects of the Strict Caste Structure

It may, however, be noted that in spite of the defects of the strict caste structure, the *Varna* as defined in this manner provided the secure and extended family life, a son of belonging to the community where the purpose of all was the same and the society was in a harmonious order.

Each individual's duty was defined; the father was not to perform the duty of a son and vice-versa. A man was not to perform the duties of the wife and similarly the wife was not to perform the duty of her husband. So in this system also there was a unity in variety. The duties of different varnas were complimentary to each other and not contradictory. Thus, the purpose of the fulfilment of the social order became harmonious and not antagonistic.

In this way each individual in different *Varnas* was shown to attain the Purpose of Life like any of the individual belonging to another *Varnas.* Therefore, in a sense the caste system also performs the basic function in a socially harmonious way and for the long time remained useful to society.

One cannot help thinking that whatever might be said of a rigid caste structure, howsoever beneficial in a certain period in the history of our country, yet the degeneration of *Varnas* with this strict caste structure and social custom was bound to be deprecated by the socially conscious people and in a renascent India it could not have been praised for ever.

However, we must note that in Tilak's ideas there has been an evolution of thinking. Whereas we shall discuss them in detail at appropriate places, we believe it is in order to briefly describe them here.

Towards the end of the nineteenth and beginning of twentieth century he started Ganpati Festival and Shivaji Festival to boost up the morale of Maraiha Nation and bring the Hindus masses on one platform through arranging these two festivals to move in the congregation.

Tilak gave a new direction to Ganpati Festival by making it a mass festival rather than individual affair. In 1894, commenting on the success of Ganpati Festival mela, he said. "The ten day Ganpati Festival sought to unite the Hindus on a pisiform of religious piety and innocent gaily."

In 1896, the started Shivaji Festival because according to him it was Shivaji who "Upheld our self-respect as Hindus and who gave a particular direction to our religion."

While travelling through Madras to Cylon in 1898 and 1899 and embarking quietly to Burmah in 1900, Tilak reflected on different experiences and concluded that "The common factor in Indian society is the feeling of '*Hindutav*' (Hindunees)."

It is alleged that in the year 1901 alongwith his trusted two col-leagues. Vasu Kaka and K. P. Khadilkar, Tilak made a plan to go to Nepal as devotees of Lord Shiva with a view to induce the Maharaja of Nepal to invade India so that Hindu Raj could be established in India. But the plan, it is said failed because the plague spread and the border of Nepal were sealed.'

To the present author it appears surprising that a reputed scholar like Stanley A. Wolpcrt should have laid this allegation against Tilak (vide his book *Tilak and Gokhale, Revolution and Reform in Making of Modern India*). This is because the only supportive evidence is provided by the biography of K. P. Khadilkar written by his nephew. It appears most probable that the nephew might have written the biography of his uncle and to boost up his uncle's image, he might have shown the association of Tilak in a 'plot' which appears fantastic. It is next to impossible that such a great leader as Tilak would have himself participated in the so-called 'plot' which on the face of it appears absurd. How could the invasion on India by Nepal would have defeated such a great military force as the British had for the protection of British India in those days!

After 1905 Tilak emerged as a national leader having no distinction between Hindus and Muslims and declared that the Ganpati Festival and Shivaji Festival brought the masses — both Hindus and Muslims — together. While addressing the congregation of Shivaji Festival in Bengal he is on record to say that a great hero like shivaji could have been a Muhammadan.

In 1916 in the Congress-League combined Session at Lucknow, be declared that he would be ready to achieve Swaraj even if the Raj was given by the British to the Muslims in India.

In April 1916 he started a Home Rule League to propagate for Swaraj so that he could achieve it as early as possible.

And finally, in 1920 he formed the *Congress Democratic Party.* The manifesto of this Party among other things said "It believes in the potency of democratic doctrines for the solution of the Indian problems and regards that extension of education and political franchise as its best weapons.' It also said that this 'party' proposes to work for Montagu-Chelmsford Reforms for what it is worth..."

This in outline provides a very sketchy presentation of the essentials of Hindu philosophy of life. In fact, several volumes and much more discussions would be needed if one wanted to work on the subject as such. We have, however, presented this sketch with the specific purpose to show the basis of the brood philosophy of life that Tilak followed in his efforts at achievement of Swaraj for the country. He also wrote and published three scholarly contributions on Hindu religion which in a broad sense of the term might be considered to be the basis of his socio-politico-economic programme of reconstruction for a free India.

We know that Tilak was a great freedom fighter and a builder of Modem India. For his cause he suffered much and the consistency and determination with which he fought for Swaraj of the country was beyond any doubt. As he was a great scholar of Sanskrit, he made masterly contribution to Vedic of research and Hindu philosophy. They all implicitly gave a message of the ancient Indian culture which was unparalleled in the sense that no other country of the world could.

However, we must note that in Tilak's ideas there had been an evolution of thinking. Towards the end of 19th and beginning of 20th century he started Ganpati Festivals and Shivaji Festival to boost up the morale of the Maratha nation and bring the masses on one platform through arranging the two festivals to move in congregation. Before 1905 his mind was preoccupied with regionalism rather than nationalism. At least one scholar W. A. Stolper, contended (even though he has not been able to supply any worthwhile documentary evidence) that Tilak wanted to establish a Hindu Slate in the country.

In 1905 Tilak emerged as a national leader having no distinction between Hindus and Muslims which is manifested by the fact that while addressing the congregation of Shivaji Festival in Bengal he is on record to say that even a Muslim could have been such a warrior as Shivaji was.

In 1916 in the Congress-League combined session at Lucknow he declared that he would be ready to achieve Swaraj if the Raj was given by the British to Muslims in India.

In 1918, he started a Home Rule League to propagate for securing Swaraj as early as possible. And finally towards the end of his life he accepted Montague-Chelmsford Reforms, which were very similar to Gokhale's last testament.

We know that Tilak was a great freedom fighter and a builder of Modern India, for this cause he suffered much and the consistency and determination with which he fought for Swaraj of the country was beyond any doubt. As he was a great scholar of Sanskrit, he made masterly contribution Vedic of research and Hindu philosophy. They all implicitly gave a message of the ancient Indian culture which was unparalleled in the sense that no other country of the world could claim to have reached such a high degree of civilization which was characterised by its dance, drama, music and the an of fine structure. The Indian culture was spread far and inside. As such Tilak believed that it was not necessary for his countrymen to learn anything from the Western culture and civilization. Except for a few other stray pieces. Tilak's principal works were *The Orion* (Published in 1893). *The Arctic Home in the Vedas* (1903) and the *Gita-Rahasya* (1915). Passing references of these have been given at appropriate places each of which broke new ground. Those who are interested in their subject matter cannot do better than study them First hand. For the general readers their arguments are presented here in Tilak's own words.

Gokhale's Place in History

It is an interesting coincidence — and perhaps more than a coincidence — that Lord Morley turned straight from his first interview with Gokhale to a renewed study of Cavour. The essential similarity between the minds of the two men may have exercised an influence, if only subconsciously, upon the thoughts of the great and wise Liberal statesman. For in studying the career and the spirit of Gokhale one is constantly reminded of Cavour.

The setting of the two statesmen's lives was of course entirely different. The Italian had the nucleus of a free Piedmont from which to start in his liberation of Italy. He had his ten years of office as minister in a responsible government. He had countless opportunities for taking, by his own choice, decisions which were of far-reaching practical importance in the actual work of nation-building. Gokhale had none of these advantages.

He started and he remained a citizen of an India under alien control. He was always in opposition. He never had an adequate opportunity (except in minor affairs, such as in connection with the Poona Municipality) to prove that he possessed the gifts of the administrator and the legislator. He died before his unceasing labour had borne fruit in the creation of a system under which the chosen representatives of the Indian people can bear the responsibilities of office.

None the less, there is an essential similarity between Cavour and Gokhale, because the two men had the same political purpose and ideal — the same determination to use what they had in their hands to the fullest advantage in order to gain more. They were both 'masters of the possible', setting before themselves limited objectives, using existing machinery, however defective attainment of those going forward, one step objective. Both of merely 'a seditionist in disguise'. But the best men amongst the officials realised something of Gokhale's real greatness, and of his significance both for India and the Empire.

Of those who came into direct contact with Gokhale in the work of the Legislature, the lesser men believed and trembled; the big men — men of the stamp of Morley, Minto and Hardinge — accepted with gladness the fact that here was an Indian leader fit to be ranked by the side of the great constructive statesmen of the world with a definite programme in view for his country's future, and with concise and concrete policies in mind whereby he might reach his objective.

For the uniqueness of Gokhale lay largely in this: that he did not merely criticise and abuse the Government, and leave it at that, as so many of his Indian opponents were — and are still-inclined to do. He saw the shortcomings of the existing system as clearly as anyone. He was instant in season and out of season at the task of pointing out those shortcomings. But he was always constructive. He always had a better method to suggest in individual cases of mal-administration; and in regard to broad general principles, he knew exactly what the next step ought to be, and where the deficiencies of things, as they were, called most urgently for practical redress.

So much was this so, that Gokhale ceased, during his later years of greatness, to be merely a leader of opposition. Technically he remained such; but in fact he became a leader — and in some relations almost a dictator — of the best elements in Government policy. His moral stature was so commanding, his personal ascendancy became so marked, that men of enlightenment and goodwill who found themselves responsible for directing the destinies of the Indian people were glad to accept his guidance wherever they could. Thus, it came about that his advice had such a far-reaching effect in regard to the Minto-Morley reforms; that his crusade on behalf of indentured labour succeeded in wiping out that shameful survival of the epoch of slavery; that his recommendations in the great Budget speeches had year after year decisive effect in shaping the financial policy of Government; that his unceasing advocacy of the Indianisation of the Services eventually bore definite fruit; that after his death much of what he had striven for was achieved in the Montagu-Chelmsford Reforms; and that in a great number of other particulars his practical idealism was justified by the formation of enlightened policies and definite measures of reform. It is true that some of his battles are not yet won, notably those in regard to free and universal education, to expenditure on the army, and to the treatment of Indians in South Africa. Nor is 'the self-determination of India', of which he dreamed, yet a reality. But in relation to these causes he initiated a movement which quite evidently can never cease till his ends are attained. 'The stars in their courses fight for him; and though he is dead, his spirit lives on in the continual progress of such liberal movements towards their destined success'.

Gokhale was above all else a champion of the poor and helpless. The unlettered peasants, the indentured coolies pining for their home-country, the victims of ignorance, exploitation, oppression, called him to an endless and zealous championship which wore him out in their service. He struggled for his country's rights primarily because he felt her to be weak and oppressed. For him nationalism was a sane and steady force for the righting of wrongs. He was a nationalist because he was a humanitarian, a friend of the helpless a tribune of the common people. He cared nothing for personal advantage. He refused a knighthood; he refused a place on the Secretary of State's Council. He did all his work for his country in the spirit in which he had taken up his first post under the Deccan Education Society, the spirit which thinks first and always of the need to be met, and which sacrifices all personal considerations to the meeting of that need.

The problems of the contact between East and West have never been more urgent than they are today. From the beginning there have been two streams of thought and activity in evidence on both sides of this world-problem. In the West there has been the spirit of exploitation, of conquest, of dominance — the spirit whose most obvious and naked embodiment was seen in the African slave-trade, but which has shown itself in all lands where the contact has taken place, whether in isolated acts of frightfulness or in settled systems. On the other hand there has been the spirit of brotherhood, expressing itself through the sense of national responsibility evinced in the trial of Warren Hastings, in the later revisions of the Charter of the East India Company, and in the Royal Declaration of 1858; and also through the great agencies, such as the enterprise of Christian Missions, which seek to give, rather than to rule or to get, in their relations with the East.

Correspondingly there has been a double spirit in evidence in the East. The Western spirit of dominance and of exploitation has led to the creation of a spirit of intransigence, of extremism, of determination to take nothing by way of a favour, but to boycott and to non-cooperate. On the other hand the better spirit of the West has found an echo in such men as Gokhale, who are willingly to take all that is given, and to use it strenuously, and in constructive cooperation with the Western rulers in order that the highest good of the country may be attained.

From this point of view Gokhale is an emblem of the brightest hope for the future contact of East and West, and therefore, for the future of humanity. He stands for the fact that West and East — or the best elements in either — can come together in a spirit of goodwill, and can cooperate for the good of mankind. He shows that the great achievement of the West, liberal methods of government, can be understood, grasped and used by the East, for the carrying through of a thousand measures of emancipation and enlightenment.

Hence, Gokhale is a beacon, of immense hopefulness for the future. One man such as Gokhale is enough to refute a thousand prophets of woe, who foretell catastrophe if Western methods of government are transplanted to the East. His speeches and the records of his life should be read and re-read by everyone who is anxious to understand the problem of the relationships between England and India, or is interested in the vast enterprise of naturalising Western methods of government in the East.

Gokhale had many faults to find with the British system in India; but he himself was, in truth, the most striking of all proofs of the fact that in the main this system has been successful methods of education, of local and national government, of imperial relationship, which in the end produced this great man — even if they had never produced any other great men — are thereby proved not to have existed altogether in vain. They have borne their fruit in him, and in the spirit which he embodied; and it is a noble fruit.

Finally, behind all Gokhale's activities, behind his deliberate sacrifice of his leisure, his health, and in the end his life, for the sake of his country, behind his unswerving resolution to take, the best which the West has to offer and use it for the uplifting and the emancipation of the East, lay a deep realisation of the meaning of our common humanity.

This expressed itself, not only in work for the downtrodden and the distressed, but in those appeals which he uttered from time to time, and always with such deep feeling, that England should remember her best self, and act generously and with sympathy by India. He had a profound confidence in the underlying kinship of humanity, both East and West, and in the fact that an appeal to the better nature, even of the governing power, would call forth a due response.

This is indeed the last word which is to be said concerning the relations of England and India — that there should be sympathy and generosity, a willingness to trust, a belief in the healing and moderating influence of liberty. Gokhale stands, and will stand (though we are not as yet far enough away from him to discern his true greatness) as, above all, a Reconciler. He takes the best that there is in the West, to interpret it and use it for the good of the East. He turns to the West, as spokesman and aspirations of the East, appealing above all for brotherhood.

With his great natural powers and force of character he might have ridden the whirlwind, denouncing the iniquities of the West, and telling a people always ready to listen to such appeals that they must separate themselves from all these abominations. Had he chosen such a course, immense popularity would have been his. He need not then have worn himself to death in the effort to adapt and transform Western institutions. But he chose the harder path, that of the Unifier, the Reconciler; and it is only as it is considered in this light that the true greatness of his work will be appreciated.

He was a great 'master of the possible', a, constructive statesman of the first rank, a bringer-together of East and West in the common service of the needy; above all an idealist, a foreseer, a prophet of a new era of inter-racial goodwill and cooperation.

The Other Side

The arduous work done by Gokhale in 1913 and 1914 for the cause of Indians in South Africa and in connection with the Public Services Commission led to a rapid increase in the diabetic trouble from which he has been suffering for a number of years. The closing weeks of his life were rendered uneasy by a controversy amongst the leaders of the Indian National Congress regarding the Congress 'Creed' or statement of political aims and objects.

Gokhale and other leaders of the Moderate group wished this creed to include a plain statement that the policy of the Congress was that of attaining self-government by constitutional means within the British Empire. They also introduced a clause regulating the appointment of delegates to the Congress; this did not find acceptance with the leaders of the more extreme party in the Congress. The controversy which arose proved very distressing to Gokhale in his weakened state of health.

Early in 1915 it became obvious that his condition was very serious and on February 19th he died. To his comrades of the Servants of India Society who were by his side at the end he said, in Marathi, 'It is time that we should go and see the other.'

5

Great Nationalist

Mahatma Gandhi, coming from South Africa in 1896, had been instantly drawn to Gokhale and spoke of him in terms of admiration to the Indian National Congress at Lahore on 29 December 1909: "He seemed to me all I wanted as a political leader: pure as crystal, gentle as a lamb, brave as a lion, and chivalrous to a fault.... It was enough for me that I could discover no fault in him to cavil at. He was and remains for me the most perfect man on the political field".

This esteem was reciprocated by Gokhale, who commented that there could be no mention of Gandhi's name "without deep emotion and pride," and called Gandhi "a patriot amongst patriots". The two men shared similar interpretations of India's needs, and both were markedly righteous in their approach to problems of Indian nationalism.

In Tune with Mahatma

Both Gandhi and Gokhale stand in marked contrast to their fiery revolutionist contemporary, B. G. Tilak. A noteworthy feature of the early Indian Nationalist Movement is the apparent ease with which it accommodated, and emphasized from time to time, the views represented by both Gandhi and Gokhale, on the one hand, and Tilak on the other.

When Gopal Krishna Gokhale died on 19 February 1915, his contributions to the Indian Nationalist Movement were widely acclaimed by both Indians and Britons. This is remarkable when one considers that he lived during a period of great unrest, as Indians struggled to achieve equality and a representative government.

Sir Verney Lovett, who spent thirty-five years in the Indian service and who made careful appraisal of the Indian Nationalist Movement, had this to say of Gokhale: "There can be no doubt that his death was a serious loss to Indian politics. He had shown himself able to adjust idealism to circumstances, and bold enough to preach common sense. At the same time, up to the day of his death, he maintained his widespread influence. His place remained empty".

Gopal Krishna Gokhale was born on 6 May 1866 in the Marathi village of Kotaluk, located in the Ratnagiri district. He was a Brahmin and a descendant of the Chitpavan clan. Historically, this middle-class clan took the role of leading social reformation, some members advocating reform within the framework of British rule and others viewing such reform only as a necessary prelude to the time when British rule would be abolished.

Gokhale's father was a tax collector in his village and a minor clerk in the local government so the family's position was superior to that of the average Indian peasant. As a younger son, however, he received little more than his college tuition and a meagre income after his father's death (Wolpert 22). Not many details are available concerning his college life at Deccan College and later at Elphinstone College in Bombay. He is pictured as a shy, diligent student, extremely proficient in English, and with a keen interest in English literature. He enjoyed poetry, and in his own poetry he seems to have been influenced by the work of Tennyson and Browning. The characteristics of his prose style have been said to show the influence of Burke, Mill, Bright, and Morley (Wolpert).

In 1885 Gokhale studied law at Deccan College and joined the faculty of the New English School at Poona as an assistant master. While at this Jesuit school he joined with its founders and supporters, including B. G. Tilak, in establishing the Deccan Education Society, whose aim was to promote education by founding schools and colleges under native Indian management.

In 1885 the society founded Fergusson College, named after the retiring governor of Bombay, Sir James Fergusson, and which continues to this day.

In the period immediately preceding the formation of the Indian National Congress the Deccan Education Society became an important political force. Its members viewed education as an effective instrument of national regeneration, and the members were encouraged to participate in political activities.

Gokhale became secretary of the Bombay Provincial Congress in 1888, beginning his career as a public figure with this appointment. During the same year he edited the English columns of the Sudharak, an Anglo-Marathi weekly.

This secular journal emphasized freedom and equality among all men as necessary conditions for reform and pointed to the role of education in India's struggle. Education, it was felt, would allow Indians to "qualify" for equal treatment.

Gokhale's first public speech was probably delivered on 1 September 1889, at Poona, on the subject of the Crawford dismissal. Protesting the dismissal of Indian magistrates implicated in the scandal, Gokhale exhorted both sides to reasonableness:

> In the interest of India and England alike. the Government of this country ought to be carried on with absolute impartiality.... if our English friends will kindly disabuse their minds of all bias against us, if they will take a calm and dispassionate view of everything, if sentiment will give way to reason, then they will find that in treating the natives of this country with courtesy, consideration, and equality, consists the best safe-guard of the British Rule.

This approach to the problem typified Gokhale's view that ill-feeling on both sides could only be increased if violence, rather than reason, were permitted to dictate policy. He was unwilling to believe that an inherent hatred could exist between Indians and Britons; his revolt against English rule was largely a moral one, for he felt that Indians should be treated with equality.

In Congress Fold

Gokhale's political activities became more important, and in 1889 he participated in the Indian National Congress. The first Congress had been called in 1885 at the inspiration of Allan Octavian Hume, a retired English civil servant who felt that the British raj had largely failed to improve Indian conditions and that there would be no improvement for the masses until Indian government became truly representative. Delegates from all parts of British India were invited to attend the Congress in order to become acquainted with each other and to decide what political action might be taken during the coming year. In the words of the announcement: "Indirectly this Conference will form the germ of a Native Parliament, and if properly conducted will constitute in a few years an unanswerable reply to the assertion that India is still wholly unfit for any form of representative institution".

At its inception the movement was Hindu-oriented and attracted middle-class intellectuals and members of the rising commercial class. The members of the Congress believed that by presenting a fair and reasonable case, and by conducting themselves according to parliamentary precedent, they could get the most pressing problems corrected and win freedom for themselves. The first Congress was conducted in English; in fact, the tradition of conducting everything in English was so strong that it was not until 1905 that Rabindranath Tagore, presiding at a provincial conference in Bengal, broke this custom by delivering a speech in Bengali (Andrews and Mookerjee 18). (Initially, the organizers of the first Congress had seriously considered asking Lord Reay, the Governor of Bombay, to preside over the meeting.)

Outwardly at least, the British seemed to attach little significance to the nationalist movement, and membership in the Congress was not considered incompatible with loyalty to the British Crown. Despite the Sepoy Mutiny of 1857, the British were not apprehensive that their administration of India would be shaken, for, as one lieutenant-governor expressed the British attitude, "good administration was like good digestion. It did its work and you heard no more about it". In 1888 Lord Dufferin remarked, at a farewell dinner marking his retirement from the vice-royalty, that the Congress party was a "microscopic minority";

even so, he did send home confidential recommendations for liberalising the legislative councils, "which is all that the reasonable leaders even of the most advanced section of Young India dream of".

Actually, much more than this was at stake. The Congress members sought reform and broadening of the powers of existing local legislative councils, but on a much larger scale than the English considered appropriate, and with the appointment of a standing committee of the House of Commons to prevent the Crown executive overruling the council's majority decisions.

When Gokhale delivered his maiden speech to the Congress at Bombay on 27 December 1889, he rose to support an amendment by B. G. Tilak that would have given provincial councils the privilege of electing members of their own bodies to the supreme legislative councils. The amendment was lost, but his participation in debate the following day (on holding simultaneous public civil service examinations) was more favourably received. This resolution, based on the Queen's Proclamation of racial equality, and intended to assure equal treatment for Indian candidates, was a recurring theme at every Congress meeting. It had to wait for nearly forty years before it could overcome official opposition.

A good example of Gokhale's style may be found in a speech that he delivered on this problem at the 1894 Madras Congress:

> We have had this question in every shape. We have examined it from ever)' point of view. Our invention has been exhausted. Reason is fatigued. Experience has given judgement. But Anglo-Indian obstinacy is not yet conquered. (Cheers.) And remember, Gentlemen, this that we have to conquer is perhaps the worst kind of obstinacy, for it is not based so much on wrong judgement; it is not based oven so much on prejudice; it is obstinacy based on the strong foundations of self-interest and love of domination.

Here we find the initial parallel simple declaratives followed by a series of similar structures before the inevitable conclusion, "But...." And there is a growing intensity in the development from *had* to *examined,* to *exhausted, fatigued, obstinacy,* and *conquered* - with both *obstinacy* and *conquered* (in a cognate) repeated for effect.

Further, the emotional words *wrong judgement* and *prejudice* are introduced in conjunction with *self-interest* and love *of domination,* applied to the "enemy," the whole section becoming a most effective use of emotional proof, of persuasive rhetoric. In many ways the composition replicates the prose of Patrick Henry's famous "Give Me Liberty" speech.

Activities beyond Congress

In addition to his association with the Indian Congress, Gokhale assumed other activities. He was secretary of the Sarvajanik Sabha, an association for political work, and edited its quarterly journal; he became a Fellow at the University of Bombay (1895) and secretary of the Deccan Education Society (1892). His work brought him into contact with many of the influential political minds of the day. Many of his ideas about economic questions came from his contacts with Mahadev Govind Ranade, the man who had been his guru since his teaching days at Fergusson College. Gokhale's idea of government initiative in economic development is hardly new to us, but at the time it was considered radical when he said:

> Is it not the duty of Government to sec that the subject population is properly fed and clothed and housed?.... Does not the security of the country lie in the real prosperity of its teeming millions?.... But 'Let alone' is the policy of Government. Free-trade, or rather political economy, is working out her laws, say they. Well! We think the laws of political economy are largely amenable to human control. The Government must take the initiative here. They should support the falling industries of the land, if they want India to be prosperous.

In 1896 such were the divergent views within the Sarvajanik Sabha that Gokhale, along with Ganade and other moderates, broke away from that group and formed another organisation, the Deccan Sabha, which they felt more adequately reflected their views of "giving to the rulers the loyalty that is due to the law they are bound to administer, but securing at the same time to the ruled the equality which is their right under law".

Gokhale was given the opportunity to explain his economic ideas directly to a royal commission appointed in 1897 to consider the state of Indian finance. He travelled to London on behalf of the Deccan Sabha, and his testimony before the Welby Commission gave him an opportunity to meet British politicians and to learn first hand the realities of English life. This was an experience not given to many of his countrymen, and Gokhale made the most of it to diminish the gap between Indians and the British. While there he had a cordial meeting with John Morley, who was later to serve as Secretary of State for India. (It is commonly asserted that Morley's favourable impressions of Gokhale were influential in his acceptance of the Indian portfolio.) The meeting also served to give Gokhale confidence in Morley and the Liberal Party.

From his stimulating and successful contacts abroad Gokhale returned to an atmosphere of hostility in India. While he was in England complaints had reached him of the conduct of British soldiers in enforcing anti-plague measures in Poona: it seems to have been what we would call police brutality. Two Indian women had committed suicide after being raped by British soldiers. Gokhale described his informants as men "whose word I can trust absolutely," and in an interview in the *Manchester Guardian* he criticized the soldiers' conduct. When challenged to produce evidence of his charges Gokhale found his correspondents unwilling to support the charges publicly, and he was driven to make an embarrassing public apology. The ostracism of the Chitpavan community and the criticism from all sides depressed him for some time. He wrote that "recent events ... have distracted me so far that my mental equipment has been for the present seriously impaired.... it will be some time before my mind will be able to return to its normal condition".

Despite his humiliation, however, Gokhale immediately took part in organising relief for the victims of the plague. In political affairs he gradually resumed his active role and was elected to the Bombay Legislative Council in 1899. During the two years that he spent as a member of the Council he was elected to represent its non-official members in the Viceregal Legislature. During both of these appointments he found himself involved in much committee work, and he delivered numerous speeches on the presentation of bills. He spoke for tax reform and vigorously opposed a bill to reform the universities, which he said would increase enormously the control of the Government over university matters and make the universities virtually a government department.

His fight against an amendment to the Indian Official Secrets Act won the support of his countrymen. The amendment would have made civil as well as military matters official secrets and their publication an offence. Gokhale charged that the bill would "Russianize the Indian Administration," and offered the following cogent defence of freedom of the press:

> The responsibility of the Government to the people in this country is merely moral, it is not legal, as in the West. There is no machinery here, as in Western countries, to secure that the interests of the general public will not be sacrificed in favour of a class. The criticism of the Indian Press is the only outward check operating continuously upon the conduct of a bureaucracy possessing absolute and uncontrolled power.

Servants of India Society

Gokhale's work with legislative bodies convinced him that politicians could not be amateurs — they must view politics as a profession and become dedicated to it. He sought to provide India with such skilled men by founding the Servants of India Society in 1905. The inspiration for the organisation came from the Society of Jesus, but the missionary seal was devoted to political and social matters rather than religious matters. The members' vows of lifelong service to India, pledging to promote their country's interests *by constitutional means,* did not necessarily mean rejection or acceptance of foreign ideas.

Emphasis was placed on purity of personal example, responsible criticism of ongoing programmes, women's emancipation, elevation of backward classes, industrial development, and political equality within the Empire: complete independence was not their goal. Gandhi became an apprentice in the society during the last year of Gokhale's life and Rajendra Prasad, who became the first President of the Republic of India, was also an early member.

Congress President

Gokhale maintained his connection with the Indian National Congress and was elected president for its session at Benares in December 1905. It was a critical time. The British had announced the partition of Bengal in October, and a wave of nationalist feeling swept over India. Tilak headed a movement to conduct a boycott of British goods as a new agitational technique. The boycott idea was not the same as Gandhi's non-cooperation, for the boycott permitted violence, which was countered by extreme repression from Lord Curzon's government, but the notion of rebellion and revolution was firmly planted in the Indians' minds. The concept of *swaraj* (self-government) spread beyond the cities to remote districts where it had never before been contemplated.

In the midst of growing trouble Gokhale went to London on 16 September 1905 to represent the Congress in an attempt to explain to the British the state of Indian public feeling over Lord Curzon's repressive acts, particularly the partition of Bengal. One of his most challenging speeches was delivered on 6 October in Manchester, where he faced an audience of textile manufacturers and workers who were distinctly hostile to the Indian boycott of their cloth. The speech emphasized that his faith in Britain had not abated, despite Lord Curzon's policies, and that "when the whole position is brought home to you, you will rise as one man and put an end to these Russian methods of administration." In London he appealed personally to Liberal leaders, particularly John Morley; his speeches seem to have been received well and mark the beginning of a change in Liberal attitudes towards India.

En route to London Gokhale occupied himself with the preparation of the speech he was to give at the opening of the Benares Congress. It was a statement that would be closely scrutinized by all sides, and he felt weighed down by the responsibility: "God knows how it will be discharged in the end," he was reported to have said. When he returned to Bombay the speech was still unfinished. The departure of Lord Curzon as viceroy made his task somewhat easier, for it permitted him to criticize administrative policies without having to face the viceroy himself in the Viceregal Legislature at Calcutta. The speech is doubtless one of the most important of Gokhale's career, for he managed to hold the Congress together in refusing to invoke the boycott. It was a narrow victory, but the same issue split the Congress the following year and set Gokhale and Tilak irretrievably apart.

The next five years were significant ones, with extremists and moderates struggling for control of Congress. John Morley had become secretary of state for India and Lord Minto was made viceroy. Gokhale travelled again to London in April 1906 to work through Morley in gaining reforms for India. Viewed in the light of history the Morley-Minto reforms were too much of the old pattern, but they had the effect of retaining the moderate element uppermost in the Congress and of delaying the time when more radical views prevailed. The difficulties of the situation were summed up by Morley in a letter to Lord Minto:

> Your way of putting this helps me to realise how intensely artificial and unnatural is our mighty *Raj*, and it sets one wondering whether it can possibly last... Will your Reform Policy, Natives on my Council, Decentralisation, Economising of Taxation, and the rest of our virtuous deeds really make a pin of difference in their feelings about British rule?

Gokhale found himself in the difficult position of trying to work with both the English and the Indians. To the British the idea of a recognized opposition point of view hardly existed; the viceroy saw Gokhale as the instrument of British authority in the Indian National Congress and was petulant when Gokhale did not play this role. As he wrote to Morley:

> As for Gokhale, if he chooses to play with fire he must take the consequences. We can't afford to let him tamper with the Army, and if he says anything to me... I shall tell him straight to his face. 1 am thoroughly disappointed in Gokhale; I had liked what 1 had seen of him and believed that he was honest at heart, but the part he has played of late has disgusted me. ... he is as big a revolutionist as the rest of them.

Gokhale persisted in his own view of his role, despite the viceroy's disappointment and the criticism of extremist elements in the Congress. In 1910 he became a member of the enlarged

Viceregal Legislature, where he continued to act as a critic of the government. Indians had expected improved conditions in the wake of Lord Minto's reforms; instead, repressions seemed to increase. The atmosphere of the times can be clearly seen in the issues which occupied Gokhale's attention: the Press Bill of 1910 (which imposed a heavy tax on operators of printing presses) and the Seditious Meetings Bill of 1911 (which limited freedom of speech).

While on the Legislative Council Gokhale used his position to present the annual Congress resolutions directly to the council. In the reforms that he urged upon them he gave great weight to education, and in 1911 he presented a bill enabling qualified districts to make education compulsory for boys between the ages of six and ten, the central government to provide at least two-thirds of the cost. Indian public opinion was solidly in favour of the measure, but the bill was defeated in spite of the proponent's lucid advocacy.

Focus on South Africa

Gokhale's attention to Indian problems extended to the suffering of indentured Indian labourers in South Africa: his friendship with Gandhi no doubt inspired this interest. Gandhi had gone to India in 1896 and sought the support of the Indian National Congress in fighting a discriminatory tax imposed upon South African Indians. As a result of their meeting, Gokhale became Gandhi's political *guru,* and Gokhale wholeheartedly supported Gandhi's stand, particularly his campaign of passive resistance. At the Lahore Congress in 1909 Gokhale successfully moved a resolution supporting the struggle in South Africa and recommending that the government of India prohibit the recruitment of indentured Indian workers. He argued a similar measure in the Council the following year, but his proposed reforms were not effected until 1917.

In 1912 Gokhale was able to visit South Africa on his return from England, where he had attended sessions of the Indian Public Services Royal Commission. It was an honour for him to have been appointed to the Royal Commission, but his health would not permit him to attend all of its sessions, and, sensing perhaps that he had little time left, he wished to influence Gandhi to return to India, where he could be prepared to assume a responsible position in the Congress. Gokhale died on 19 February 1915, before the work of the Commission was finished. His death may be viewed as having brought an end to the dominance of the moderate element in Indian politics and its policy of logical analysis rather than vehemence as advocate or adversary in public policy debate.

In reviewing the strengths and weaknesses of Gokhale we find ample testimony to his command of both spoken and written English and to the efficacy of his use of the language. As Wolpert says, "Gifted as he was with a unique command of the spoken and written English language he could most effectively fashion his protests, petitions, and pleas, and by the end of his life the weight of Gokhale's influence upon British official opinion was unsurpassed by that of any Indian".

Even Valentine Chirol, whose criticism of the Indian Nationalist Movement was at times vitriolic, had this to say of Gokhale's conduct on the Viceregal Council:

> Though often an unrelenting critic of the Administration, he struck from the first a note of studied moderation and restraint to which most of his political friends attuned their utterances. He naturally assumed the functions of the leader of His Majesty's Opposition, and he discharged them, not only with the ability which every one expected of him, but with the urbanity and self-restraint of a man conscious of his responsibilities as well as of his powers. His was, amongst the Indian members, not only the master mind, but the dominant personality.

Gokhale's friends' "utterances"—their informative and persuasive public speeches, their council debates, their courtroom presentations, their interpersonal deliberations —apparently exhibited the strong ethical proof of their leader, whose quiet reasonableness, general equanimity, and unwavering fidelity were admired.

Gokhale's devotion to the cause of Indian nationalism is evident in all aspects of his work. He refused to compromise his belief in the equality of all men and clung to the belief that Indian reform should be evolutionary. His righteousness and straightforwardness sometimes forced him into situations where he faced unpleasant alternatives, as in the apology incident. In that instance the blow to his pride was considerable, but his comment later was, "The best part of our nature is manifested not in what we enjoy; but in what we endure".

His education and his personal contacts with political leaders in England inclined him towards a sympathetic view of Britain that was not shared by many Indians. Perhaps his views made him seem rather remote. Although he was politically "thin-skinned"—he suffered agonies over the dilemmas he found himself in—he attempted to face problems in a logical, a rational fashion rather than retreat into religious mysticism.

Gokhale's photographs generally show him in Western dress with a long scarf around his neck and a red silk-covered Maharashtrian hat. He wore a moustache, which was at the time an essential mark of virility, but he did not shave his hair, as was the Brahmin custom. His face seems placid, yet as his biographer Wolpert has pointed out, his benign appearance hid a temperament that was often contradictory: "he was a rationalist who believed in astrology, a statesman who founded a monastic society, a poet who taught mathematics".

An Unmatched Speaker

Of his speaking voice and his delivery, little seems to have been written. We read that he was soft-spoken, mild in his manner, reticent, and not particularly at ease with crowds: he is pictured as "too vulnerable to endure long the strain of political controversy and public responsibilities". Despite any physical limitations, Gokhale did not spare himself, and we read of the taxing round of activities he imposed on himself. When he decided to stand for the Bombay Legislative Council he campaigned throughout Maharashtra in the sweltering heat.

Yet Gokhale addressed many large outdoor gatherings on his trip to South Africa and in connection with his efforts for the Indian National Congress; but of the physical conditions which prevailed under these circumstances there is little direct evidence. His effectiveness in interpersonal communication was widely acknowledged and his rapport with British Liberals has already been noted.

We find two interesting descriptions of the parliamentary situation in which Gokhale spoke, both of which are from English sources. The first is from accounts of the Viceroy's Legislative Council originally appearing in the *Times* [London]:

> The old Council Chamber at Government House presented a very significant spectacle.... The round table at which the members of the Viceroy's Legislative Council used to gather, with far less of formality, had disappeared, and the 59 members of the enlarged Council had their appointed seats disposed in a double hemicycle facing the Chair. The}' sat for the most part according to provinces, and the features as well as, in some cases, the dresses, of the Indian members showed at a glance how representative this new Council really was ... if the voice of the Indian National Congress did not predominate it had certainly not been reduced to silence.

Not a few official members ... were inclined at first to rely exclusively upon their written notes, and there was indeed, from beginning to end, but little room for the rapid thrust and skilled parr' of debate to which we are accustomed at Westminster. Most of the Indian members themselves had carefully prepared their speeches beforehand, and read them out from typed or even printed drafts before them. In many cases the speeches had been communicated two or three days ahead to the Press, and sometimes a speech was printed and commented upon in the favoured organ of some honourable member, though he had ultimately changed his mind and preserved silence....

The florid style of eloquence cultivated by the leaders of the Indian National Congress fell distinctly flat in the calmer atmosphere of the Council-room, as indeed Mr. Gokhale warned some of his friends it was bound to do...

Amongst Indian members it was the politician, and especially the more "advanced" politician, who figured most prominently in the discussions. The more conservative Indians were usually content to listen, with more or less visible signs of weariness, to the facile and sometimes painfully long-winded eloquence of their colleagues. When they did intervene, however, their speeches were usually short and none the less effective.

The second, a comment on the Indian National Congress, is provided in an editorial of the *Times:*

> We have produced an extensive class of talkers, and equipped them with a great deal of second-hand knowledge of English history and literature. Such a Congress as that which sat last year in Bombay, or is now sitting in Calcutta, is composed of delegates from all these talking clubs who focus the valuable results of their perennial activity.

It should be remembered that conservative Englishmen thought that the Congress was an organisation founded to preach sedition; with the passage of the Seditious Meetings Bill of 1911, Congressmen may have risked imprisonment for statement of their views.

No doubt Gokhale wrote out his speeches as did other members of the Congress, and his advice to fellow Council members shows that he had quickly learned to adapt his speeches to the audience and also to the demands of the speaking occasion. In his lifelong participation in public life as a member of the Indian National Congress and the Viceregal Legislature he had ample opportunity to develop his speaking abilities. He frequently found that he had to take a position between extremes, and this necessity apparently demanded that he prepare his speeches with great caution and care; but he was facilitated in preparing even long orations before deliberative assemblies by his excellent command of English, by his familiarity with the great British orators, by his appreciation of parliamentary exigencies, by his knowledge of the intricacies of parliamentary procedure, and by his grasp of historical contexts and the relevant precedents.

He liked to argue by analogy (other colonies and dominions) where appropriate and also to proceed from easier decisions and not disturb settled matters; but he frequently expressed the view that the rulings handed down in previous judicial decisions often contravened the ordinary principles of justice as he understood them. He was, it was apparent, able to argue quickly, analytically, and incisively and phrase his thoughts in a style that was appropriate for the audience, the subject, and the occasion, not infrequently rising to the high style.

These characteristics can be seen, for example, in his speeches to the New Reform Club, London, on 14 November 1905, and on the Press Bill to the Imperial Legislative Council on 8 February 1910—both challenging audiences—the complete transcripts of which are to be found in the volume *Speeches and Writings of Gopal Krishna Gokhale.*

Despite the fact that Gokhale was speaking to the Reform Club on a subject of great personal importance, the general tone of his speech is controlled; the speech is not lengthy or effusive, but straightforward. The speaker opens with a short introduction that is simple and establishes his goodwill. Mindful of the honour of such an invitation, he views this opportunity to speak as "a sign, a most gratifying and unmistakable sign, of another awakening, the awakening of England to the claims of India." He next states the reason for his address:

> For the last twenty years the Indian people have been agitating for a greater voice in the affairs of their country, through the Indian National Congress. The bureaucracy, however, pays little attention to what we say in India, and so my countrymen thought it desirable that an appeal should now be addressed direct to the electors of this country.

The body of the speech contains his analysis of the causes and effects of India's problems. It is, he asserts, Lord Curzon "on whom the chief responsibility for the repression of the last three years mainly rests ... his main aim has been to strengthen the position of the Englishman in India, and weaken correspondingly the position of the Indians," and that "this reaction and this repression ... has driven my countrymen to a position bordering on despair." Continuing to ascribe blame to Curzon, Gokhale says:

> Lord Curzon is no believer in free institutions, or in national aspirations.... He has tried to fetter the Press.... he has transferred the control of [higher education] to the hands of the officials and to such Indians as will

> always agree with him... he has abolished competition, and made everything dependent upon the pleasure of the officials.... he has tried to take away, especially in Bengal, a portion of that self-government which had been given to the people a quarter of a century ago.

Gokhale regards Lord Curzon's repudiation of the Queen's Proclamation as particularly injurious. Although he calls the Proclamation a "legal fiction," he says it was nonetheless "a very important thing as laying down in theory the policy of a great nation towards a subject people."

Gokhale built a causal relation between India's bitter despair and the reactionary measures of the viceroy. He then extends the source of blame to British bureaucracy, for "it is your system of administration in India that has enabled him to attempt all this repression...." An efficient administration of India had been the government's goal, but this would not fulfill Britain's public pledge of eventual Indian self-government, for "the higher efficiency, which comes of self-government... you can never secure under a bureaucratic system."

The effects of over-zealous pursuits of bureaucratic efficiency are such that "nobody in the Government ... is permanently identified with the interests of the people," and because of the exclusion of the educated class from power, "The interests of the services are thus allowed to take precedence of the interests of the people." Such a policy produces a people "full of bitterness,' whose despair is compounded by comparison of themselves with even Japan, where "the whole weight of the government has been thrown on the side of popular progress." Thus he specifies the evils of British rule.

Having left his hearers with a definite understanding of the coerciveness and short-sightedness of British policy in India, he concludes his speech with an appeal for self-government as the only feasible solution. He concedes that the task is difficult, but "after all they [the bureaucrats] are only the servants of the British people, and when you have definitely made up your minds, they will be bound to carry out your policy." The time is late, but he has faith that the audience will make the right judgement.

In this speech we see Gokhale using the available means of persuasion that are to be found in ethical, emotional, and logical proofs. He increases his credibility in the introduction by showing due regard for the importance of the occasion and by ascribing to his audience the virtues of wisdom and justice in their desire to learn of Indian problems. He condemns Curzon's policies but maintains that his "personal feeling towards Lord Curzon ... is one of respect" and adds, "I am anxious to be fair to Lord Curzon." In this attempt to separate the polities from the man, Gokhale is establishing his own good moral character, his ethical proof. He reiterates this approach later in the speech when he says, "My quarrel, therefore, is less with him (Lord Curzon) personally ... than with this system."

The speaker ascribes the viceroy's lack of insight to the "limitations imposed upon him by his temperament and his training," and he increases his own *ethos* when he shows that he knows the facts about India's economic condition: "On this point, 1 claim some right to speak, for I have been studying this phase of the question for nearly twenty years now." He does not use ethical proof extensively in the speech, but it does serve to make his arguments more acceptable to his audience.

Closely related to ethical proof is the concept of emotional proof, and Gokhale uses this persuasive device in moderation. (It might be observed that his judicious use of ethical proof itself produces a favourable emotional response.) Throughout the speech he seeks to arouse the audience's sense of fair play by showing Indians as undeserving victims of oppression. The appeal to justice is one of the strongest that can be made to an English audience, and Gokhale reaches the high point of his emotional proof in his description of Lord Curzon's repudiation of the Queen's Proclamation. He recalls that the viceroy said of the working of the Proclamation, "It says that you will have equality when you are qualified for it. Now, here we have certain qualifications which can only be attained by heredity or race. Therefore, as you cannot acquire race, you really cannot have equality with Englishmen in India as long as British rule lasts."

Lord Curzon's deliberate misrepresentation of the intent of the Proclamation must have incited in the audience feelings of shame that an Englishman would be so lacking in integrity. Gokhale underscored the point by continuing:

> Now, apart from the question of your national honour being involved in this—this explaining away *of* a 'Sovereign's word,' look at the unwisdom, the stupendous unwisdom, of the whole thing, telling the people of India that unless they were content to remain permanently a subject race in their own country, their interests and those of British rule were not identical. After this, how can any Englishman complain if my countrymen regarded ... your rule in India as maintained ... for a selfish purpose?

Throughout the speech the language is moderate. There are no stinging denunciations, no fiery tirades. With Gokhale's audience, this temperance was probably effective and appreciated.

The restrained emotion and judicious use of ethical proof make Gokhale's arguments readily acceptable. He uses cause-to-effect reasoning to establish a relationship between the misery of the Indians and the policies of the British government; he judiciously bases his case on the premises already held by the audience. For example, in assigning blame for India's condition, he builds on the idea, agreed upon by all, that a subject people cannot alone be held responsible for their own condition, so his logic is unassailable: since India is a subject nation and Great Britain controls her government, Great Britain must accept the blame for India's plight.

Again, in urging the audience to accept self-government as the solution to India's problems, Gokhale uses the premise that there can be no stability for any country unless it has a government—whether imposed or indigenous. Since the imposed government (the British *raj)* has failed, the alternate form of government (Indian *swaraj)* must be tried. These enthymemes are supported with illustrative examples and the personal experience of the speaker; there is no doubt of the speaker's intimate acquaintance with the facts. His comparison of India's backward state with Japan's prosperity serves to support his contention that India must have self-government. In the long run his idea of self-government did take root; however, his method of attaining self-government by almost imperceptibly gradual means was rejected.

When Lord Curzon's oppressive administration ended and Lord Minto arrived in India as viceroy, Indians hailed the beginning of "an era of responsible association." However, the first measure considered by the Reformed Indian Legislature was the Press Bill, devised to curtail sedition by enabling the Government to impose a heavy tax (5,000 rupees) on anyone owning a printing press and to seize their property if, in the authorities' opinion, their publications were seditious. (An appeal could be made to a board of three judges, but there was no trial.) The effect of the measure was to force small Indian publishers out of business, thus effectively silencing some of the most outspoken Indian critics, who depended in large measure on the printed texts of their speeches to convey their ideas beyond the immediate locality.

Gokhale's position in the legislature was a difficult one, for he was a member of the select committee that reviewed the bill. The other Indian member, Saryendra Sinha, was on the Viceroy's Executive Council and was responsible for introducing the bill and steering it through the Council. The bill was morally wrong as far as both were concerned, but differences of opinion arose over what course of action to take. Sinha was unable to secure any amelioration of the harsh terms of the bill before he presented it; as an Indian he felt unable to present it, so he offered his resignation.

Gokhale felt that Sinha's resignation would be an irresponsible rejection of Lord Minto's programmes before they had any test. Further, as Sir C. Y. Chintamani commented, "If the first Indian admitted into the Governor-General's executive council after a long struggle on the part of the Secretary of State threw up the office in less than a year after the appointment and did so on a political issue, it would produce a disastrous impression on public opinion in England". Gokhale persuaded Sinha to stay, and in return he agreed to move amendments to the bill.

These comments on the situation surrounding Gokhale's speech show that the real issue here was probably not the Press Bill itself but what role an Indian member of the government should take. Gokhale's problem was not so much to judge the contents of the Bill as it is to weigh the overall effect of his own behaviour in this instance. Karve and Ambekar write that "the general reaction within the country to Gokhale's attitude towards the Press Bill was naturally unfavourable. This was not unexpected, and, therefore, for Gokhale it was a calculated cost".

The thesis of his speech is that there is no need for the bill: "the Penal Code is amply sufficient to punish sedition and ... the special legislation of last year can effectively put down incitements to violence." Gokhale notes the "irony of fate that the first important measure that comes before the Reformed Council is a measure to curtail a great and deeply cherished privilege which the country has enjoyed, with two brief interruptions, for three-quarters of a century," an effective argument from precedent. He questions the hasty consideration of the bill "by suspending the standing orders and without giving the country practically any opportunity to express its opinion on it."

Gokhale maintains that if the bill is put into effect, the punishment, "so far from restricting the area of sedition, actually widens it by reason of the unhealthy excitement it causes." Unfortunately, the government permitted the existing penal code "to remain practically a dead letter," but "a proposal to amend ... would have made its operation more simple and expeditious [and] would have caused less disturbance."

Subsequently, Gokhale indicates his reluctant readiness to accept the bill. Resuming his train of thought, he places responsibility for sedition on previous British repressions: "the crop of violence that has now come to the surface had its ground prepared five years ago." The provocative writings in a section of the Anglo-Indian press are also blamed "in turning so many of my countrymen against British rule. The terms of race arrogance and contempt... of the Indians ... cut into the mind more than the lash can cut into the flesh. Many of my countrymen imagine that every Anglo-Indian pen that writes in the Press is dipped in Government ink." Powerful metaphors.

Advocacy for Reason

His conclusion is simply stated as an appeal for a return to reason, moderation, and justice:

> My Lord, I feel bound to say that this Bill by itself cannot achieve much. It is oven possible that the immediate effect of its passing will be to fill the public mind with a certain amount of resentment... the evil which they are intended to combat may only be driven underground. Force may afford temporary relief, but it can never prove a permanent remedy— It is only in the co-operation of all classes and the steady pursuit of a policy of wise conciliation on the part of Government that the best hopes of thoughtful men on both sides for the future of this land must lie.

Gokhale's use of ethical proof is manifest when we understand the circumstances surrounding the speech as well as the ideas expressed in it. In supporting the bill Gokhale has deliberately chosen a difficult course, and he states his position very carefully:

> My Lord, in ordinary times I should have deemed it my duty to resist such proposals to the utmost of my power.... But in view of the situation that exists in several parts of the country today, I have reluctantly come, after a careful and anxious consideration, to the conclusion that I should not be justified in opposing the principle of this Rill. It is not merely the assassinations that have taken place, or the conspiracies that have CORK to light ... that fill me with anxiety. The air in many places is still thick with ideas that are undoubtedly antagonistic to the unquestioned continuance of British rule, with which our hopes of a peaceful evolution are bound up; and this is a feature of the situation quite as serious as anything else.

He gives two reasons for his reluctant support: the increasingly violent activities of Indian extremists and his desire to see the activities of "certain sections of the Press" curtailed. This ambiguous reference is not to the Indian press, but to the Anglo-Indian press; and to the extent that the Press Bill would curb the excesses of those journalists, Gokhale is willing to support it. His reasoning satisfies his own purposes, but is probably too subtle for his

Indian audience, who wish to see a forthright rejection of the Bill. He realizes that his stand will be acceptable to the English; his problem is to maintain his own integrity and the confidence of his Indian supporters by not appearing to capitulate to the British demands. In my estimation he is not successful, and the Indians felt he was too conciliator)'. In the subsequent application of the Bill it was obvious that official British opinion towards India had hardly changed.

The task of presenting Indian policies in an essentially hostile situation, before the viceroy himself, must have been tremendously difficult. Gokhale's whole temperament and training made him respect and even admire the ideals that the British government was supposed to represent. He wished to be worthy of his position yet expressive of the needs of his own people. The precariousness of his situation may explain the oblique rationalisation he makes for supporting the bill.

He appears anxious throughout the speech to conciliate Lord Minto ("I entirely share the view which was so clearly and firmly expressed by your Lordship ... despite repressive measures to which you have been driven"), and he expresses his own dilemma when he comments that "the juncture is a most difficult and delicate one, (calling for) the utmost tact and conciliation."

In using argument Gokhale's basic approach is to apply the considerations of need, practicality, and desirability to the problem: (1) there is no need for the bill; (2) the bill would be impractical because it would not "prove a permanent remedy" and would "not overcome the evil altogether"; (3) the bill would be undesirable because it would incite new violence.

The intrinsic difficulties of his position seem to affect the "reasonableness" of his arguments. In the first place the statement of his position is abruptly thrust into the middle of his arguments, as though the necessity of clarifying his stand has preoccupied his mind to the extent that he disregards normal methods of order and arrangement. Some of his ideas are contradictory. He asks the government not to adopt the Press Bill because it will create further violence, yet he agrees to support it because of likely manifestations of violence in the community. On one hand he indicates that Indians are beginning to realize the dangers of sedition and violence and are able to impose self-control; on the other, he says, "I am prepared to let the Government apply to the situation even the drastic remedies contemplated by this Bill."

It should be said that there are a number of factors that influenced Gokhale's development as a speaker. Chief among these are his education and later associations with British and Indian political leaders. His character and personality were shaped by these influences so that, as a speaker, he tried to be responsible to both points of view. Realising the frequent incompatibility of such different outlooks, his answer was to propose that Indian reform should be accomplished gradually. Whether such an approach was the wisest, or the most useful, is a question that can not be answered categorically from the present vantage point. Gokhale was a Brahmin, and that fact doubtless dictated respect for the past and moderated instinctive urges for modernisation; but he was not a spokesman for Hinduism. He was a scholar and a traditionalist and saw his role as a spokesman for evolutionary politics; he was fortunate to have enlisted as a follower no less than Gandhiji himself, whose great achievement was Indian nationhood.

The chief emotional appeal that Gokhale makes is to the wisdom of expediency. This appeal operates in the arguments of the speech that have already been set out, but when he warns the English audience of the effects of the repressive Press Bill, he is playing on their fear and arguing from exigency; in his conclusion he is exhorting them to be wise and just.

6

Economic Reforms

Gokhale dominated the Supreme Legislative Council by his thorough grasp of the problems he handled and by his luminous, masterly and convincing manner of exposition. He was armed with facts and figures which he could marshal with consummate skill and perfect confidence. He was steeped to his finger-tips with the knowledge of the political and economic problems of India and could draw upon the rich store with ease. His knowledge had been completely assimilated, and Gokhale, by constant study and though formulated definite principles of reform for which he fought with rare persistence and courage.

His reading was wide and up-to-date, and the inspiration for reform had come to him through his study of the political and economic history of western countries and a constant pondering over the condition of his motherland. Intensely patriotic and national in his ideal, he had enriched his mind and widened his outlook by steady observation and thought. Though he died prematurely, he had devoted more than twenty five years of his life to the passionate study of Indian problems and his knowledge, experience, talents, eloquence and patriotism combined to place him in the foremost ranks of his countrymen and made him a towering personality in the Imperial Legislative Council. Such was the impression he had made upon that legislative body that

Gokhale was sorely missed when he was, owing to illness, prevented for two years, in 1913 and 1914; from taking part in its debates. His absence was particularly felt at the time of the discussion of the financial statement and the Finance Member thought that without Gokhale the Viceroy's Council acted Hamlet with the part of the Prince of Denmark left out.

Gokhale's Unique Position

Towards the latter part of his career, Gokhale occupied a unique position in the public life of his country. He enjoyed the confidence and the regard of his countrymen in a higher degree than any other Indian leader, except Dadabhai Naoroji, and his life of service and sacrifice won him universal admiration. He came to be regarded as the most faithful and reliable exponent of Indian feeling and opinion, both by Government and people, and his pure motives, his statesmanship and his patriotism were warmly recognised.

Closing the budget debate at a meeting of the Viceregal Council, on 24th March, 1913, Sir Guy Fleetwood Wilson remarked: "It is difficult for those who served in previous Councils to express to those who are new to this Council what a greet blank Gokhale's absence creates. It seems to be the play of Hamlet without Hamlet, and I think we all agree in wishing him a return to good health and a return to the Council next year."

Gokhale was looked upon as the leader of the Opposition in the Supreme Legislative Council and performed the duties of that office with unprecedented success. But he never acted in the spirit of party and faction as leaders of opposition do in other countries. Popular representatives in our legislative bodies cannot, in fact, emulate the policy of the latter in as much as they cannot, under the existing Indian Constitution, hope, by their opposition; to get into power which is permanently fixed in the hands of the officials. However, strongly they may criticise the policy and measures of Government, they find it difficult to make an impression on the official attitude. Gokhale's criticism was invariably well-informed and delivered in the interest of reform and progress, although the members of Government could not openly admit its reasonableness, they had quietly to carry out some of the measures the people's leader threw out. Gokhale's agitation for economic reform, in the Supreme Legislative Council, we shall show how his labours were constructive and fruitful when he hammered away, year after year, at the problems of financial and material progress of India. It will be sufficient here to record the testimony of one of the officials who had often to bear the brunt of Gokhale's attacks on the policy of Government and who had to yield to their vigour, persistency and reasonableness.

In 1912, Gokhale moved a resolution in the Viceroy's Council urging the necessity of strengthening the financial position of Local Bodies and recommending the appointment of a committee for enquiring into the matter. In the course of his reply to his remarks, the Hon'ble Sir James Meston observed: "Whenever Gokhale advocates a policy to which he attaches much importance, I am irresistibly reminded of the Indian juggler who sows a mango seed in a flower pot and covers it over with a cloth. In an extraordinarily brief space of time he removes the cloth and behold there is a goodly mango tree in full bearing! So it is with Gokhale. He advocates a certain reform. We give him the mild answer which turned away wrath, and we think we have before us an appreciable breathing time. But Gokhale has sown his little seed in his little flower pot; he has covered it over with his little cloth, and within an incredibly short space of time he removes his little cloth and presents to our astonished vision a tree bearing not only leaves, not only buds and flowers but a goodly crop of wholesome fruit."

In repudiation of the charge of incapacity and unfitness of Indians to fill responsible positions in the administration, Gokhale had once challenged the critics to try the experiment and confidently assured them that men like Ranade and Mehta would have creditably discharged the duties which great ministers in foreign countries performed. A similar remark might be made of Gokhale himself who, everybody said, would have made an ideal Finance Member of the Government of India.

Whatever truth there may be in the story that was at one time circulated that he was consulted as to his acceptance of the Finance Membership and that, for obvious reasons, he declined that offer, it shows the public estimate of his capacity. As critics of the policy and measures of Government, Indians are at a great disadvantage. They have no access to the sources of information which are open to European officials and non-officials, and they have no opportunities of getting first-hand knowledge of the machinery of administration. But Gokhale had overcome this difficulty by making him thoroughly acquainted with the details of every question he took up and in this matter he could give points even to official members of the Legislative Council. When he was on his legs to speak, the officials were very uneasy as they knew Gokhale would hit the weak joints in their armour.

He was never superficial, never ill-informed, and never inaccurate and had no difficulty in demolishing the case made out by his opponents in favour of their measures or attitude. The story is told how, on one occasion, "Lord Kitchener privately asked him the points on which he wished to touch so far as military expenditure was concerned, and, out of consideration for the great soldier who was no debater, Gokhale did not emphasise certain points as much as he would have liked to." Such predominance in an assembly like the Supreme Legislative Council, which had not the backing of official prestige or authority, was the result solely of Intellectual eminence, impressive eloquence, sustained and painstaking study of public questions and a reputation for sincerity of purpose and purity of motive.

Ranade's Influence

Very few of the people who admire Gokhale realise how in his early years he toiled and laboured for equipping himself for the life lie had selected for himself. Endowed with a strong memory, lie developed that faculty with the greatest assiduity, and the nervous English and the incisive eloquence of which he was a master, had been laboriously required. When he was called upon to teach classes in Fergusson College he was entrusted, at the outset with Mathematics, English, History and Political Economy. Though he taught all these subjects satisfactorily he shone in the last two and they came to have a peculiar fascination for him. The public life of Maharashtra was at that time very stirring and movements for all kinds of reform, social, political and industrial, were remarkably active. The late Justice Ranade was the soul of these movements, and his influence was all-pervading. He attracted and attached to himself all sorts of men, young and old, and inspired them with a desire to do some work for public good. Ranade exercised peculiar magnetic influence over all who surrounded him and imparted to them a touch of his own public spirit and enthusiasm in the cause of progress.

He could detect with a singularly unerring eye the aptitudes of men and make them put forth their for the benefit of the country. Young, earnest and aspiring, Gokhale could not resist this force of attraction and was soon drawn into the orbit of Ranade's influence. And he proved himself an apt pupil of the great master from whom he picked up many of the qualities which characterised him in later life. His optimism, catholic sympathies, liberal tendencies, gentleness, urbanity, devotion to the study of public questions, breadth of vision, moderation and other traits of his character and career may be traced to this source. In the tribute he paid to his departed guru at the memorial meeting held in Bombay.

In July 1901, Gokhale thus remarked: "My friend, Sir Bhalchandra, has already referred to the extraordinary quickness with which Ranade discerned and encouraged all earnest workers in the country. He had a wonderful faculty in this respect and, as a result, he was, to many young men, scattered all over the country, like the central sun from whom they derived their light and warmth, and round whom they moved, each in his own orbit and at his own distance. The feeling of devotion that he was able to inspire in such men was most marvellous and to those young workers who were privileged to come in intimate personal contact with him, his word was law and his approbation their highest earthly reward. Ranade, in fact, possessed in the highest degree the ideal attributes of a great teacher."

Even when he had himself become a great man, Gokhale often frankly and openly acknowledged his deep indebtedness to Rao Saheb, as Ranade was popularly called, and it is difficult to convey a correct idea, of how much the pupil owed to his master. This contact of the two earnest and kiwi-red souls began at a time when the Indian National Congress had just been started and filled the country with a newborn enthusiasm and when the condition and the political and economic problems of India were being discussed with peculiar zest in the press and on the platform. We have this fact from Gokhale himself who addressing the Bombay Congress of 1904,011 the question of surpluses with which the Indian Treasury overflowed during the regime of Lord Curzon, said: "Gentlemen, it was more than sixteen years ago that I first imbibed a love for the study of financial questions at the feet of my great master, Ranade, and since then, I may claim to have been a fairly close student of Indian finance". It was thus about the year 1888-89 that Gokhale's apprenticeship commenced and his progress, as may be expected, was extraordinarily rapid. He was eager to learn, possessed the capacity to take infinite pains and had good opportunities for the exercise of his faculties.

The Sarvajanik Sabha of Poona was then a very active public body, interesting itself in the well-being of the people and representing to Government, from time to time, their views, grievances and needs. Turning over the pages of the Quarterly Journal of the Sabha one is struck with the record of the active work the Sabha did, its memorials to Government, the correspondence it carried on with the officials on the questions of the day, and its discussion of the various administrative and legislative measures which affected the interests of the public. The Journal also published essays and papers on political and economic questions contributed by writers like Ranade and Rao Bahadur G. V. Joshi, which even at this distance, make instructive reading. One sighs for the days when such public activities were possible in Poona. For about six years till 1896 when Gokhale severed his connection with the Sabha, he was the editor of the Journal and must have done a good deal of work in drafting the memorials of the Sabha and in other ways.

He took part in public meetings and made speeches on the burning topics of the day on the Congress and other platforms. This was a period of Gokhale's apprenticeship to public life and he worked hard to make a way for himself to public leadership. Many of our aspiring young men forget that the path to eminence in public life is toilsome and rugged and that no one who wants to serve his country can do so without laborious training and painful experience. Ranade was uniformly courteous to everybody, but Gokhale was often made to feel when he read out to his guru or wrote to his dictation that he was in the presence of a task-master. No true greatness is possible without preliminary training and discipline, and Gokhale had these in their due measure. We lay special stress on this point' for the benefit of the rising generation, most members of which are anxious to shine and become great but unwilling to pay the price of that greatness. They applaud Gokhale's abilities and his knowledge, but scarcely realise that these were acquired by hard and incessant labour.

Gokhale's advocacy of financial and economic reform bore fruit as much as the earnest and persistent pleading of an Indian member of the Viceregal Council of his position tumid influence could bear it, and the financial statements and the proceedings of that Council bear ample testimony to this fact. In them we clearly see what it was that Gokhale fight for, what were the directions in which he sought financial progress and what were the aims of his policy. His speeches in the Supreme Legislative Council emphasise certain definite principles which, according to him, ought to have animated the policy of Government, and they are as it were, so many chapters in a textbook on the financial position and development of India.

His views are reiterated, enforced and amplified, from year to year, so that they sink into one's memory on account of repetition of statement, vigour of expression and lucidity of exposition. But he had not the same scope in the Bombay Legislative Council, where the questions he dealt with were of provincial interest and of limited magnitude, though problems like the land revenue policy of the Local Government, supplied him with good material. And before the year 1900, when he became member of the Bombay Council, he had no opportunity to criticise the measures of Government at the same board as the highest responsible officials and thus to ventilate and, in a measure, educate public opinion. His evidence before the Royal Commission on Expenditure in India is indeed a remarkable performance and pointed him out as a leader with great possibilities in him.

Before 1897, Gokhale was, by no means, an unknown quantity in Indian public life, having been already hailed as the rising star of the Deccan. Some of his speeches at and before this time bear the characteristic marks of his genius, but the decade which preceded his appearance before the Welby Commission was a period more or less of preparation, and using the terminology Gokhale has chosen to describe the members of his Servants of India Society before they are admitted to the full status of membership, we may say that during these ten-years he was a leader. As he was in no way connected with the work of legislation or the discussion of the Indian budget, we cannot get a connected and full view of his ideas about economic and financial reform. And we have to content ourselves with the occasional glimpses we obtain in the speeches he made on the Congress platform and elsewhere.

Character of the Times

The period of Gokhale's apprenticeship was a period, as we have said above of a newborn popular enthusiasm and witnessed the agitation for reform started by the National Congress. From the point of view of finance, it was the time of great stress and storm and of additional taxation. Lord Lytton's regime was marked by distress caused by widespread famine, by the prosecution of an aggressive military policy on the northwestern frontier and by the consequent financial embarrassment, aggravated by a fall in exchange. In 1877-78 famine still raged in southern India. "During the following three years the Government had to meet the heavy expenditure of the Afghan War, which amounted to over 16 crores, exclusive of the contribution made by England, while in 1878-79 there was a further fall in exchange."

For three consecutive years there were heavy deficits. But with the advent of Lord Ripon as Viceroy, came a brief spell of financial prosperity. The revenue jumped up with a bound and when the Provincial settlements were revised in 1882-83, assignments to Provincial Governments were increased and taxation was reduced in the United Provinces at a cost of 24 lakhs. But a wave of deficits and depression came on again and enhancement of the burden of taxation followed. In 1884, the finances were in practical equilibrium, but two of the following four years showed a heavy deficit, and in the remaining two, a small surplus was secured only by the suspension of the famine insurance grant. The Madras famine of 1877 led Lord Lytton's

Government to create, by imposing new taxes, a Famine Relief and Insurance Grant. The object of the grant was declared to be the provision of an annual surplus of crore and a half for famine relief and famine insurance. To the extent to which, in any year the amount was not spent on relief, it was to be spent solely on reduction or avoidance of debt. A pledge was given that the proceeds of the new taxes would not be expended for any other purpose than the one stated.

And yet the grant was often suspended for meeting deficits. Lord Duffierin was then Viceroy and the policy of the Government of India as of the Government in England was dictated by the spirit of imperialism. The financial situation of the time is tersely but vividly brought out in the following passage: "In 1885 occurred the Punjab incident on the Russo-Afghan border and the conquest of Upper Burma. The imminent danger of war with Russia involved an outlay on military preparation of two crores, and the Burmese war cost 60 lakhs. In neither case did the matter stop with the initial expenditure. The progress of a great European power towards the borders of India made it necessary to reconsider the military position. The army was increased and larger sums were spent during several years on strategic railways, fortifications, and other works on the frontier. The restoration of order in Upper Burma, and the administration of the Province, also entailed a large net outlay until, after several years, the newly acquired territory begun to development its revenues to expand. The arrangements so careful elaborated during Lord Lytton's royalty broke down under the strain of this accumulated expenditure; and recourse was had to fresh taxation. In January 1886, the license tax was converted into a general tax on non-agricultural incomes in excess of Rs. 500 per annum, and in 1887-88, it was found necessary to enhance the salt duty from Rs. 2 to Rs. 2.8, and to impose an import duty on Petroleum."

Gokhale himself gave the Viceroy's Council a brief but graphic description of this financial position in the following words — During the first 1.2 years of this period, from 1885-86 — when Sir Auckland Colvin told the Council in his financial statement almost in prophetic terms that affairs were 'passing into a new phase', necessitating a reconsideration and revision of the fiscal status established in 1882 — down to 1896-97, there was one continued and ceaseless struggle on the part of the Finance Department of the Government of India to maintain, at all risks and hazards a strong financial position', in the face of a rapidly changing situation, and provide by anticipation against all possible dangers near and remote, fancied and real; was full and not a year passed — literally speaking — but heralded some change in the financial arrangements of the country. The famine grant was suspended for three successive years, 1886-87 — 1888-89, then reduced for two more and permanently so in the last year of the period.

Twice during these twelve years were the Provincial contracts subjected to drastic revision (1887-88 and 1892-93), and the total gain secured to the Imperial Treasury on such a contraction or Provincial resources 10 crores (64 lakhs in 1887-88 and 46 lakhs in 1892-95). Further more, during the period, thrice (in 1886-87, 1890-91, 1894-95) were the Provincial Administrations called upon to pay special contributions in aid of Imperial revenues. But the chief financial expedient employed to escape the supposed embarrassment of the time was continuous additions to the taxation of the country. Nine years out of these 12 witnessed the imposition of new taxes.

First came the income tax in 1886, and then followed in rapid succession the salt duty enhancement of 1887-88 (June, 1888), the petroleum and Patwari-taxes and extension of the income tax to Burma in 1888-89, customs on imported liquors increased in 1889-90, the excise duty on Indian beer in 1890-91, the import duty on salt fish in Burma in 1892-93, the reimposition of the 5 per cent, *ad valorem* duties on imports, excluding cotton goods, in 1893-94, and the extension of import duties to cotton goods In 1894-95- In 1896 there were changes in the tariff. The 5 per cent, import and excise duties on cotton yarns were abolished and the import duties on cotton goods were reduced from 5 to 3 per cent involving a sacrifice of 50 lakhs of rupees as a concession to the clamour of Manchester, but a countervailing excise of 3 per cent, was imposed on cotton goods of all counts manufactured in Indian mills.

This is rather a lengthy extract, but it is calculated to give the reader an excellent idea of the 'time of extreme stress and anxiety' through which India passed towards the close of the last century so far as the finances were concerned, and it was also a time, as has been stated before, when a new spirit and impulse vibrated through the class of educated people in the country. The first session of the National Congress was held in Bombay in December 1885, in the beginning of which year, Gokhale had joined the Deccan Education society, and it was attended, among others, by the late Ranade, Prof. R. G. Bhandarkar, Principal V. S. Apte and Prof. G. G. Agarkar for all of whom Gokhale entertained the highest regard during" the whole of his life and the last two of whom were his colleagues. This very first Congress passed resolutions on the growth of military expenditure and on fiscal reform and gave a stimulus to the discussion and agitation of public questions. Gokhale seems to have appeared on the Congress platform for the first time in 1889, and his interest in economic problems began to grow.

He became editor of the Quarterly Journal of the Sarvajanik Sabha and plunged deeper into public life. Poona had become the centre of remarkable public activities, and the example of Messrs. Ranade an G. V. Joshi, who were devoted students of questions relating to Indian economics and finance and who used to give out to the public the results of their studies must have inspired and stimulated Gokhale a great deal, Many of his papers on Indian economics and of the promotion of indigenous industries were written by Ranade about this time, and in them and in his speeches he brought a fresh, independent and discriminating eye to bear upon the economic condition of India. He delivered at the Deccan College in 1892 on 'Indian Political Economy' has become classical, and Ranade may be looked upon as the Adam Smith of the Indian school of economic thought.

He analysed the political and social situation in India, examined the strong and the weak points of his countrymen and indicated the direction in which salvation lay. At the inaugural address, Ranade delivered at the first Industrial Conference held in Poona in 1890 he observed: "We have been all along like most ancient nations. But our contact with the world outside, and the freedom of exchange which has resulted in consequence, have produced one most undesirable result. They have aggravated the situation by making us mere than ever dependent upon a single and precarious resource. The industry and commerce of the country, such as it was, is passing cut of our hands, and except in the large Presidency towns, the country is fed, clothed, warmed, washed, lighted, helped and comforted generally, by a thousand arts. Industries in the manipulation of which its sons have every day a decreasing share. Foreign competition, not because it is foreign, but because in the competition of nature's powers against labour — it is the competition of organised skill and science against ignorance and idleness — is transferring the monopoly not only of wealth, but what is more important, of skill, talent, and activity to others."

Salt Duty Question

Such was then the situation when Gokhale entered upon his apprenticeship to public life. Political and financial reform was in the very air of educated India and he was strongly attracted to economics as a subject to which he might devote special attention. The appointment of the Finance Committee of 1886 was announced by the Viceroy on 4th January of that year in the Imperial Legislative Council. Military operations on the North-West frontier and the continued fall in exchange Tendered the financial position most embarrassing. Reduction of expenditure effected in 1885 gave only temporary relief and a thorough-going enquiry into expenditure with a view to the division of economies, was urged upon Government, and the appointment of the Finance Committee followed.

Sir Elliot was President, and Ranade was one of its members. The saving, the economies recommended by it, would have effected; could not enable Government, however, to face the financial situation which the conquest and annexation of Burma created. Burma proved the White Elephant of Lord Duffierin's administration, and even the Secretary of State for India had to admit that financially, Upper Burma has been so far a disappointment; and lie candidly stated that the annexation had of thrown on the revenues of India a heavier charge than was expected Westland, the Finance member, was confronted with a deficit of £11 million and Lord Duffierin's Government decided to fill up this void in the national revenues by enhancing the duty on salt. There were other ways open but they were examined and rejected as unsuitable. It was felt that by economy and retrenchment a sufficiently large saving might have been secured and if that had not been enough, the income tax might have been raised or some tax falling upon those who were able to bear the burden, might have been imposed. In 1886, at the time of the imposition of the income-tax, Sir A. Colvin and Lord Dufferin had pleaded against increasing the burdens of the mass of the population and in favour of: taxing the rich and the well-to-do. Assurances had also proceeded from high quarters that there would be no further addition of taxation in India. But in spite of all this, Westland, the Finance Member, thought that enhancement of the duty on salt was the only practicable and the least objectionable resource of revenue that could be tapped by Government He said: "The figures show also that the extra duty of eight annas may be expected to bring in an extra revenue of Rs. 1,60,00,000 and considering the improvement in all means of communication and the generally improved condition of the people, we may reasonably hope that the burden of a duty of Rs. 2-8 will not now have any effect in restricting the rate at which the consumption is increasing."

No tax in India has been more strongly objected to as oppressive to the masses as the duty on salt, which is a necessary of life with the poor man, and the first measure of relief to the tax-payer urged by Gokhale in Lord Curzon's regime of financial prosperity, was the reduction of the duty.

The poor man's salt ought to be regarded as an object of taxation only by a desperate Finance Member who has exhausted all other fiscal expedients and is driven by an overwhelming necessity to tax even that necessary of life. When in 1886, the enhancement of the salt duty was proposed as an alternative to the income-tax, Lord Duffierin expressed himself thus: "The only alternative open to us was to re-enhance the salt tax; but though this would have been an indirect tax and consequently not so unpopular as the one we are about to impose its operation would have chiefly affected the poorer masses of the community. New, I am very far from wishing to say that in the presence of any overwhelming necessity, such as that of a great war, or a great famine, it might not be necessary to raise the duties upon salt. But commercial and other interests were up in arras against any proposal to touch the pockets of the wealthy, and they were

Indifferent as to the imposition of a burden upon the shoulders of the poorer classes. Before 1892, there were no elected representatives of the people in the Legislative Councils and there were consequently no serious budget debates. The people's view did not find adequate expression in the Councils, and is the case of the enhancement of the salt duty In 1838 even a formal assent of the Viceregal Council was act necessary. The Indian Salt Act of 1882 had empowered the Governor General in Council to impose a duty not exceeding Rs. 3 per ton of 82 pounds avoirdupois, on salt manufactured in, or imported into, any part of British India, and to reduce or remit any duty so imposed, and reimpose any duty so reduced or remitted. This clause of the Salt Act conferred upon the Executive Government of the day an extensive and enormous reserve of staring power under a legislative enactment, by which it can at its own will and pleasure at a moment's notice add to its current revenues no less a sum than full 3 crores without further application to the Legislature for sanction to that addition.

Armed with this power, the Executive Government notified the public on January 19th, of their having raised the duty on salt and later on, though not bound to do so, Westland referred to the question in his speech in the Legislative Council, in the course of the discussion on the taxing bills before it. In his paper on The Burma Deficit and the Enhancement of the Salt Duties, Joshi wrote: "But even a deficit of nearly 2 millions now as is the estimate, is a very serious affair for a poor country like India. Optimistic writers in the press assure us that the Government of Lord Duffierin need not be appalled by this crisis. The course adopted by Government, however, is that of working along the line of least resistance.

They dare not touch the import duties, because of the British clamour it would raise; they dare not ask the English Government to bear part of the expenditure incurred to keep forward English interests; they will not reduce expenditure lest, the services rebel; they therefore come down upon the silent millions who cannot speak and levy a poll tax of 2 annas per head by raising the duty 25 per cent upon the cost of manufacturing salt in the exercise of the powers vested in it under the Salt Act of 1882, section 7,

Government has thought fit by a Notification in the Gazette of India Extraordinary to raise that duty OR salt from Rs. 2 to Rs. 2-8 in continental India and from 3 annas to Re. 1 in Burmah, making thereby a sudden permanent addition at a moment's notice of nearly two crores to its annual revenue. It is superfluous to add that this measure created great commotion and dissatisfaction m the country, and a reduction of the-salt duty was pressed upon the attention of Government from year to year, till they thought it fit to grant the relief in 1903 when surpluses in the over-flowing treasury left BO excuse for withholding the reform."

Appearance on the Public Platform

At the Calcutta Congress of 1890, Gokhale spoke in support of a resolution pleading a reduction of the duty on salt, and he briefly but culture brought out the points in favour of the measure-noticed above, He said: "He say that the measure for the enhancement of the duty on salt in January 1888, by a mere executive order of the Government of India was a cruel departure — I might almost say a criminal departure from the wise policy long since laid down by the Government of India and reaffirmed are strange as it may seem, when Lord Lytton was our Viceroy and Sir John Strachey our Finance Minister, namely the policy of raising a revenue from salt by a low rate of duty and unrestricted consumption instead of by a high rate of duty and restricted consumption. I say that this new departure — was extremely unjust, that as a measure of statesmanship it was extremely impolitic that its consequences have been simply disastrous ..." Gokhale went on to demonstrate the truth of this statement, and in a touching peroration, drew a vivid picture of the misery of the mass of the people affected by the enhancement of the salt duty. Already in 1889, Gokhale had made a speech at the Bombay Congress in seconding the fifth resolution voicing the popular dissatisfaction created by the orders of the Secretary of State for India on the re sort of the Public Services Commission. The document was extremely disappointing and the Secretary of State's orders were more disappointing still this subject has an economic as well as a political aspect, and the employment of Indians in the higher services of the country has been urged as much on financial grounds as on those of justice and expediency. But we have only to call the attention of our reader here to the systematic-manner and lucidity of Gokhale's exposition of every topic he handled. These qualities of his bespeak the care with which Gokhale studied and thought out problems to him. There is no confusion of ideas and no vagueness — Precision and pointedness were the characteristic features of the facts and arguments marshalled, which came one after another in their orderly array. As an example we give here an extract from the above speech. Said Gokhale — "It had intended to review the whole question but time is short and I am afraid of abusing the almost fatherly indulgence of the President. My point is two-fold. First, that the Commission, which was appointed with such a flourish of trumpets, left us in a worse position a great deal than did the Commission's report. I want to draw your attention to three points. First, there were competitive examinations before the Commission sat and before the Secretary of State issued his orders. Secondly, there was the statutory system whereby one sixth of the posts reserved by the enactment of 1861 for the Government Service were to be given to Indians. Thirdly, what is called the Provincial Service or the Uncovenanted Service, was theoretically at least almost exclusively ours, the natives of India. With regard to these three points, let me tell you what the Commission did and what the Secretary of State has done."

To the great misfortune of the country, Gokhale did not live to see the completion of the work of the Islington Commission on the Public Services, of which he was a prominent member. He had carefully studied the whole question and gave expression to his views on the public platform from time to time. Another problem to the solution of which he so passionately devoted himself, later on, seems to have engaged Gokhale's attention at an early date and it was the problem of mass education. His campaign against illiteracy will ever remain a memorial of the earnestness and persistence with which he fought for reform. Speaking in support, of the eighth resolution in the Congress of reciprocating a diminution of educational grants and advocating an enquiry into the industrial condition of the country, Gokhale observed: "India is the least advanced in the matter of education. I have statistics with me but will not quote them. You will find that in the countries of Europe, 90 per cent of the school-going population attend school; but in our own country the proportion is only 11 per cent,

I have also statistics with regard to expenditure; but I will mention only a few. In Europe, in the most backward countries as far as education is concerned no less than 6.5 per cent of the public revenues-goes towards the expenses of education, whereas in India the proportion is about 1 per cent." The intimate relation between education and national progress made such a profound impression on Gokhale's mind that, towards the close of his public-career, he bent all his energies to the question of free and compulsory education, and it was always unimportant plank in his programme of reform. The seven or eight years preceding his appearance before the Welby Commission in 1897, we have somewhat arbitrarily characterised as a period of Gokhale's apprenticeship to public life. The Commission recorded very valuable evidence, though it narrowed the scope of its enquiry against the declared intentions of those who appointed it. Before proceeding to unfold the financial and economic situation and needs of India as reflected in that enhance and the case for reform made out by Gokhale and the other Indian witnesses as also by the writers of the, minority report, it is necessary to give the reader an idea of the general position of affairs in this country.

Falling Exchange

These last ten years constitute a period of transition in the history of Indian finance as in the story of Gokhale's life-work. They were years of heavy deficits, of a falling exchange, a dwindling opium revenue and of two of the most disastrous-famines that have ever occurred in India. This decade was succeeded these years of anxiety and depression, viz. the beginning of the present century, found exchange established upon a firm basis, the

Treasury of the Government of India over-flowing with continuous surpluses and the State in a position to undertake new schemes of expenditure and to remit taxation. The forward policy on the frontier-entailed heavy non-recurring and recurring expenditure and increased the serious difficulty which falling exchange and decreasing opium receipts had created. The deficits had to be met by the imposition of additional taxation and even the resumption of a portion of the growing revenues of the Provincial Governments. The total gross revenue of India and the total expenditure charged against revenue.

As to opium receipts, which have now become practically extinct, they had been steadily declining in the last quarter of the nineteenth century, In 1876-77 opium yielded 16 per cent., and in 1902-03 only 7 per cent., of the total net revenue. But the cause of the greatest disturbance and anxiety in Indian finance was the continuous fall in the gold value of the silver rupee and the consequent increased amounts which the Government of India had to find to meet the 'home charges'. Exchange fell since 1883-84 from 19,536 to 1,300 per rupee in 1895-96, and the loss on Home remittances increased in consequence from Rs. 5,37,37,000 to Rs. 13,11,63,000 — a net increase of about 91 crores.

To make this point clearer it may be mentioned that in 1873-74, before the fall in the exchange value of the *rupee* commenced, the amount of Home remittance, in line of payments the Secretary of State makes in England, on behalf of the Indian Government, of such charges as interest on debt raised in civil and military pensions, salaries, the price of stores was about £13 millions, which at a rate of exchange 10,351 was represented by Rs. 14,26,57,000. During 1892-93, the amount remitted was £16 millions which, at the average rate of exchange in that year, viz. is 2,985, required payment of Rs. 26,47,84,150. If this could have remitted at the rate of exchange of the year '74, it would have needed only Rs. 17,75,19,200, means that there was a loss of Rs. 8,72,64,950 upon India by the falling exchange.

Currency System

It is necessary to state here that before the gold value of the rupee was fixed, there was great uncertainty as regards the amount which the Government of India had to remit to the Secretary of State from year to year. The Indian revenues are raised in silver rupees and the foreign remittances have to be made in gold. The lower the gold values of silver, therefore, the higher the amount which the Indian Government must spend for meeting the home charges. In fact, the drop of one penny in this exchange value added more than one crore to the amount of rupees that had to be provided for procuring the necessary amount of gold to meet the home charges in England. It is by means of bills of exchange, which the Secretary of State sells to British importers of Indian goods, who have to make remittances to this country that he draws the funds needed to meet the home charges, and this method dates from an early part of the last century. Down to 1872-73, the rate of exchange at which the Secretary of State was able to sell his drafts upon the Indian treasuries did not fall much below. There began then a decline which continued down to the end of the century. In 16 out of the 27 years ending in 1898-99, the Secretary of State was unable to realise the budgeted amount of home charges. The downward movement of the gold value of silver began with the demonetisation of the white metal by Germany after the Franco-German War.

The metal thus discarded found its way to America and India, whose currency systems stood upon a silver basis. By the Bland Act of 1878 and the Sherman Act of 1890 it was made compulsory for the American Government to make large purchases of silver with a view to raising its value, and yet the metal fell per ounce, the average of 1878 to 43 in 1890 and later on to 374. The continuous fall in exchange was the cause of extreme embarrassment to the Government of India, as we have pointed out above, and there was no prospect of improvement.

The deficits which the falling exchange combined with military and other expenditure to cause from year to year were met by the imposition of fresh taxation and the limits of the tax-paying capacity of the people seemed to have been reached. The unsteady, uncertain and fluctuating tendency of the exchange imparted to trade the character of gambling and speculation, and merchants loudly complained against those evil as much as European officials who had to make remittances abroad. An agitation was started by people interested in a steady and high exchange rate against the existing currency system and they urged immediate reform upon the attention of Government.

As early as 1876, the Bengal Chamber of Commerce and the Calcutta Trades Association, alarmed at the fall in the value of silver, memorialised the Viceroy, urging the temporary suspension of the compulsory coinage of silver by the Indian mints. The Government of India was not at that time disposed to view the proposal with favour. They declared that a sound system of currency must be automatic or self-regulating and decided that

' up to the present there is no sufficient ground for interfering with the standard of value. But their growing difficulties made the Government change their mind and they addressed a dispatch to the Secretary of State in 1878, suggesting, among other things, the introduction of a gold standard and gold currency into India and the limitation of the free coinage of silver in the Indian mints. The proposals were, however, stoutly opposed by the Lords Commissioners of the British Treasury to whom they had been referred for opinion ... and they stated that the relief to the Indian Government, and to civil servants and other Englishmen remitting money to England, which, it was supposed, would attend the adoption of the proposals, would be given at the expense of the Indian tax-payer and with the effect of increasing every debt or fixed payment in India including debts due by ryots to moneylenders. Writing to the India Office, in 1886, the Treasury observed: "It is impossible to regard this question from the point of view either of the Indian exchequer or of the Anglo-Indian official without a corresponding regard to the general effect of the fall in the gold price of silver upon the trade and prosperity of the great mass of the population."

The Treasury seems to have accepted the general belief that the fall of the rupee was rather to the advantage of Indian manufactures. The continuous fall of the rupee, however, at last induced the British Government to depart from the policy it had so long maintained on behalf of the Indian tax-payer and the Indian industries. The question of the Indian currency was therefore referred to a Committee presided over by Lord Herschell, then Lord Chancellor, and they were asked to consider whether, having; regard to the difficulties which confronted the Government of India through the heavy fall in the price of silver, it was expedient for His Majesty's Government to allow them to stop the free coinage or silver. From the evidence that came before it, the Committee concluded that the evil complained of as to the effect of a falling exchange was genuine, that economy, though desirable as a remedy, was impossible and that the limits of taxation in India had been reached. The Committee reported in 1893 in favour of the closing of the mints and an Act was accordingly passed immediately, stopping the mints in the face of the free coinage of silver.

The chief complaint against this measure was that it sacrificed the interests of the Indian people to the clamour of a small section of self-interested agitators and that the true remedy lay in retrenchment and economy and not in a tampering with an automatic system of currency. A hue and cry was raised throughout India when the announcement regarding the closure of the mints was made by Government. Men of experience and acquaintance with local conditions vehemently protested against the measure and characterised it as a death-blow to the Indian export trade. But during the long number of years that have intervened; the people of have been thoroughly accustomed to the change and the trade has not only recovered any set-back which it may have temporarily sustained at the time but has, since, made rapid strides. This view is now largely shared in India, and critics of the currency policy of Government have reconciled themselves to the change of 1893 as far as undergone still further developments and is not likely to be reversed.

The main object of the closing of the mints was to make rupees scarce and thus to enhance their price by rendering impossible their competition with the Secretary of State's drafts on the Indian Government. This was attained forthwith; and it rose steadily from 1.3-15 per rupee in 1894-95 to 16.0 in 1898-99. Now the Government of India wished that the policy of 1893 should be carried to its logical conclusion, that the gold value of the rupee should be permanently fixed and that a gold standard should be adopted. The Secretary of State, therefore, appointed another Committee, with Sir Henry Fowler as chairman to deliberate and report upon the monetary system in force in India, Though such witnesses as Sir Robert Giffin strongly objected to the artificial system set up in India and recommended economy and the reduction of certain heavy charges which were unfairly imposed upon this country, as cures of its currency ills, the Committee did not open the question of general policy.

Sir Henry Fowler's Committee submitted its report in 1899 and recommended that the British sovereign should be made a less tender and in current coin and that without undertaking to give gold for rupees at that rate, Government should accumulate a gold reserve out of the profits they would receive on the coinage of rupees owing to the difference between the intrinsic and the face value of the silver token, and that this gold should be made available for foreign remittances when a fall of exchange rate made such help necessary. Thus, the policy of currency was definitely laid down and accepted by the Government of India.

Cotton Duties

Before the Mutiny there was a general import duly of 5 per cent, on all commodities coming into the country, it was raised during the next few years. In view of the heavy expenditure the Government had to meet. But very short the tendency commenced towards of the tariff so by the beginning of the last quarter of the nineteenth century the import duties stood at 5 per cent. About this time, however, the question of abolishing the customs duties began to be discussed. The Government of India desired to give the fullest play to free trade principles, and the Lancashire cotton manufacturers finding a serious competitor in the growing Indian industry, were pressing for the removal of the artificial advantage given to the latter by the 5 per cent.

The House of Commons pressed, at the instance of Lancashire manufacturers, a resolution in 1877 to the effect that, in the opinion of this House, the duties now-levied upon cotton manufactures imported into India, being protective in their nature, are contrary to sound commercial policy, and ought to be repealed without delay, as soon as the financial condition of India will permit," Lord Salisbury, who was then the Secretary of: State, pressed upon the Indian Government the urgency of a repeal of the import duties on cotton goods and yarn on the ground that they had a protective effect, and Lord Lytton's Government was prepared to submit to all demands unconditionally, though they were strongly opposed by high officials and the public in India.

In 1878 and 1879, certain duties on cotton imports, which were supposed to have an unfavourable effect upon the Lancashire industry, were removed. "The duty was actually repealed when Southern India had not yet recovered from the Madras famine of 1878; when new cases on land had recently been added to the land revenue; when the Famine Insurance Fund created by special taxes had disappeared; when the estimated budget showed a deficit; and when troubles and a vast expenditure in Afghanistan, brought about in quest of a scientific frontier, were impending. It was not wise to have sacrificed a large source of revenue; especially at time of falling exchange, recurring famines and growing military-expenditure. When, under Lord Ripon, however, financial prosperity temporarily returned, the Government abolished the remaining import duties in 1882 in a fit of generosity. For the twelve years 1882-1894, no fresh import duties were levied, except a small duty on petroleum in 1888.

But the falling exchange and rising military expenditure once more forced Government to resort to fresh taxation. In 1894 they were confronted with a deficit of about two crores, and as other methods of filling up the void were considered as impracticable, (the Herschell Committee having pointed to the customs as the only source available) a duty of 5 per cent, *ad valorem* was imposed generally on all articles with a few exceptions. Cotton yarns and fabrics were, of course, exempted to satisfy the free trade conscience and Lancashire interests. To the outcry that arose against this measure Lord Elgin, in passing the Tariff Act in March 1894, threw out a hint that it was not a final arrangement. In December of the same year, a fresh Act was passed subjecting cotton fabrics and yarns to a 5 per cent, duty, but propitiating Manchester, at the same time, by imposing a countervailing excise duty of 5 per cent, upon yarns produced in Indian mills which, it was thought, would compete unfairly with those of Lancashire.

The British manufacturing interests were not, however, satisfied and they clamoured for more favours. Lord George Hamilton who had, on the accession of the Conservatives to power in 1895, become Secretary of State for India, urged the Indian Government to modify the tariff so as to leave Lancashire no ground for complaint. Lord Elgin's Government accordingly introduced into the Viceregal Council next year, the Indian Tariff Amendment Bill and the Cotton Duties Bill, which imposed a 3 per cent duty on all woven goods and exempted all yarns but which still subjected all cotton goods produced in Indian mills to a 3 per cent duty. The measure met with strong opposition from all sides and was condemned by officials and non-officials, Europeans and Indians. Twenty years have passed since then and the outcry against the iniquitous excise duties has been hard and persistent. As an instance of fiscal injustice the Indian Act of 1896 is unexampled in any civilized country in modern times. The excise duty remains as a lamentable memorial of the subordination of Indian interests to those of Lancashire and of the fiscal dependence of the Government of India on the will of the Secretary of State whose policy is swayed by extraneous considerations and exploded theories.

Famines

After having enjoyed comparative immunity from any serious famines for about eighteen years, India had, in 1896 and again in the last year of the Nineteenth century to pass through the ordeal the severest that had ever been sent to her to try her patience and staying power. The last calamity, in particular, was very wide spread and caused enormous distress. Government's machinery of famine relief was severely tried and the famine taught the State many a lesson in administration... The first of the two famines of this decade "occurred in 1596-97 during Lord Elgin's administration and was chiefly felt in the United Provinces, the Central Provinces, Bihar, Bengal and portions or the Punjab. In the Central Provinces the difficulties or famine relief were very great and the famine operations were, on the whole, defective. A Famine Commission was afterwards appointed under the presidency of Sir James Lyall and its report had just been prepared when Lord Curzon landed.

The-second calamity which overtook the country three years later, was more widely spread and caused greater havoc. Lord Curzon, who had toured round the famine-stricken parts and seen the distress with his own eyes, summed up some of the features of the famine in the following words: "It was not only a crop failure, but a fodder famine on an enormous scale followed in many parts by a positive destruction of cattle — both plough cattle, buffaloes. In other words, it affected and may almost be said to have annihilated, the working capital of the agricultural classes. It struck some of them when they were still down from the effects of the recent shock, it struck others who had never before known what calamity was and who were crushed and shattered by the suddenness and directness of the blow...... For a India Under Curzon and After by Lovat Fraser year it never left hold of its victims and one half of the year had not elapsed before famine; had brought its familiar attendant furies in its train; and cholera dysentery and fever had fallen upon an already exhausted, enfeebled population. This is the picture of suffering that India has presented during the past year". The loss of human life and of cattle due to this famine, was enormous and this cost to Government and the Native States for providing' direct relief and for remission of land revenue was extremely heavy. As we have remarked above, the famines taught Government many a lesson as to their causes and their cure and also as to the proper organisation, of relief.

Measures for prevention and treatment were gradually developed in the light of experience and of the recommendations of the Famine Commissions. But before the close of the last century, the famine policy and measures of the State gave cause for serious criticism and in supporting, at the Calcutta Congress of 1896 a resolution appealing to the Government to apply the Famine Insurance Fund more largely to the immediate relief of the famine-stricken people Gokhale said: "There was a time when Government held that it was no part of its duty to bring relief to the distressed people, and that the Government would leave the natural economic laws to work out their own relief. Happily, however, that time has long passed; Government has now made the fullest and amplest admission of its responsibilities."

He then proceeded to pass a scathing criticism on the inadequate and unsatisfactory character of the relief measures taken by Government in his own Presidency and the hardships which those who received relief had to suffer. These poor creatures he said, "have lied from starvation and death these poor creatures are starved also in the relief works when complaints of their treatment are made to the Government, they are coolly told that if they are not satisfied they may complain to their superior officers, or if the prefer it, leave the work." At the time of the famine of 1877, an appeal for assistance had been made to British charity and had received a noble response, bringing about a crore of rupees into this country from England. A similar appeal on the occurrence of the last great calamity of the century was equally fruitful. But Gokhale emphasised the importance of charity beginning at home and appealed to his countrymen, rich and poor, high and low, to "come forward to bring help and consolation in order that as many lives as possible might be saved and in order that the evil effects of the famine might be averted us far as possible." Fortunately for us, India has not been overtaken by calamities of this terrible type during the past fifteen years, though scarcity, in one part of the country or another, is ever-with us. Famine relief machinery has likewise greatly improved and both government and people have come to realise their; responsibilities in the matter. Organisation or private relief to supplement the efforts of Government has been found necessary and has proved very beneficial. And it may be noted that the members of Gokhale's Servants of India Society have taken a commendable part in the organisation of this kind of relief.

Home Charges and 'Drain' Theory

There is one very important subject which requires notice before we bring the present chapter to a close, and it is the much-misunderstood and misrepresented question of: what has become famous as 'drain'. Dadabhai Naoroji persistently hammered at this subject and advocated such administrative and economic reforms as would tend to stop what he called the material and moral drain to England. It indeed betrays a lamentable lack of the knowledge of the laws of Political Economy to suppose that a country which exports more than it imports and which borrows capital in foreign countries, or pays highly the services of foreign experts it employs, is in a parlous state and is bound to go to ruin.

Some such notions seem to lie tit the bottom of the criticism of those who maintain that all the payments which are made abroad on behalf of India for interest on the capital borrowed, for civil and military salaries and pensions and for the stores purchased, constitute a drain of her wealth and are, as such responsible for her economic decadence. These payments are not gratuitous and are made for benefits received. If we want railways for the development of the resources of the country and cannot raise the necessary capital, we must borrow it in London where it is obtainable at cheap-rates. We want an army and a navy for the defence of the country and must pay for it. Foreign countries and the self-governing colonies borrow very largely in the London market and cheerfully bear the charge of interest. It is foreign capital that has made the economic development of these countries possible, and payments for services received cannot be characterised as a tribute. These considerations-ought to be borne in mind to those who indiscriminately condemn the Home Charges as a drain of India's: wealth, and the fact that the blessings of British, rule cannot be had for nothing and that no country can escape the payment of a value equivalent to the advantages enjoyed, must not be lost sight of.

If this is the misconception of the charges India pays in England on the one side, there is on the other side, an equally serious apprehension of the position of those who advocate the reduction of such charges on the ground that they stunt the material and moral development of the people. Taking up the material aspect of the question, it must be stated that borrowed capital invested in railways and irrigation works, is certainly a beneficent factor in the production of wealth. And it ought to be freely admitted that European experts have to-be imported and highly paid too. But the aim of the-policy of the State ought to be to train the people themselves so that the charges paid by India may-turn out a really good investment.

For several years to come, we shall require the services of experts of various kinds for our development. Our effort must; however, be to substitute Indian agency in the place or the foreign agency in all departments. The British Government has so often declared It to be the aim of its policy to prepare the people to govern themselves and generally to bring them up to the British standard. The demand of the Indian people that the high civil and military posts should be thrown open to them, especially now that they have demonstrated their capacity, whenever opportunities have been given to them, is based upon this principle, and not only will Home Charges be reduced if this reform is introduced but the moral development of the people will likewise be stimulated. If the growth of indigenous industries is similarly promoted by the State wealth, production in India will increase and the profits which at present go out of the country, will remain to fructify in the pockets of the people and to form the store of capital necessary to build up nascent industries. Dadabhai Naoroji and others have never fallen victims to the fallacy that India's trade with foreign countries is detrimental to her prosperity. On the contrary, they have contended that the larger the wealth produced by the people, the larger will be their imports of foreign goods and the happier will they be. That is why they have insisted upon the desirability of the accumulation of capital in the country and the more extended employment of Indians in the public service. The analogy of foreign countries and the Colonies which borrow in London, is misleading in as much as they pay only interest upon their loans but retain all the profits. This India is not able to do and much of the wealth produced in the country goes out in one form or another. The prayer of: the people to Government, therefore, is that they should equip the country in such a way that it will be enabled, to manufacture its own raw materials, accumulate more capital and promote its material welfare. There is a well-founded complaint that the administration of India is very costly and if the reforms suggested are carried out, there will be a great saving to the immense benefit of the people.

Latterly a good deal of improvement is visible in the attitude of Government; but it is extremely and unjustifiably slow. As regards the public services Dadabhai says: "Beyond the positions of Deputy Collectors or Extra Commissionaires, or similar subordinate positions in the Engineering, Medical, and all other services (with a very few somewhat better exceptions), all experience and knowledge of statesmanship, of administration or legislation, of high scientific or learned professions, are drained away to England, when the persons possessing them give up their service and retire to England." These exceptions, it must be frankly admitted, are nowadays becoming more frequent, but there is absolutely no justification for the hesitation and caution. Dadabhai, who was a member of the Welbey Commission, brought out the material aspect of the problem we are considering, in his cross-examination of Gokhale. The question at issue was the extreme dependence of the people upon land and the decay of Indians industries. Gokhale stated that there was a universal feeling in the country that protection was the remedy for the economic decadence.

7

Significant Speeches

Budget Speech

Gokhale's Budget Speech of 1906 was again a vigorous plea on behalf of retrenchment and economic and administrative reform. He bitterly complained of the lavish expenditure upon the Army and the utilisation of the large annual surpluses for the construction of works which ought to be built out of borrowed funds.

> "And as regards the new Secretary of State for India, what shall I say? Large numbers of educated men in this country feel towards Mr. Morley as towards a Master, and the heart hopes and trembles, as it never hoped or trembled before. He, the reverent student of Burke, the disciple of Mill, the friend and biographer of Gladstone—will he courageously apply their principles and his own to the Government of this country, or will he too succumb to the influences of the India Office around him, and thus cast a cruel blight on hopes, which his own writings have done so much to foster?" He said.

The saddest part of the whole thing, he said, 'is that in spite of this superabundance of money in the Exchequer and the resultant growth of administrative expenditure, the most pressing needs of the country in regard to the moral and material advancement of the people have continued for the most part unattended to, and no advantage of the financial position has been taken to inaugurate comprehensive schemes of State action for improving the condition of the masses.'

Gokhale then went on to indicate the lines along which reform was urgently needed, *viz.*, educational expansion, sanitation, relieving the burdens of the ryots and so forth. On April 14, 1906, Gokhale again left for England on a political mission to press for a redress of grievances and the concession of Council and other reforms. Behind him, in India, particularly in Bengal, things were going from bad to worse. The partition of that Province had caused a deep wound in the minds of the people and the blundering acts of the executive were most harsh and exasperating.

The harsh, unwise and short-sighted policy of Government aggravated the evil to such an extent, that a section of the population was swept off its feet. People became pessimistic and lost faith in constitutional political agitation. A boycott of British goods and of all Government institutions was preached and practised. A party of Extremists thus arose in the country consisting of men who saw no good in the Congress as it was then constituted. People who till then had done little constructive work and had given no promises of a capacity to do any, suddenly shot into fame and became self-constituted leaders.

Their propaganda was practically anti-Congress. Their mock-heroic phrases caught the ear of a large section of the public and the fate of the Calcutta Congress hung in the balance. When reverence for authority, age and experience had vanished and the new doctrines of so-called self reliance and nationalism were gaining ground in the country, it is no wonder if a number of raw and inexperienced people fell victims to the infection of the movement.

The work of the responsible leaders of the political movement became very difficult and all progress seemed to be threatened. The charm of the personality of Dadabhai Naoroji, who was induced to preside over the Calcutta Congress, somehow staved off the disruption of that body. But the Extremists became every day more clamorous and framed a political programme of their own, which was at daggers drawn with the traditional aims and methods of the Congress. They wanted that body to adopt Swarajya or unrestricted Self-Government and, a universal boycott as the main planks of its programme, and they seemed to be bent on thus mending, or ending, the Congress. Constructive work was not in their line and they all but succeeded in wrecking the Congress at Surat when they found they could not capture it.

As a sincere and selfless patriot and a keen-eyed statesman, Gokhale was deeply pained by the way things were developing and - with a view to explaining the real situation to his countrymen, he undertook in the early part of 1907 an extensive tour in the United Provinces and the Punjab, in the course of which he delivered speeches at various places and attempted to define and elucidate the work which educated Indians had to do for the uplift of their country.

We shall not recount the incidents of 1907 and 1908 which showed that the poisonous exotic of anarchism, which years of vigilance and determined action have not succeeded in wholly exterminating, had taken root in the Indian soil, that forces of violence were gaining strength and that new political doctrines subversive of all progress were being imbibed by the unwary, the inexperienced and the impression able folk. The voice of reason, of true patriotism and of statesmanship was drowned in the frenzied clamours of the exponents of Extremism.

As it was, the unfortunate Surat incident left no choice to the responsible leaders of the Congress but to place it oh a sound basis and to frame a Constitution and rules for its guidance though this might keep out from that body several people who were once its adherents. Self-Government within the Empire was made the fundamental article of faith of the Congress aid it was under this Constitution that the session was held at Madras. Thus, the leaders displayed on this critical occasion rare courage and capacity for Constructive, work, and the even course of the Congress has committed to run smoothly. These were most anxious times for Gokhale who was consistently misrepresented and vilified by his detractors and yet who was manfully doing his onerous duty by his countrymen. The country was not yet pacified, the repressive policy of Government went on unabated and the high hopes entertained of the Morley regime seemed to be dashed to the ground.

Nothing could have been more disappointing and disconcerting to Gokhale than the situation in the country, the persistence by Government in a policy which intensified the unrest among the people and the consequent block in the path of progress.

After urging, as usual, various financial, economic and administrative reforms, in his budget speech of 1907, Gokhale observed:

> "Since last year, the impression has prevailed that the Government has at last decided to move forward and that important concessions are contemplated. I earnestly trust that this impression is well-founded. I trust also that |the proposed reforms, when announced, will be found to be substantial and conceived in a generous spirit. My Lord, it is of importance that there should be no unnecessary delay in this matter. The public mind is in a state of great tension, and unless the concessions are promptly announced and steps taken to give immediate effect to them, they will, Hear, lose half their efficacy and their grace. The situation is an anxious — almost critical low, and unless the highest statesmanship inspires the counsels of the Government, difficulties threaten to arise of which no man can foresee the future."

In the next year's Budget Speech also Gokhale referred to this point and appealed to government to stem be times the tide of unrest and impatience, which was fast spreading throughout the own ratty and becoming stronger every day, by-line adoption of a statesmanlike and satisfactory policy.

Hiving dealt with the questions of the utilisation of surpluses, of the causes and effects of the prevalent high prices, and having pointed out how disappointment and discontent were getting a firm bold of the young generation, Gokhale said:

> "My Lord, the Government will no doubt put down — I It must put down — all disorder with a firm hand.

> But what the situation really requires is not the policeman's baton or the soldier's bayonet, but the statesman's insight, wisdom and courage. The people must be enabled to feel that their interests are, if not the only consideration, at any rate, the main consideration, that weighs with the Government, and this can only be brought about by a radical change in the spirit of the administration. Whatever reforms are taken in hand, let them be dealt with frankly and generously. And My Lord, let not the words too late be written on every one of them."

The reforms came at last, but though they carried our constitutional progress one step further, they did not give much satisfaction. Yet there they were and represented a move forward in the right direction. It was in this spirit that Gokhale wanted his countrymen to take the reforms, to make the best of them and to prepare for further advance. In his Budget Speech of 1909, that being the last year of the pre-reform Councils regime, Gokhale offered a few observations of a general "character, mainly reviewing the political situation in the country. He expressed his strong disapproval of the repressive policy of Government, which three months before had dictated the deportation of nine Bengalee gentlemen under an old Regulation of 1818.

He then referred to certain features of the new reform scheme, which was being adversely criticised from different standpoints in the Indian, the Anglo-Indian and the British press. Gokhale felt it his obvious duty to express his countrymen's gratitude Lord Minto and Lord Morley for the good work they had done in introducing the reforms under conditions of extraordinary difficulty. He paid a handsome and well deserved tribute to both which is epitomised in the following two sentences in his Budget Speech:

> "My Lord, I sincerely believe that your Lordship and Lord Morley have between you saved India from drifting towards what cannot be described by any other name than chaos. For, however strong a Government may be, repression never can put down the aspirations of a people and never will."

In the meantime, in spite of the reforms secured by India through the initiative of the two liberal-minded statesmen, the course of crime and violence which had been adopted by a few political fanatics and anarchists, went on and made the position most anxious and embarrassing. In a speech delivered at Poona under the auspices of the Deccan Sabha, on 4th July, 1909, Gokhale expressed in the strongest terms the horror and indignation with which the dreadful news of the assassination of Sir William Curzon-Wyllie and Dr. Lalkaka by an Indian student in London had just been received in this country and emphatically denounced people who spread wild and non-sensical ideas about independence and whose noxious propaganda unsettled the minds of the young generation in the country.

Seven days later he delivered another speech in which he dealt with the question of special representation on the Legislative Councils which had created an amount of soreness in the minds of a large section of the people of the country. He explained the special difficulties that surrounded the question of Muslim representation, but strongly opposed special treatment of any community as such. In October, 1914, Gokhale gave an address at the annual meeting of the Students' Brotherhood, Bombay, and while urging the necessity of our students studying political problems under proper guidance, warned them against the Extremist teaching which had become the bane of the country.

From the commencement of the reformed councils epoch, Gokhale steadily availed himself fully of the new opportunities to move resolutions on important subjects and to criticise in an effective and helpful way the financial policy of the Government.

Though the fat surpluses, which were a feature of the time of Lord Curzon, tended to diminish in later years, Finance Members showed great anxiety to budget for a surplus and expended the funds thus obtained on works which should have been provided for out of loans. Gokhale's position was perfectly sound, and it was that surpluses meant a higher level of taxation than was justified by the needs of the country and as the money represented by the surpluses came but of the pockets of the people, it should be devoted to reforms designed to ameliorate the condition of the people.

In his speech on the budget estimates for 1910-11, Gokhale took a comprehensive review of the financial situation and the steady rise of expenditure for the previous ten years, and suggested the necessity for an enquiry into the growth of civil and military expenditure during that period.

So seriously heavy was the increase in public expenditure that Gokhale hammered at the question next year and moved a Resolution in the Legislative Council in January, 1911, recommending that Government should order a public enquiry by a mixed body of officials and non-officials into the causes which had led to the phenomenal rise.

> "How large and how unprecedented," he said, "this growth of expenditure has been, may be seen from the fact that two years ago; of a sudden and without any warning, we came to a heaviest deficit that the known since the Mutiny. And last year the Hon'ble Member, as if to emphasise the gravity of the situation, felt himself driven to impose additional taxation to the tune of about a million and a quarter in a perfectly normal year, free from famine, war or any of those other disturbing circumstance which in our mind have been associated with increased taxation in the past."

Gokhale's speech on this occasion is one of the finest expositions that have been given in the Council Chamber of the Indian financial policy, which has allowed an enormous growth of public expenditure, civil and military. His speech in connection with his proposal about an Opium Fund is equally illuminating and interesting. In fact, all his latter speeches on economic and financial questions make most instructive reading.

He handles figures with an ease that even on the official side it is rare to meet with. He has an extraordinarily firm on his subject, his insight is deep and clear, and his principles sound and unassailable. Gokhale's knowledge, his capacity and his grip of principles, were so wonderful that it would be no adequate compliment to him to say that he would have filled the place of the Indian Finance Minister with distinction.

We are sure we shall not be charged with using the language of exaggeration if we observe that he would have made a successful Chancellor of the Exchequer in England. Referring to his absence, due to ill-health, Sir Guy Fleetwood Wilson observed in 1913, that it had created a blank in the Council and that Hon'ble Members, who had experience of previous Council meetings must think that day they were playing Hamlet with the part of the Prince of Denmark left out.

By constantly pressing for retrenchment, economy and more liberal expenditure on schemes calculated to ameliorate the condition of the people and to District Advisory Councils. This reform he urged for the purpose of securing a close association of the people with district officials in the administration of the country. The proposal was, of course, stoutly opposed by Government but Gokhale's resolution showed his anxiety to improve the administrative machinery at the bottom, where it came into direct and everyday contact with the mass of people. Ill-health and work in connection With the Public Services Commission did not allow Gokhale during 1914 to take part in the deliberations of the Supreme Legislative Council, and this was felt as a serious loss to that body and to the country generally.

In two important matters Gokhale rendered invaluable service to his country, and they were his advocacy of the introduction of free and compulsory elementary education, and his espousal of the just cause of Indians in South Africa. As the reader must have seen, the expansion of mass education was always one of the objects he had at heart. In March, 1910, he placed the following Resolution before the Supreme Council:

> "That this Council recommends that a beginning should be made in the direction of making elementary education free and compulsory throughout the country, and that a mixed Commission of officials and non-officials be appointed at an early date to frame definite proposals."

In speaking to this Resolution, Gokhale made out a strong case in favour of his proposal, but he had to content himself with an assurance from Government that the matter of the expansion of primary education would receive their serious and sympathetic consideration. Next year he introduced his Elementary Education Bill, which was warmly supported by people throughout the country. It was a very cautious measure, and Gokhale had been very careful in framing the Bill to meet the various difficulties he was sure to encounter in making it acceptable to Government and different classes of people concerned. The measure did not try to achieve the impossible by seeking to introduce free and compulsory education universally and all at once, but provided for gradual yet definite expansion. He introduced the Bill in a powerful speech full of convincing facts, figures and arguments.

> "My Lord, one great need of the situation, which I have ventured again and again to point out in this Council for several years past, is that the Government should enable us to feel that, though largely foreign in personnel, it is national in spirit and sentiment; and this it can only do by undertaking towards the people of India all those responsibilities, which national Governments in other countries undertake towards their people. We too, in our turn, must accept the Government as a national Government, giving it that sense of security which national Governments are entitled to claim, and utilising the peace and order, which it has established, for the moral and material advancement of our people. And of all the great national tasks which lie before the country, and in which the Government and the people can cooperate to the advantage of both, none is greater than this task of promoting the universal diffusion of education in the land, bringing by its means a ray of light, a touch of refinement, a glow of hope into lives that sadly need them all. The work, I have already said, is bound to be slow, but that only means that it must be taken in hand at once. If a beginning is made without further delay, if both the Government and the people persevere with the task in the right spirit, the whole problem may be solved before another generation rises to take our place. If this happens, the next generation will enter upon its own special work with

> a strength which will be its own security of success. As for us, it will be enough to have laboured for such an end — laboured even when the end is not in sight. For, my Lord, I think there is not only profound humility that also profound wisdom in the faith which says:
>
> 'I do not ask to see the distant scene:
>
> One step's enough for me.' "There was an animated debate on the Bill, and Gokhale bad no reason to be dissatisfied with the reception which it met with at the hands of the members of the Council. He also expressed his gratitude to the Honourable Mr. Butler and to the Government for the most sympathetic attitude they had adopted towards the Bill, the motion to introduce which was put and agreed to."

The country was enthusiastically in favour of the Bill. Meetings held in various parts accorded of heir support to the measure and thus strengthened Gokhale's hands. Gokhale himself was active and spoke in Calcutta and elsewhere on the question of compulsory education, removed misunderstandings, tried to conciliate opponents. He was thus encouraged to move in the Viceregal Council on 18th March, 1912, that the Bill to make better provision for the expansion of elementary education be referred to a Select Committee. On this occasion he analysed the opinions recorded upon his Bill by Local Governments, Municipalities, District Boards, and officials, European and Indian, and attempted to meet the objections which some of them had raised.

Mr. Gokhale then went on to criticise the unfavourable opinions that had been expressed in the Council on his motion, and his running commentary makes interesting reading, especially remarks about the unexpected and sudden conversion to official views and methods of the Hon'ble Dadabhai.

But all his figures, his reasoning and his arguments were of no avail. A stone wall of opposition had been erected by the Provincial Governments against the passage of the Bill, and the Government of India, had it been inclined to accept Gokhale's motion, Was utterly helpless. The motion, to the disappointment of the whole country, was negatived by a majority of 25 votes. Yet one effect of the agitation in favour of compulsory education has been that the wheels of the Government machinery have begun to move a little more speedily. But the people cannot be satisfied with this: they want primary education made compulsory and free and definite schemes to be framed for the purpose. In short, public opinion wants an Education Act of the type proposed by Gokhale, to whom the country is indebted for the splendid work he did in that cause.

This is not the place for enlarging upon the South African problem. The grievances of Indian settlers in South Africa, their oppressive treatment at the hands of the white population, the attitude adopted by the Union Government and the utter helplessness and apathy of the Imperial Government in the matter, are all too well-known now in this country to require mention here. From the very first Gokhale felt most deeply for his countrymen and country-women, in South Africa and did what he could to help them.

Seeing that the very system of indentured labour was immoral and degrading, Gokhale moved a Resolution in the Viceregal Council on 4th March, 1912, recommending that the necessary steps should be taken to prohibit the recruitment of Indian labourers under contract of indenture, whether for employment at home or in any British Colony. Two years before such recruitment for Natal had been stopped by law, but Government were not prepared for the prohibitory suggested by Gokhale.

The position in South Africa, had in the meantime, gone from bad to worse, and Gokhale decided to visit that country to study the question on the spot and collect facts. But while in London, it was suggested to him by high authorities that he might seek an opportunity to discuss the Indian question personality with the ministers in South Africa. It "is needless to say, Gokhale utilised the opportunity to the full but the problem bristled with difficulties of a serious nature and the task of the peacemaker is proverbially thankless. He was most warmly received by his countrymen wherever he went, was entertained and presented with numerous loving and grateful addresses which may now be seen adorning the walls of the Associates' room in the Servants of India Society's Home in Poona. Gokhale's position in South Africa was one of extreme delicacy and responsibility.

With a full sense of this he tried to do what he could to bring the Union ministers and the white population to look at the position of the Indians in the proper perspective. Unfortunately Gokhale's attitude was misunderstood in certain quarters in India and was subjected to hostile criticism. Addressing a crowded public meeting in the Bombay Town Hall on 14th December, 1912, on his return from South Africa, he completely answered this criticism by pointing out how those who passed it did not show any real grasp of the problem. The supreme question for the Indian community in South Africa, he said, was not to urge, a policy of the open door for more Indians to come there, as certain ill-informed critics thought, but to secure such an amelioration of the conditions under which they lived that their lot might become more bearable, and they might have opportunities of growing into an important part of a self-governing community. If he had stood out for the open door, the cause of the Indian community could not have been furthered in any way. His position was the position of Gandhi who certainly understood and cared for the, interests of Indians in South Africa better than their countrymen out here. The tribute Gokhale paid to Gandhi is most touching and inspiring.

He said:

> "In all my life I have known only two men who are affected me spiritually in the manner that Mr. Gandhi does — our great patriarch, Dadabhai Naoroji and my late master Ranade — men before whom not only are we ashamed of doing anything unworthy, but in whose presence our very minds are afraid of thinking anything that is unworthy. The Indian cause in South Africa has really been built up by Mr. Gandhi. Without self and without stain, he has fought his great fight for this country during a period now of twenty years, and India owes an immense debt of gratitude to him."

While Gokhale was devoting his attention to the political and educational advancement of his country he did not forget the great need there was for its social and industrial regeneration. In regard to social reform his attitude was definite and pronounced.

He was often grieved to think of the differences' of caste and creed which divided our countrymen, and he lost no opportunity in pleading for the eradication of these distinctions. The wretched condition of the depressed classes made a profound impression on him and on many occasions he was intensely distressed over their miserable lot. He said on one occasion, "it is so deeply deplorable that it constitutes a grave blot on our social arrangements," and it is "deeply-revolting to our sense of justice."

But all too suddenly has the noble career come to an end. The strenuous work in which Gokhale had been engaged began to tell upon his health. The South African tour and the work on the Public Service Commission had almost worn out his physical frame though his spirit was as untiring and fresh as ever.

On the evening of Thursday the 18th Feb., 1915, the papers announced the telegraphic message that the Hon. Gokhale had been suddenly taken ill with cardiac asthma and that he had to cancel his trip to Delhi to attend the meeting of the Imperial Legislative Council. The morning dawned with the news that he had passed away. At once there spread a terrible gloom over the country from which it has not yet recovered fully. Gokhale was cremated in his own native city, where men of all parties met and expressed their most deep-felt sorrow at his untimely death. The grief was not felt in India alone. England too and the Colonies testified to their sorrow at the death of this great Indian. From all quarters of the Empire, from the King, from Secretaries of State, from Viceroys, from Provincial Governors and the Ruling Chiefs, poured in messages of condolence to the bereaved family. Meetings were held in India and in England to offer men's sorrowful tribute to the departed statesman. Bombay and Madras voted for permanent memorials in the form of statues, while All India was eager to strengthen The Servants of India Society by subscribing liberally towards its upkeep.

All through his strenuous life Gokhale thought and spoke on the political destiny of India, and he seldom failed to impress on his countrymen the need for sustained effort. Gokhale used to say that "we must muse by day and dream by night" of the future of our motherland and he practised his precept literally. For almost the last act of Gokhale was to frame a scheme of post-war reforms for India. This document now known as Gokhale's last political testament was published in August 1917 by H. H. the Agha Khan. It is included in this collection.

Within the short span of life allotted to him he has achieved so much that it is difficult to cite the example of another Indian to compare him with.

A graduate at eighteen, Professor at twenty, Editor of a journal like the Quarterly of the Poona Sarvajanik Sabha at twenty-one, Secretary of the Provincial Conference at twenty-five, Secretary of the National Congress at twenty-nine, leading witness before a most important Royal Commission at thirty-one, Provincial Legislator at thirty-four, Imperial Legislator at thirty-six, President of the National Congress at thirty-nine, National Envoy to the Imperial Government and founder of institutions at forty — what a truly marvellous and brilliant career has it been and how mournful it is to think that a life of such "singular gloriousness" had been so soon cut short! We feel "that a sudden darkness has fallen upon our lives." We cannot resist the thought that he was "a man whose death would leave humanity the poorer in any age and in any part of the world." An embodiment of public spirit and self-sacrifice, "without self and without stain," he sacrificed himself at the altar of the motherland. His strong sense of duty, his devotion to his *guru,* his disinterested pursuit of patriotic ends caring for neither wealth nor station, his sweet reasonableness and transparent sincerity, his singleness of purpose, his mastery of detail and lucidity and cogency of argument, and, above all, his saintly character — these will make his name for ever remembered by all lovers of India. Gokhale often impressed it on his countrymen that "public life must be spiritualised." And he lived the life he preached.

We have lost the outstanding figure in the great transition stage of modern India; a man whose abilities brought him to the forefront, and whose sense of right forced him into controversies of which we have not yet seen the end. But at this moment the dominant feeling among all who were brought into contact with him is that the value of a life and personality such as his — a record of single-minded devotion to an unselfish ideal and of ceaseless labour in its service over an almost unlimited field of activity — stand above and apart from all controversy.

One of the many remarkable characteristics of Gokhale was the degree to which he was able to combine enthusiasm for reform with a patient industry not too often found in close association with the first quality. But he never allowed hit idealism and his infinite capacity for taking pains to interfere with one another; rather, they both served as a joint inspiration to the work he set before him. The result was that, whether one agreed or disagreed with him, he gave a sense of practicalness in his dealings which seemed to sweep away half the difficulties at the outset. He impressed one as being among the most candid and unassuming of men and he was equally ready to give or to take advice where it seemed most serviceable.

His mind possessed the qualities ascribed to statesmanship without overlosing the fire of its enthusiasms or its warm human interests. We feel that his loss touches deeply not only India but the Empire and the whole world of men whose thoughts move in harmony, whether they know it or not.

Elevation of the Depressed Classes

[At the Dharwav Social Conference held on April 27th, 1903, the Hon. Mr. Gokhale moved the following Resolution on the elevation of the depressed classes. In doing so, he said].

Mr. President and Gentlemen — The proposition which has been entrusted to me runs thus: That this Conference holds that the present degraded condition of the low castes is in itself and from the national point of view unsatisfactory, and is of opinion that every well-wisher of the country should consider it his duty to do all he can to raise their moral and social condition by trying to rouse self-respect in these classes and placing facilities for education and employment within their reach.

Gentlemen, I hope I am not given to the use of unnecessarily strong language and yet I must say that this resolution is not as strongly worded as it should have been. The condition of the low castes — it is painful to call them low castes — is not only unsatisfactory as this resolution says — it is so deeply deplorable that it constitutes a grave blot on our social arrangements; and, further, the attitude of our educated men towards this class is profoundly painful and humiliating. I do not propose to deal with this subject as an antiquarian; I only want to make a few general observations from the standpoint of justice, humanity, and national self-interest. I think all fair-minded persons will have to admit that it is absolutely monstrous that a class of human beings, with bodies similar to our own, with brains that can think and with hearts that can feel, should be perpetually condemned to a low life of utter wretchedness, servitude and mental and moral degradation, and that permanent barriers should be placed in their way so that it should be impossible for them ever to overcome them and improve their lot.

This is deeply revolting to our sense of justice. I believe one has only to put oneself mentally into their place to realise bow grievous this injustice is. We may touch a cat, we may touch a dog, we may touch any other animal, but the touch of these human beings is pollution! And so complete is now the mental degradation of these people that they themselves see nothing in such treatment to resent, that they acquiesce in it as though nothing better than that was their due.

I remember a speech delivered seven or eighty ears ago by the late Mr. Ranade in Bombay, under the auspices of the Hindu Union Club. That was a time when public feeling ran high in India on the subject of the treatment which our people were receiving in South Africa. Our friend, Mr. Gandhi, had come here on a brief visit from South Africa and he was telling us how our people were treated in Natal and Cape Colony and the Transvaal — how they were not allowed to walk on footpaths or travel in first-class carriages on the railway, how they were not admitted into hotels and so forth.

Public feeling, in consequence, was deeply stirred, and we all felt that it was a mockery that we should be called British-subjects, when we were treated like this in Great Britain's colonies. Mr. Ranade felt this just as keenly as any one else. He had been a never-failing adviser of Mr. Gandhi, and had carried on a regular correspondence with him. But it was Mr. Ranade's peculiar greatness that he always utilised occasions of excitement to give a proper turn to the national mind and cultivate its sense of proportion. And so, when every one was expressing himself in indignant terms about the treatment which our countrymen were receiving in South Africa, Mr. Ranade came forward to ask if we had no sins of our own to answer for in that direction. I do not exactly remember the title of his address. I think it was "Turn the search-light inwards," or some such thing. But I remember that it was a great speech — one of the greatest that I have ever been privileged to hear. He began in characteristic fashion, expressing deep sympathy with the Indians in South Africa in the struggle they were manfully carrying on.

He rejoiced that the people of India had awakened to a sense of the position of their countrymen abroad, and he felt convinced that this awakening was a sign of the fact that the dead bones in the valley were once again becoming instinct with life. But he proceeded to ask: Was this sympathy with the oppressed and down trodden Indians to be confined to those of our countrymen only who had gone out of India? Or was it to be general and to be extended to all cases where there was oppression and injustice? It was easy, he said, to denounce foreigners, but those who did so were bound in common fairness to look into themselves and see if they were absolutely blameless in the matter. He then described the manner in which members of low caste were treated by our own community in different parts of India. It was a description, which filled the audience with feelings of deep shame and pain and indignation. And Mr. Ranade very justly asked whether it was for those who tolerated such disgraceful oppression and injustice in their own country to indulge in all that denunciation of the people of South Africa. This question, therefore, is in the first place a question of sheer justice.

Next, as I have already said, it is a question of humanity. It is same times urged that if we have our castes, the people in the West have their classes, and after all, there is not much difference between the two. A little reflection will, however, show that the analogy is quite fallacious. The classes of the West are a perfectly elastic institution, and not rigid or cast-iron like our castes. Mr. Charnberlain, who is the most masterful personage in the British Empire today, was at one time a shoemaker and then a screw-maker. Of course, he did not make shoes himself, but that was the trade by which he made money. Mr. Chamberlain today dines with Royalty, and mixes with the highest in the land on terms of absolute equality. Will a shoemaker ever be able to rise in India in the social scale in a similar fashion, no matter how gifted by nature he might be? A great writer has said that castes are eminently useful for the preservation of society, but that they are utterly unsuited for purposes of progress.

And this I think is perfectly true. If you want to stand where you were a thousand years ago, the system of castes need not be modified in any material degree. If, however, you to emerge out of the slough in which you have long remained sunk, it will not do for you to insist on a rigid adherence to caste. Modern civilization has accepted greater equality for all as its watchword, as against privilege and exclusiveness, which were the root-ideas of the old world. And the larger humanity of these days requires that we should acknowledge its claims by seeking the amelioration of the helpless condition of our downtrodden countrymen.

Finally, gentlemen, this is a question of National Self-interest. How can we possibly realise our national aspirations, how can our country ever hope to take her place among the nations of the world, if we allow large number of our countrymen to remain sunk in ignorance, barbarism, and degradation? Unless these men are gradually raised to a higher level, morally and intellectually, how can they possibly understand our thoughts or share our hopes or cooperate with us in our efforts? Can you not realise that so far as the work of national elevation is concerned, the energy, which these classes might be expected to represent, is simply unavailable to us? I understand that great thinker and observer — Swamy Vivekananda — held this view very strongly.

I think that there is not much hope for us as a nation unless the help of all classes, including those that are known as low castes, is forth- coming for the work that lies before us. Moreover, is it, I may ask, consistent with our own self-respect that these men should be kept out of our houses and shut out from all social intercourse as long as they remain within the pale of Hinduism, whereas the moment they put on a coat and a hat and a pair of trousers and call themselves Christians, we are prepared to shake hands with them and look upon them as quite respectable? No sensible man will say that this is a satisfactory state of things. Of course, no one expects that these classes will be, lifted up at once morally and intellectually to a position of equality with their more-favoured countrymen.

This work is bound to be slow and can only be achieved by strenuous exertions for giving them education and finding for them honourable employment in life. And gentlemen, it seems to me that, in the present state of India, no work can be higher or holier than this. I think if there is one question of social reform more than another that should stir the enthusiasm of our educated young men and inspire them with an unselfish purpose, it is this question of the degraded condition of our low castes. Cannot a few men - five per cent, four per cent, three, two, even one per cent — of the hundreds and hundreds of graduates that the University turns out every year, take it upon themselves to dedicate their lives to this sacred work of the elevation of low castes? My appeal is not to the old or the middle aged — the grooves of their lives are fixed — but I think I may well address such an appeal to the young members of our community — to those who have not yet decided upon their future course and who entertain the noble aspiration of devoting to a worthy cause the education which they have received. What the country- needs most at the present moment is a spirit of self-sacrifice on the part of our educated young men, and they may take it from me that they cannot spend their lives in a better cause than raising the moral and intellectual level of these unhappy low castes and promoting their general well-being.

Farewell to Fergusson College

[On the eve of his retirement from the Fergusson College, the students presented Mr. Gokhale with a farewell address, on Friday, the 19th September 1902, to which he replied as follows].

Mr. Principal, Brother-Professors and Students of the College: It is not possible for me to rise without deep emotion to reply to the address which has just been read, and to return thanks for the great, the overwhelming kindness with which you have treated me today. All parting in life is sad, but where the heart's deepest feelings are involved, the severance of old ties, and the necessity of saying good-bye, is about as trying an ordeal as any that a man can be called upon to go through. For eighteen years now, I have tried, according to the humble measure of my capacity, to give the best that was in me to this Society. Through good report and through evil report, through sunshine and through storm, it has been my endeavour to work for this institution with a single aim to its welfare, till at last it has become impossible for me to think of myself as apart from this College. And now, when the time for my withdrawing myself from all active work in this institution has come, my heart is naturally stirred by conflicting emotions, in which a feeling of intense thankfulness is mingled with a feeling of deep sadness. I feel thankful, profoundly thankful, that it has pleased Providence to give it to me to discharge the solemn and onerous obligations of a vow taken so many years ago under the influence of youthful enthusiasm, and that no matter what happens to me in the future, I shall always be able to look back with pleasure and pride on this part of my career, and say to myself: " Thank God, I was permitted to fulfil my pledge."

But, gentlemen, side by side with this feeling of thankfulness, there is a feeling of deep regret, that my active work for this great institution is now at an end. You can easily understand what a wrench it must be to me to thus tear myself away from an institution, to which my best work hitherto has been given, and which always has been first in my thoughts and affections, no matter in how many fields it was my lot to work. Some of you here may, perhaps, be tempted to ask, as other friends have already asked — why do you retire from the College, if you feel the parting so keenly? My answer to this question is, that my decision has not been arrived at without a long and anxious examination of the whole position. In the first place, my health is not now what it once was.

During the last term, it was a matter of anxiety to me from week to week, and almost from day to day, how I should be able to finish my work without breaking down in the middle of the term. Even then, as many of you are aware, I was not able to perform my duties in the College with that strict regularity, with which my colleagues were performing theirs, and one cannot help feeling that this is a very unsatisfactory position to be in, though never a word of complaint was heard from my colleagues. And I felt I had no right to put such a strain on their indulgence. You know the golden rule that when you sit down to a repast, it is always well to rise a little hungry or when you go to a friend's house, you should rather leave before your time than overstay his hospitality even by a day, I know my colleagues do not think that the illustrations apply. All the same, having worked for eighteen years more or less under high pressure I thought it was best for me to retire and leave the field to other workers.

This, however, is, not my sole reason for withdrawing from the College and some of you are apt to think that it is not a very conclusive one either, and I will frankly tell you that another reason has influenced me in making up my mind, quite as much as this one. Years ago I remember to have read the story of a man, who lived by the side of the sea, who had a nice cottage and fields that yielded him their abundance, and who was surrounded by a loving family. The world thought that he was very happy. But to him the sea had a strange fascination. "When it lay gently heaving like an infant asleep, it appealed to him; when it raged like an angry and roaring lion, it still appealed to him; till at last he could withstand the fatal fascination no longer. And so having disposed of everything and put his all into a boat, he launched it on the bosom of the sea. Twice was he beaten back by the waves — a warning he would not heed. He made a third attempt when the pitiless sea overwhelmed him. To a certain extent this seems to me to be my position today.

Here I am with a settled position in this College, and having for my colleagues men with whom it is a pleasure and a privilege to work, and whose generosity in overlooking my many faults and magnifying any little services I may have rendered, has often touched rue deeply. And yet, I am giving up all this to embark on the stormy and uncertain sea of public life. But I hear within me a voice which urges me to take this course, and I can only ask you to believe me when I say that it is purely from a sense of duty to the best interests of our country, that I am seeking this position of greater freedom, but not necessarily of less responsibility. Public life in this country has few rewards and many trials and discouragements. The prospect of work to be done is vast, and no one can say what is on the other side — how all this work may end. But one thing is clear. Those who feel in the matter as I do must devote themselves to the work in a spirit of hope and faith and seek only the satisfaction which comes of all disinterested exertions. This is not the place where I may speak of my future hopes or lines of work.

But one thing I know, and it is this: Whether I am permitted to press onwards and prove of some little use to the public in another capacity, or whether I have to return a weather-beaten, tempest-tost, shipwrecked mariner, my thoughts, as you have said in your address, will constantly be with this institution; and, on the other hand, I shall always be sure of a warm and hospitable welcome within these walls, whenever I choose to come here. And, now, before concluding I wish to say one thing to the students of this College. I hope and trust that they will always be proud of this institution. I am about to leave you and so I can speak on this subject now with less reserve. I have been nearly all over India and I have naturally felt special interest in the educational institutions of different places. Nowhere throughout the country is there an institution like this College of ours.

There are other institutions better equipped, and also with older traditions; but the self-sacrifice of men like my friends, Mr. Paranjpye and Mr. Rajawade, surrounds this College with a halo of glory all its own. The principal moral interest of this institution is in the fact that it represents an idea and embodies an ideal. The idea is that Indians of the present day can bind themselves together, and putting aside all thoughts of worldly interests work for a secular purpose with the zeal and enthusiasm which we generally find in the sphere of religion alone. The ideal is the ideal of self-help, that we may learn slowly but steadily to rely less and less upon others, however willing to bear our burdens, and more and more upon ourselves, I trust that you, the students of this College, will keep this character of the institution steadily before your eyes — that your devotion to it, your enthusiasm for it, will be commensurate with the nobility and importance of its work, that even when you feel disposed to criticise it, you will speak of it with that loving solicitude with which we mention a parent's faults, and that you will always do what lies in your power to further its interests and enlarge the sphere of its usefulness and influence. And now nothing remains for me but to say "good bye." I know I have given but feeble utterance to the thoughts that are at this moment uppermost in my mind, but nothing that I can say will express them adequately. I wish you well — individually and collectively. In leaving you as I am doing, I feel I am leaving the best work of my life behind me. I trust I may meet some of you hereafter as co-workers in other fields, that we may also occasionally meet within the walls of this College. God bless this College and bless you all.

Bombay Land Revenue Bill

[At a meeting of the Bombay Legislative Council, held at Mahableshwar, on Thursday, the 30th May 1901, His Excellency Lord Novthcote presiding, the Hon. Mr. J. Monteath moved the reading of the Bill to amend the Land Revenue Cede, 1879. In opposing it, the Hon. Mr. Gokhale spoke as follows].

I am sure the Council has listened with great interest to the very lucid and comprehensive speech which the Honourable Mr. Monteath has made in introducing this Bill. In the course of the speech, the honourable member explained to us how it was that Government came to take the somewhat unusual course of summoning this meeting at this hill-station. But I fear the explanation will hardly satisfy those who are of opinion that only the greatest urgency can justify a choice of time and place which cannot but be more or less inconvenient to some of the members. My Lord, I do not think it can be said that the introduction of the present measure was a matter of such extreme urgency.

The only reason which the honourable member has mentioned for bringing forward the Bill at this time and place and in its present form is, that the Honourable Mr. Lely considers that the present juncture is favourable for taking an important step forward towards the solution of the much-vexed agrarian problem in the Presidency. Now with all respect for Mr. Lely, I feel bound to say that this question is so important and so complicated that even his great authority is not sufficient to make us accept without careful examination a measure which, though apparently a small one, may not be as innocent as it looks. And the proper course for Government to adopt is, I venture to submit, to defer this kind of legislation until and careful and comprehensive enquiry has been instituted into the whole Land Revenue problem, the pressure of assessments, the extent of the indebtedness of agriculturists, the extent to which lands have gone out of their possession, the cause of relinquishments and forfeiters, the effect of the rigidity of the State demand and the general condition and resources of the agriculturists. Last year Your Excellency, in speaking of a suggestion made by the Honourable Mr. Mehta, was pleased to state at a meeting of this Council that the Famine Commission, then about to be appointed, would among other things enquire into the land revenue policy of the Bombay Government.

It is true that Sir Antony MacDonnell's Commission did make in some places assort of enquiry into the incidence of State demand and the question of suspensions and remissions, but the enquiry was not systematic, and moreover, the report of the Commission has not yet been published, so that the public is in the dark as to the conclusion at which the Commission has arrived in these matters. Mr. MacConochie's report is also not yet out. And thus even such help as would be available to the public after the publication of their reports informing its judgement on these important questions is not at present available. My Lord, there is another reason for which I respectfully press for a general enquiry before such legislation is undertaken. All those who have any acquaintance with the land revenue administration of the Presidency feel that it was time that Government undertook a general revision of the Land Revenue Code.

The grievances of the Inamdars, which my honourable friend the Chief of Ichalkaranji has been pressing on the attention of the Council for some time past the provisions about the collection of revenue, about suspensions and remissions and various other matters, all these require amendment, and I think it is not all desirable that, when such a general revision of the Code is needed, Government should bring forward, and that in such hurry, an amending Bill dealing with one point only. I submit, my Lord, that such a course is nothing better than a mere tinkering with the problem. The honourable member has made a lengthy statement on the subject of the indebtedness of the peasantry and the incidence of the State demand.

I do not propose to follow him in that discussion today. I will say something about these matters at a later stage of the Bill, but to one statement of his I think I must demur at once. The honourable member is of opinion that the peasantry of the Deccan was even more involved in debt before British rule began than it is today. I do not think that there is any warrant for that statement. It is true that Mr. Elphinstone and other authorities have stated that there was a good deal of poverty and even indebtedness among the agriculturists before the Deccan came under British rule. But the Deccan Ryots Commission, after a careful examination of the question, has, if I remember right, recorded its deliberate opinion that the extent of the agriculturalists' indebtedness has much increased since British rule began.

And two causes contributed very materially to this result. One was Mr. Pringle's unfortunate settlement, which in the opinion of competent authorities simply ruined the peasantry of the Deccan, and the other was the facilities given by the British Government to the money-lending class in the matter of the recovery of debts. The evil of the wrong start given by Mr. Pringle's settlements to the peasantry, aggravated by the action of the Civil Courts and the embarrassment and the consequent helplessness of the peasantry, has gone on increasing with time. I do not think, therefore, that the British Government can fairly claim to be free from responsibility for the present extent of the ryots' indebtedness in the Deccan. The honourable member also observed that the State demand has nothing to do with the indebtedness of the agriculturists. I submit this is an unsafe position for any one to take after what several Commissions have recorded on the subject.

The rigidity of the State demand and the theory of averages are in no small measure responsible for driving many agriculturists into the hands of the money-lenders, and I think this a point on which not much difference of opinion should be possible. Having made these few general observations I may now proceed to indicate very briefly, I think I need not do more than that at this stage of the Bill, my view of the measure which has just been introduced. And I may say at once that, as regards this proposal to restrict free transfers in the case of waste and forfeited lands which may be given on lease, I have an open mind. I admit that the proposal, as far as it goes, interferes with no vested rights. I also admit that under certain conceivable circumstances - such restriction may be the lesser of two evils. But have such circumstances, I ask, arisen? What evidence is there to show that they have? I listened very attentively to the honourable member's speech and I confess I have not been convinced by it. I confess I am very doubtful as to whether this proposed restriction by itself will confer any benefit on those who will be affected by it. Perhaps more light will be thrown on the point when the Bill comes to be considered by the Select Committee, and till then I will continue to have, as I have already said, an open mind on the subject. On one point, however, in this connection I think it necessary to say a word. The Bill does not state what restrictions are proposed to be imposed on free transfers. The whole thing is left to the discretion of the Collector. Now this is not what the Punjab Act does, and I mention the Punjab Act because the honourable member has mentioned it.

The Punjab Act provides for three kinds of mortgages and for these the permission of revenue officers is not needed. The Punjab Act also provides for free sales between agriculturists under certain circumstances, and under the Act, therefore, an agriculturist knows what he may do of his own free choice and for what he must obtain the previous sanction of the revenue officer. The Bill before us makes no such detailed provision, but leaves everything to the unfettered discretion of the Collector, which, I think, is very unsatisfactory. As regards the proposal to give short leases, that to my mind appears to be the most objectionable feature of the Bill.

I submit that absolutely no case has been made out for this departure from the established policy of granting leases in perpetuity, subject to revision of assessment every thirty years. The Statement of Objects and Reasons says that sometimes, when land requires long intervals of fallow, it entails a loss of revenue on Government, if under the perpetuity tenure such land is not taken up, while, if it is taken up by anyone, it may occasion loss to him. If this is the only reason for proposing short leases, I think the difficulty may well be got over by the simple expedient of granting leases in perpetuity and remitting the assessment as a matter of course in years of fallow. Moreover, in the case of forfeited lands, there is no shadow of justification for substituting short leases for the present survey tenure.

There is no question of fallow in the case of such lands, and there is no reason why the new occupants should have only short leases granted to them. My Lord, the perpetuity tenure is a matter of the most vital importance both in the interests of the agriculturists and for the sake of the improvement of land, and I submit it should not be lightly disturbed. What interest will the holder of a short lease have in the permanent improvement of his land? Moreover, what is there to prevent the Collector from raising the assessment every time a new lease is granted? It may be said that the Collector will ordinarily use his discretion well, but I for one would not confer such wide discretionary powers on him when lands are forfeited, when neither the ryot nor the sowcar cares to prevent the land from going back to Government.

I think it is a fair presumption that the assessment is excessive in comparison with the productive capacity of the soil, and the remedy for this state of things must be sought, not in the substitution of short leases for the perpetuity tenure but in the abatement of the State demand. I earnestly trust, therefore, that Government will drop this proposal about giving land of short leases. My Lord, I do not think I need detain the Council longer. I regret the introduction of this measure at this time and place and in its present form. I fear it can do but little good. I also fear it is capable of doing a great deal of harm.

[At a meeting of the Bombay Legislative Council held at Poona on the 23rd August 1901, Lord Northcote presiding, when the Hon. Mr. Monteath had moved the second reading of the Bill to amend the Bombay Land Revenue Code, 1879, the Hon. MY. P. M. Mehta moved an amendment to the effect that the Bill be referred for opinion to various gentlemen and public bodies and reconsidered by the Select Committee in the light of the opinions received The Hon. Mr. Gokhale supported the amendment in the following speech].

Your Excellency — I rise to support the amendment which has been moved by my honourable friend Mr. Mehta. My Lord, it is with a deep sense of responsibility that I do so. I have now been for fifteen years in public life — I mean such public life as we have in this country — arid I can sincerely assure Your Excellency that I have never seen the public mind so profoundly agitated as over this Bill. The Honourable Mr. Monteath complained yesterday that the Bill had been widely misunderstood and misrepresented. But has the misapprehension been all on one side? Is it not a fact that Government themselves had to issue a special resolution shortly after the Bill had been introduced to correct the misapprehension of one of their own Collectors. But, my Lord, I go further and I say that the honourable mover of the Bill himself and also the Honourable Mr. Lely have shown by their speeches of yesterday that they are themselves under a great misapprehension as to what the Bill can do and what it cannot.

If no misapprehension had existed in their minds, much of what they said yesterday — however true it might be as descriptive of the agrarian situation in the Presidency — would have remained unsaid as irrelevant to the discussion of the present measure. The Honourable Mr. Monteath said that the Bill was intended to bring relief to those who were only nominal occupants of their holdings, i.e. whose lands were in the hands of the sowcar and who were practically his serfs. The Honourable Mr. Lely cited a number of instances of families that have been ruined by the unrestricted right of transfer under the survey tenure and whose lands are now in the hands of the Bania. As I sat yesterday listening to these instances — some of them very pathetic and all of them interesting — while I felt sincere admiration for the patient labour with which my honourable friend had collected his data, I could not help saying to myself — "All this is entirely beside the point." If the Bill could really bring relief to those who are practically the serfs of their money-lenders, I admit that, whatever there might be to be said against the measure, there would also be a good deal to be urged in its favour. But, my Lord, it is absolutely impossible that the Bill can do anything of the kind. What is it that is proposed to be done under the Bill? Its principal provision, which has exercised the public mind so much, is that Government may re-grant forfeited lands without the power of free alienation.

Government intend to re-grant such lands as far as possible to old occupants. This is not in the Bill itself, but I will assume for my present argument that they will do so. Now let the Council mark what is the true scope and character of this provision. Before a holding can be brought under the new tenure, it must first be forfeited which means that the assessment in respect of it must be withheld. The Bill will be simply inoperative in the case of those lands the assessment of which is paid. Now under the Land Revenue Code the assessment can be paid not only by the occupant in whose name the holding stands, but by any one interested in the holding, including the mortgage, i.e. the sowcar, and under the present Bill, Government are bound to give at least 15 days notice before forfeiture, so that any one who is interested in the holding may pay the assessment. The sowcar, therefore, can pay the assessment when the occupant does not, and when this happens the Bill will be absolutely powerless to help the ryot, however much he may be the serf of his money-lender.

Now, my Lord, whatever else the sowcars may be, they certainly are not simpletons, and it is inconceivable that they will ever allow any land which is mortgaged to them to be forfeited when they can prevent the forfeiture by simply paying the assessment. Even under existing arrangements, the assessment is in most cases paid by or realised from them when the occupant is unable to pay it, though it is true that at present they try to secure, if possible, remissions in the name of the occupant. When the present Bill becomes law they will, no doubt, take good care to pay the assessment in all cases, but that only means that the collection of land revenue will be more stringent than at present — it will bring no relief whatever to the ryot who is the sowcar's serf. Mr. Lord, in vain the net is spread in the sight of any bird.

A sowcar here and a sowcar there may perhaps be caught napping — where, for instance, he is gone on a pilgrimage, or is a minor and has no one to look after his interest, but such instances will be extremely few. My honourable friend, Mr. Desai, has perhaps seen this point, and that was, I think, why he regretted yesterday the provision contained in this Bill that at least fifteen days' public notice should be given before forfeiture. He would like to give no notice whatever and thereby he hopes to be able to take a larger number of sowcars unawares.

Now, my Lord, whatever results Mr. Desai's method in this particular might achieve, that method is not, I submit, consistent with our notions of the dignity of the British Government or the sense of justice and fair play which we have been accustomed to recognise as forming part of its character. And I am sure the

British Government will never come to such a pass unless men like my honourable friend have more to do with its legislation than they have at present. But I will ask Mr. Desai this — Supposing you are able to catch a few sowcars this way, do you think that thereby you will be able to free the ryots concerned from their liabilities?

When the lands of these ryots are forfeited and are regranted to them under the new tenure, the sowcars will, no doubt, not be able to get the lands back into their own hands. But the personal liability of the ryots for the old debts remains in full force and, therefore, the moment the harvest is gathered and the crops brought home, the sowcar can seize them and thus he will be able to exploit their labour as much as ever. And that is really all that he does even at present as pointed out by the Honourable Mr. Aston. He does not till the lands himself. All he cares for is to exploit the ryot's labour. In the first place, therefore, no sowcars will allow the lands in their possession to be forfeited, which means that this Bill will be inoperative, and, secondly, even if a few sowcars are caught napping and the lands in their possession are forfeited and re-granted to the old occupants under the new tenure, the personal liability of these ryots for their old debts will remain in full force, and thus the sowcars will be able to exploit their labour as much as ever.

Even if these ryots are taken from their old holdings and put on new lands, and Government go so far as to pay them a bounty for cultivating lands which otherwise would remain uncultivated, the crops on these new lands will be liable to be attached, just the same as the crops raised on the old lands. Unless, therefore, the Civil Courts are closed to the so wears and it is enacted that their contracts whatever their nature, are all invalid and cannot be enforced, you cannot get a ryot, who has once got into a sowcar's clutches, out of those clutches till the debt is paid off, and the present Bill can bring him absolutely no relief. My Lord, the Honourable Mr. Monteath threw down to me yesterday a challenge with reference to the drafting of a certain section.

Now challenges, as Burke says in one place, are rather serious things. But, for once, I will set aside Burke's advice and follow the example of my honourable friend, and I will make him this offer: If he will satisfy me — and I hope I am not quite unreasonable

— If he will satisfy me that this Bill will bring any the least relief to those ryots whose lands are already in the hands of the sowcars, I will at once abandon all further opposition to this Bill, I will vote for the second reading, and I shall even feel happy when I am pilloried in the columns of the press for my change of opinion. My Lord, I repeat, the Bill can bring no relief to the ryot who is indebted. And is it for those who are themselves under a misapprehension in so important a particular to complain of the misapprehension of others? But I have something more to say on this question of misapprehension and I will speak freely today, and even bluntly — for on an occasion of such gravity, blunt speech is a duty, however much it might be liable to be misconstrued.

I admit, my Lord — I have admitted in private conversation and I make the admission openly in this Council today that there has been a certain amount of excited writing in the columns of the press on the subject of this Bill. But may I ask what steps Government took to prevent or check a misapprehension of their intentions beyond the Resolution of June 18th, which was intended simply to recall the steps taken by one of their own Collectors? I feel bound to say that in this matter everything which should have been done was left undone, and whatever should not have been done has been done. I was once given to understand that the Press Committees, about which so much was said at one time, had been established not so much for keeping a watch on the conduct of newspapers as for the purpose of noting the grievances ventilated in their columns and correcting misapprehensions wherever such correction was necessary.

Was this agency of the Press Committees used in the present instance to prevent or remove misapprehensions? Did Collectors or such other officers arrange anywhere to meet native gentlemen of education and influence and talk the matter over with them with the object of dissipating their fears? Was any attempt to explain to the ryots the true scope and character of the present Bill? But whilst none of these things were done, mark what the Government did do. At a time when the agriculturists of the Presidency had just passed through a period of the greatest privation and suffering, when Government has already done so much for them and so much more had been promised which had aroused in them feelings of deep gratitude, when, in fact, the relations between the two races were better than they have ever been for years past and were every day growing more cordial, when Your Excellency had won all hearts by your own profound sympathy — and may I add that of the noble lady who is your partner in life — with the poor in their distress, this bomb was suddenly thrown into our midst; and because people got scared and began to run about wildly — some shouting perhaps more excitedly than was necessary — the honourable member turns sharply on them and says — "Oh, it was only a harmless explosive, and you had no business to get so frightened." Then again, look at the manner in which the Bill is being rushed through the Council. It was first published on 18th May, and it came on for first reading on 30th May, almost before anyone had time to grasp its true meaning and character.

Even the statutory provision, requiring the publication of the Bill fifteen days before its first reading, was not complied with, and though Your Excellency, by suspending the standing orders, legalised what otherwise would have been illegal, that did not increase the time allowed to the members of this Council for studying the measure. The first meeting of the Select Committee was held the very next day after the meeting of the Council, 31st May, and the second meeting, which was also the last, was held on the 24th June, i.e. before a single memorial from public bodies or anyone else had reached the Council. The deliberations of the Select Committee were thus closed before the public had any opportunity to submit a single suggestion or a single criticism to that Committee. Now, my Lord, I do not subscribe to the doctrine that the official classes alone understand what is in our interests and what is not. And, I think, the public are entitled at least to be heard before a Select Committee appointed by the Council makes up its mind as to what it shall recommend.

In the present instance, however, all the numerous petitions that have poured in upon the Council have been simply brushed aside. It is true that a few of them were considered by Government in their executive capacity, and a reply, too, was given to one of them. But that is not the same thing as this Council considering them; the Select Committee alone can act on behalf of the Council, and so far, therefore, as this Council is concerned, the memorials against the Bill have been merely so much waste paper. These petitions — the huge mass of papers — were laid on the table only the day before yesterday, and it was physically impossible for any member of this Council to go through them before the honourable member rose to move the second reading of the Bill. Can any one seriously maintain that there is not a single suggestion, a single hint, in all these papers which this Council might usefully consider? I submit, my Lord, this extreme precipitation and this indifference to public petitions is as responsible for any misapprehension of the intentions of Government as anything else. My honourable friend, Mr. Chunilal, told us yesterday that agriculturists who were in the beginning favourable to the Bill are now opposing it owing to the misrepresentations of certain people. And he mentioned how he had a talk with two agriculturists who are heavily indebted to sowcars, and who welcomed the measure as beneficial when he explained its true nature to them.

Now, I ask my honourable friend, what did he tell the two agriculturists? Did he tell them that the Bill would free them from the power of the sowcar — that their land would get out of his hands after this Bill was passed? If he said this to them, I say he has misrepresented the Bill — I do not say consciously — he has misrepresented the Bill to them. How can this Bill help any one who is already in the hands of sowcars? I would request my honourable friend, when he goes back to Broach, to have another talk with those agriculturists, and I would ask him to tell them that, so far as ryots in that condition were concerned, the Bill was not capable of bringing any relief. I would then like to know if these two agriculturists would still regard the Bill as likely to prove beneficial to them.

My Lord, I am amazed that members should talk of misrepresentation and misapprehension, who do not yet seem to realise what this Bill will do and what it cannot do. I will try to make it clear to this Council that this Bill cannot confer the least benefit on agriculturists; but that, on the other hand, it will do large numbers of them great harm. But, before I deal with that question, there are one or two other points on which I wish to say a word. I have with regret seen it suggested by some of the official supporters of the measure that the educated classes are not really in touch with and do not understand the true wishes and feelings of the great body of agriculturists in this matter, and that their opinion on this Bill is not entitled to any weight. Such a suggestion, I submit with due deference, is inaccurate as a statement of fact and questionable in point of taste. How would these gentlemen like it, if we turned round and said — what do these Collectors and Assistant Collectors really understand of the true feelings of villagers? When they happen to go to a village, in the course of their official duties, what actually takes place is this: they pitch their tent at some distance from the place, unless there is a traveller's bungalow any where near, make a few enquiries of the village or taluka officials that are always in attendance, and visit, perhaps, a few spots in the neighbourhood.

Their knowledge of the vernaculars no more qualifies them to enter into a free conversation with the villagers than does the English of Johnson and Macaulay which we study enable us to understand without difficulty the vigorous language of a British or Irish soldier. Meanwhile, it is the interest of the village officials that as few complaints should reach these officers as possible, and that they should go away well pleased, and the termination of the visit of inspection is regarded with feelings of genuine relief. I think such a way of putting the matter has in it just that amount of truth which makes the whole description look plausible. But I feel bound to say it is grossly unfair to a large number of very deserving and very conscientious officers of- Government. The truth, my Lord, is that the English officials in this country understand the ryot from one standpoint, and we understand him from another, and between the two our knowledge of him is certainly not the less deep or instinctive or accurate.

Then, again, it has been stated that only the sowcars and their champions are opposing this Bill, and, to our great regret and astonishment, we find the Seciretary of State for India declaring in Parliament that it is all a moneylending agitation. Now all I can say is, in this matter, that there cannot be a more complete or a more grievous misapprehension of the true facts of the situation, and the circumstance that the Secretary of State should have lent the weight of his authority to this misapprehension shows to my mind how entirely out of touch those who are responsible for advising him are with the real sentiments of the agricultural population. My Lord, the agitation against the Bill is emphatically not a money-lending agitation. Why should it be thought that men like the Honourable Mr. Mehta would ever associate themselves with an agitation started in the interest of money-lenders and against those of the ryots? We are not money-lenders ourselves, and there is no earthly reason why we should champion the interests of the money-lender more than those of the ryot, even if the instinctive sympathy which ail human beings feel for the weaker party in any struggle were to be withheld by us from the poor ryot. And speaking for myself, if Your Excellency will pardon the egotism of a slight personal reference, I will say this: that it was my privilege to receive my lessons in Indian Economics and Indian Finance at the feet of the late Mr. Justice Ranade, who, as Your Excellency so truly observed at the Bombay Memorial Meeting, was always a friend of the poor ryot, and who, it is well known, greatly interested himself in the passing and the subsequent successful administration of the Deccan Agriculturists Relief Act, It is not, therefore, possible, unless I am prepared to prove false to the teachings of my departed master, that in any agrarian discussion I should range myself against the interest of the ryot or be swayed by a special feeling of partiality for the money-lender.

No my Lord, it is because I believe, and very firmly believe, that this Bill will prove disastrous to the best interest of the agriculturists and not because it is likely to do any harm to the money-lender — which I do not think it really will, as I will show later on — that I deem it to be my duty to resist the passing of this measure to the utmost of my power. If it is true, as I have heard it alleged, that the agriculturists themselves do not dislike this Bill, may I ask how it is that, while the petitions against the Bill have poured in upon the Council in a manner perfectly unprecedented — and many of them are signed by large number of agriculturists — there is not a single petition from any agriculturist in favour of the Bill? If it be said that the agriculturists are too ignorant to formally submit an expression of their views to Government or that they have not yet had time to do so, my answer is that the first contention cannot hold good in view of the numerous petitions purporting to be in favour of the Khoti Bill submitted by khoti tenants in the Ratnagiri District during the last three or four years; and, as regards the second contention, it only adds strength to the eloquent appeal which my Honourable friend, Mr. Mehta, has addressed to this Council to postpone this measure for six months. This will give the agriculturists time to petition in favour of the Bill, and then the position of Government will be immensely strengthened, for the ground from under the, feet of those who are opposed to the Bill will be cut. My Lord, to my mind it is the most natural thing in the world that the agriculturists of the Presidency should have received this Bill with feelings of consternation and dismay.

How could it be otherwise when we consider the nature of the Bill, the time selected for its introduction and the feelings and prepossessions of our agricultural community? I can only regard it as an instance of the malignity of fates that at a time when Government had done so much to save the agriculturists from actual starvation and when they had been encouraged to expect specially liberal treatment in the matter of suspensions and remissions, and when in consequence they were feeling profoundly thankful to Government, this Bill should have come upon the community like a bolt from the blue, undoing, so to say, in a moment the splendid work of months, if not of years, and substituting distrust and alarm, in place of growing attachment and warm gratitude.

From a return laid on the table yesterday, we find that in May last, when the Bill was introduced, the amount of arrears in the Presidency was about 2 crores, of which Government had already decided to suspend or remit 15 crores. Seeing that these arrears were practically for two famine years, and seeing how extensive had been the crop failure on both the occasions, I do not think the arrears were at all excessive, especially when we bear in mind that in many places the intended relief had not been definitely announced to the particular individuals concerned and, therefore, many more persons were in a state of expectancy than would have been the case if the requisite announcement had been previously made. The extent to which the Bill has frightened the people may be gauged from the fact that out of these arrears 45 lakhs have been already paid, and probably more would have been realised but for the announcement of Government made in June that no forfeiters would be made before the passing of the Bill, and that, even after the Bill became law reasonable time would be given to the occupants to pay up before forfeiters would be ordered. My Lord, the ordinary Indian peasant is so tenaciously attached to his proprietary rights over his holding, and he finds the full enjoyment of these rights so useful in actual life, that there is nothing he will not do, if it is in his power to ward off what he regards as a direct or indirect attack on those rights.

And is it difficult to understand that a proposal to take away from him his power of alienating, when necessary, his holding should appear to him to be a most serious encroachment on his rights? When the Survey Act of 3865 was passed, it was claimed on behalf of Government that the conferring of the survey-tenure on those who have been *upari* tenants previously practically added to the wealth of the agricultural community nearly £35,000,000 sterling. If this was not a mere idle assertion, it follows that, when it is proposed today to withdraw from a portion of the land of the Presidency the power of free transfer, it is equivalent to withdrawing a portion of the wealth that was claimed to have been added to it in 1865, and that has since been enjoyed by the survey occupants. The agriculturist feels that his power of transfer enables him to raise a loan in times of difficulty; when the difficulty passes away he, in many instances, tries his best to repay the loan; but the struggle is very hard and he of ten finds redemption beyond his power.

All the same, he values his power of transfer and will not relinquish it if he can. Suppose Government were to declare tomorrow that Government Securities were not transferable and that the holders were entitled only to receive interest from Government. How many of us will like such a restriction? I only mention this illustration to show how, human nature being what it is no one would like to part with a power which means a command of resources in times of need. Whether such unwillingness on the part of the ryot to part with his power of free transfer ought to deter Government from a course which they think to be necessary in his interests is another question.

My present point is that it is not in the nature of things — possible that the agriculturists could like this Bill — except, perhaps, those among them who under a misapprehension may imagine that it will enable them to get rid of their debts to the sowcar. I have so far tried to show to the Council that, whatever value Government may attach to the present measure as likely to ameliorate the condition of the ryots, the opposition to it is a genuine and spontaneous opposition, and is strongest among those for whose benefit the Bill is avowedly intended, namely, the agriculturists themselves. I will now come to the question whether the Bill is really likely to do any good to- anybody. My Lord, I am strongly of opinion that, so far as the agriculturists of the Presidency are concerned, it cannot do them the least good and that it will do large numbers of them great injury. Our agriculturists may be divided into four classes: (1) Those who are yet free or virtually free from debt; I believe these form a small proportion of the total number; (2) those who have already got into debt, but not to such an extent as to be hopelessly involved and who are making honest efforts to keep their heads above water — these I believe constitute a large class; (3) those who are so heavily indebted as to be hopelessly involved; these also constitute a large class and they are, I believe, at present practically serfs in the lands of sowcars; (4) and, lastly, those whose lands are so poor and over-assessed that the cost of cultivation and the Government assessment eat up the whole gross produce, if indeed it suffices for the purpose, and who, therefore, are unable even now to raise any money on the security of their lands. This class is, like the first, numerically a small one. Let us now consider how the Bill will affect the interests of each one of these four different classes.

As regards the first class, it is obvious that those agriculturists do not need Government intervention. They have so far used their credit well and Government themselves have often declared that they have no desire to interfere with the freedom of action of those men. But if the Bill is passed, this class will be very prejudicially affected by it in one respect. These men are, at present like other agriculturists, entitled to the relief of suspensions and remissions in times of famine. But it has been stated on behalf of Government that the proposed legislation will enable Government to determine without difficulty who should get the benefit of suspensions and remissions and who should not: a man's readiness to come under the tenure being accepted as a test of his deserving the required relief. And as men of this class will never care to part with their power of free transfer for the sake of a year's assessment it is clear that their position will become worse when the Bill is passed, in that they will not practically get the benefit of suspensions and remissions to which they are at present entitled. My Lord, I submit it is very hard that a class which has deserved so well of the Government by reason of the judicious use that it has made so far of its credit should thus be marked for injury.

The assessment of Government, as is well known, is based in the Deccan — at any rate on an average of seasons, the standard being, that in three years one is good, one bad and one indifferent. When, however there is a succession of bad seasons, as has been the case during the last five or six years, Government are morally bound to remit a portion of the assessment as a matter of course. And it is unfair to make this relief dependent upon the applicant accepting a change in tenure which he does not like. As regards the second class, that is those who have already got into debt, but who are not yet hopelessly involved, their position, too, will be made much worse by this legislation.

A case within my own personal experience will illustrate what I say Government has appointed me to administer the estate of and minor in Poona. My ward's father, a sardar of the Deccan, who is used to lend money to agriculturists on the security of their lands, had advanced about 7 years ago a sum of Rs. 900 at 10 per cent, to one man, whose holding will fetch, if sold in the market, about Rs. 2,000 in ordinary times. This holding has to pay an assessment of Rs. 108, and deducting that, it brings- to the holder a net income of about Rs, 150, out of which, however, he has to pay us Rs. 90 a year as interest.

Now for the last five years the seasons have been continuously unfavourable, and this man has not been able to pay us anything on account of interest. He managed to pay the Government assessment, somehow or other, till two or three years ago, and since then he has been in arrears. Now till June last this man was under the impression that his arrears would be remitted, when all of a sudden he received a notice that, unless he paid up, his shortage would be forfeited. The man at once came to me in great fright and asked me to advance the amount required to pay the arrears. I asked him how I could advance any more money to him when he had not paid us the interest for the last five years. The man, however, begged hard. He said he would give me a new bond for the original Rs. 900 plus Rs. 500 — the amount of interest unpaid to the two hundred and odd rupees required for paying up Government arrears, or altogether for a sum of nearly Rs. 1,700. As this sum was to bear the same interest as the original amount, i.e. 10 per cent, the man's proposal practically meant his utter ruin, as he would, after the new transaction, have to pay Rs. 170 a year as interest with an income of only about Rs. 150.

Fortunately, the last Government Resolution on this subject has come to his rescue, and for the present, at any rate, I believe, he will have no more trouble. Now this is a typical and not an insolated case, and it will illustrate how agriculturists of the second class mentioned above will be harmed by this Bill. These men will not accept the new tenure, if they can help it, and will go on adding to their debts in bad times in order to pay the Government assessment and even if in a few stray cases they are inclined to take advantage of the new tenure, the sowcars who have already advanced to them money will not, as I have already showed, allow the land to be forfeited, but will pay the assessment themselves and thus add to the liabilities of the occupants. The third class is of those who are hopelessly involved and whose lands are at present in the hands of the sowcars.

I have already shown that this class will not be touched by this Bill at all, though some members are under a misapprehension that it will bring them relief, and I do not think I need say anything more about these men now. Finally, as regards that class of agriculturists who cannot raise any money on the security of their lands, even at present, by reason of the poor character of the soil and the heaviness of Government assessment, why, my Lord, these lands are practically inalienable even now, since no money can be raised on their security, and so I do not see how the position of these men will be improved by the passing of this Bill. Thus, then, of the four classes into which the agriculturists of the Presidency may be divided, and, it will be admitted, my division is exhaustive — the first two classes, i.e. just those who are entitled to the fullest sympathy and protection of Government, will be very prejudicially affected by the Bill. The third class, which requires the special assistance of Government, if it is to be helped out of its present hopeless condition, and if the question of agricultural indebtedness is to be really faced, will not virtually be touched by this Bill at all; while the position of the last class will remain just what it is at present — only they will feel that their status in life has been lowered. The Bill thus will do absolutely no good, and must, on the other hand, do a great deal of harm to the agricultural community.

Then, again, the apprehensions of so wears have now been aroused, and if the Bill is passed into law, a considerable number of them will arm themselves with decrees and compel the sale of the occupancies at present mortgaged to them, which they will try to buy themselves. And thus the expropriation of the peasantry, so far from being prevented, will, in fact, actually be hastened by this Bill. As regards the sowcars themselves, I think it is quite clear that the proposed measure cannot really injure their interests except, perhaps, in so far that where the new tenure comes to be substituted — which, I believe, will now be on an exceedingly small area — they will not be able to engage in loan transactions to the same extent as elsewhere. But this really is no loss as in course of time an adjustment is bound to take place, and these men will find other openings for investment.

The only party whose position is improved by the Bill are the Government themselves. I do not mean to say that the framers of the Bill have this object in view. But that cannot alter the fact that this will be the result of the proposed legislation. In the first place, as my honourable friend, Mr. Mehta, has already pointed out, the Bill constitutes an emphatic assertion of the theory of State landlordism, and this is bound to have far-reaching consequences. The Bill means a nationalisation of forfeited lands, which alters completely the character of the land tenure in the Presidency. The

Honourable Mr. Monteath expressed his surprise yesterday that I should call the Government scheme a measure for the nationalisation of forfeited lands. I do not know in what sense the honourable member understands the word nationalisation, but if he takes it in the sense in which political economists use .the term, I do say, and I say it emphatically, that the Bill constitutes a scheme for the nationalisation of forfeited lands. The honourable member will remember that the Relief Act Commission of 1891 discussed in their report the question whether Government might not buy lands themselves instead of letting the sowcars secure them and then re-grant them to agriculturists as tenants of State without, of course, the power of alienation. They pronounced the proposal a good one if it could be carried out; but they considered the cost would be prohibitive and there were other difficulties also in the way.

What they thus considered was unattainable by reason of its excessive cost, Government now propose to achieve by foregoing merely a year's assessment when the average price of land according to the Honourable Mr. Monteath's own testimony is twenty-five times the assessment And what is this, my Lord, but nationalisation of land for a most trifling amount? Then, my Lord, the wide discretionary powers, which Government propose to take under the Bill, will enable them whenever they like — though this is nor desired at present — to grant short leases or take land for public purposes without any compensation, or allot it to whomsoever they please.

This, my Lord, is a real danger, because the tendency of revenue officers generally is to put the widest possible interpretation on the powers of Government for the purpose of enhancing the Government revenue in every possible way. Take, for instance, the question of building fines and assessments; who would have thought before 1865, when there were neither building fines nor special assessments for building sites, that in a few years Government would advance their claims from point to point in such a manner as to end by claiming for themselves the entire non-agricultural market value of unalienated land? It has been stated that Government intend the Bill to be in the nature of an experiment. But, I think, there are grave objections to Government embarking upon an experiment which, it is quite clear, is bound to fail and which will bring needless discredit on the policy of restricting the power of alienation, which, under certain circumstances may prove useful. If Government really want to make an experiment which has reasonable chances of success, let them select at first a small area, take over in that area the debts of the ryots from the so wears to themselves by effecting a settlement of some sort, start agricultural banks to provide for the ordinary needs of the agriculturists who are thus taken out of the hands of the sowcars, and then declare their lands inalienable without their sanction. This would be facing the question in the only manner in which it ought to be faced, and many of our countrymen will support Government in such a policy.

Government will then be incurring some risk, and will, therefore, so to say, earn a right to make an experiment in this matter. What the ryot needs is money, or, what is nearly the same thing, cheap money. And if you do not reduce what he pays at present to the so wear or do not advance anything from the coffers of Government for helping him, how can you give any relief to the ryot? It is, I submit, not possible to improve the position of the agriculturist by a mere manipulation of the legislative- machine.

My Lord, I have said what I had to say about the Bill I will now say a few words in reply to certain remarks which have fallen from the Honourable Mr. Monteath and the Honourable Mr. Lely in the course of this debate. The Honourable Mr. Monteath, if he will pardon my saying so, spoke with somewhat unnecessary warmth about certain observations contained in my minute of dissent. The honourable member told us that I was not correct in saying that in no other province of British India has the executive such wide discretionary powers about waste forfeited or relinquished lands, as the Bombay Government are seeking to acquire by means of this Bill, and he went on to say that in every other province the executive already possessed such powers and that Bombay alone was behind them in this respect.

Now, my Lord, I do not know where the honourable member has obtained his law from? The statement in the minute of dissent was not made without a careful enquiry, and I claim that I am right in the view I have taken, and the honourable member is quite mistaken. I repeat that in no other province has the executive got the power of transferring land from one kind of tenure to another in the exercise of its own discretion. Waste lands to which the survey settlement has been extended, as also forfeited and relinquished lands are, at present, in this Presidency under the survey tenure, i.e. they can be granted to occupants only in perpetuity and with the full power of alienation. Under this Bill Government seek to obtain the power to change the tenure of these lands whenever and wherever they please. If the honourable member will be so good as to show me his authority for his statement, I shall be glad to modify my view of the matter.

Then again, my Lord, I was amazed yesterday to hear what he said about the present law as to the disposal of forfeited lands. The minute of dissent states that at present forfeited lands are sold to the highest bidder, except in certain exceptional cases, such as a combination not to buy the land at a fair price. And when these sales take place the proceeds, after deducting the arrears of land revenue and the expenses of sale, are credited to the defaulting occupant. It is only in those exceptional cases where sales cannot take place for certain specified reasons, that the Collector has power to dispose of the land in any other way — of course, without changing the character of the tenure under which it is held.

The honourable member said yesterday that, whatever might be the present practice, this was not the present law on the subject. Now, my Lord, it is almost presumptuous on my part to pit myself in this matter against the honourable member, who is well known for his great abilities, who has been a Revenue Officer all his life, and who presides at present over the Revenue Department of the Presidency. Still, my authority for my statement is unimpeachable. Here I hold in my hand the Land Revenue Code of the Presidency, and I make bold to say that a reference to the provisions contained in it, on the subject of the disposal of forfeited lands and especially to Rule 60, will show that my view of the matter is absolutely correct.

My honourable friend also challenged me yesterday to draft a section — and he offered to give me a certain amount of time to do it in — so as to limit the discretionary powers of Government, as we desire to limit them, and yet to provide for all those cases for which he says, provision is necessary. Now, in the first place,

I think this is not a fair challenge to throw down to me. Are the drafting resources at the disposal of Government so inadequate to the work of framing a small section such as would meet all requirements? Cannot the Advocate-General who occupies so high a position in the Bombay Bar or the Legal Remembrancer, who is already recognised to be one of the ablest Civilian Judges in the Presidency, help the honourable member in this little matter, that he should ask me, who am no lawyer and have only my own plain commonsense to guide me, to do this work? However, my Lord, as the honourable member has thrown down the challenge I make bold to accept it and I venture to assure him that with the assistance of my lawyer friends, I will produce such a section as he suggests if he will give me the necessary time that he has already promised. Surely it cannot be difficult to frame a section which provides that, when land is given for a temporary non-agricultural purpose or is given to wild tribes for agricultural purposes, the perpetuity tenure should not apply.

Now, that I have accepted his challenge, I hope the honourable member will not proceed further with the Bill today. The Honourable Mr. Lely, in the course of his remarks, regretted that men of education and of undoubted patriotism should confine themselves to the work of mere criticism and should oppose so small a measure framed in the interests of their poorer brethren. He seemed to think that our energies would be much better employed if we gave up this negative work of mere criticism and came forward to initiate measures of reform. Now, my Lord, in the first place, it should be remembered that in all countries with strong centralised Governments the work of initiating important measures naturally devolves upon the Government.

Moreover, what opportunities have we for initiating important measures? Put men like the late Mr. Ranade or my honourable friend Mr. Mehta on your Executive Councils. Place them in a situation of real power and responsibility, and then we undertake to show that we can initiate measures as well as anyone else. It is because you have power to carry out your ideas and we have not, that we appear to you to be engaged in unpractical or academic discussions while you claim for your efforts the character of practical or constructive work. We are not, to use the words which

Lord Curzon once applied to the Liberals in speaking of the Cretan question, so empty of suggestion and full only of denunciation, as some people imagine. But perhaps it is not the part of wisdom to talk of what cannot be. Let not the Council misunderstand me. I say this in no spirit of discontent, but merely to repel a charge which we think we do not deserve. I freely recognise — what the late Mr. Ranade so often used to impress upon our minds — that though there may be less field for personal ambition and less scope for the display of individual talent under the present regime, there is ample compensation and more than that in the blessings of peace and of order well established, in the larger possibilities of enlightenment and progress secured to the mass of our countrymen, in the higher ideals of civic arid national life to which we have been introduced and in the rousing of the moral energies of our people.

And now I come to the concluding portion of my speech. I earnestly implore the Council to accept the amendment of my honourable friend, if not in the form in which it is proposed, in some other form which may be more acceptable. And I base my request on two grounds. In the first place this voluminous mass of petitions has not been so much as looked at by any one on behalf of the Council. I have already pointed out that the Select Committee's deliberations had come to a close before a single one of these petitions had reached the Council. Of what use, my Lord, is it for the people to petition, if those to whom the petitions are addressed will not even care to look at them? It was not thus that the Honourable Sir Charles Ollivant dealt with the numerous petitions, against the District Municipal Bill. It is not my object, my Lord, to praise one member of the Government at the expense of another — that would be unworthy artifice — but I mention this because it illustrates my idea of how a measure should be considered by Select Committee.

Sir Charles Ollivant used to go himself through the petitions, as far as possible, and, if he had no time, he asked us to go through them and bring the principal points to his notice. He was always ready to enter into our feelings, to accept whatever suggestions appeared in the course of the discussion to be good and always ready to meet us at least half-way. He was not wanting in strength.

The iron hand, we felt, was always there; but he ever took care to put on the velvet glove. I submit it is not right to strike us with the mailed fist after the manner of a certain high potentate. My second ground for asking for a postponement is that the reason which was mentioned by the Honourable Mr. Monteath at Mahableshwar for rushing the Bill through the Council no longer exists. The honourable member told us at Mahableshwar that it was intended to make the new experiment on a large scale, and it was necessary to pass the Bill before the beginning of the new Revenue year, i.e. the 1st of August last.

Well, the 1st of August is already past; and as regards the area on which the experiment can now be tried, the resolution recently issued by Government directing that no forfeiters should take place for one year, practically settles that question. You will get only an exceedingly small area — if you get any at all — for trying your experiment on. I submit, therefore, that there is now absolutely no justification for proceeding with this measure so precipitately. My Lord, the late Mr. Ranade, in a lecture which he delivered some years ago at the Deccan College, on some Aspects of Indian Political Economy, referred to the curious phenomenon of Anglo-Indian Administrators, who are strong Conservatives in English politics, developing radical and even socialistic tendencies in dealing with certain aspects of Indian Administration.

I asked a high officer of Government for an explanation of this phenomenon a few days ago. He said: It is because we are able to take £ more impartial view of things here than in England, having no personal interest to think of. I think, my Lord, this explanation is true as far as it goes, but it does not state the whole truth. I think it is also because too much power has produced a sense of irresponsibility. Does any one imagine that a measure of such far-reaching tendencies would have been introduced in England and rushed through Parliament with so much precipitation in spite of the unanimous protests of the people? And I submit that the deliberation which becomes in England a duty of Government, owing to the power of the electors, should also be recognised by the British Government in India as a duty under a sense of self-restraint. My Lord, what is the position here today? We the elected members of this Council are absolutely unanimous in resisting this Bill, and though our voting power is not large enough under the Constitution of this Council to prevent the passing of any measure which Government are determined to carry, we represent, when we are unanimous, a moral force which it is not wise to ignore.

For better for worse, you have introduced the elective element into your Councils, and according to your own English ideas, you must now accept us as speaking not for ourselves individually but in the name of those who have sent us here. And if a standing majority has been secured to Government under the Constitution, its real purpose, I take it, is not to enable Government to ride roughshod over our unanimous expression of opinion, but to prevent the non-official members from combining and overthrowing anything that Government may have done. This, I submit, is the only true interpretation of the present Constitution of this Council. My Lord, the Government with their superiority in votes can pass this measure here today, but let them remember the words of the poet:

> Oh 'tis excellent to have a giant's strength,
>
> But 'tis tyrannous to use it like a giant.

Nothing can fill us with greater sadness than this spectacle of Government trying to carry a measure in such haste and without proper deliberation, measure that is bitterly resented by the agriculturists, that has roused the apprehensions of the sowcars and that is condemned by the educated classes with one voice and in no uncertain terms. Is it fair, is it wise that Government should reduce us, the elected members, to a position of such utter helplessness that our united appeal should not secure even a brief postponement for a measure of such great importance? My Lord, I appeal to Your Excellency personally in the matter. Your Excellency has come fresh from a land where political opponents receive greater consideration and better care is taken of the several conflicting interests that must be harmonised in every important legislative measure. Your Excellency is free from what the Honourable Sir Charles Ollivant called the other day deteriorating limitations. I appeal to Your Excellency to pause — pause before it is too late, pause in spite of anything Your Excellency might have said yesterday.

During the brief time Your Excellency has been at the head of the Administration in this Presidency, you have taught us to look up to you, not only with respect — that is due to all Governors — but also with confidence and, if I be permitted to say so, with feelings of deep attachment. The people of the Presidency look up to Your Excellency, even at this last moment, to come to their assistance, and I fervently hope and trust that they will not look in vain.

[When the amendment was declared lost, the Hon. Mr. Mehta, the Hon. Mr. Khare, the Hon. Mr. Parekh, and the Hon. Sir Balchandra Krishna withdrew from the Council Hall. Before following them, the Hon. Mr. Gokhale spoke as follows].

Your Excellency — May I offer a word of personal explanation? In the remarks which I made this afternoon I did not like to say anything as to the course I should take if the amendment were lost. I think it my duty, my Lord, now to say that I must follow the course which has been taken by some of my honourable colleagues. I take this course with the greatest reluctance and regret. I mean no disrespect to Your Excellency or your colleagues personally. It is only an overwhelming sense of duty which urges me to take this step because I am not prepared to accept even the remote responsibility of associating myself with this measure which my farther presence here would imply.

Mofussil Municipalities Bill

[At a meeting of the Bombay Legislative Council hold on Tuesday the 12th February 1901, His Excellency Lord Northcote presiding, the Hon. Sir Diaries Ollivant moved the second reading of the Bill for the better management of municipal affairs in mofussil towns and cities. The Hon. Mr. G. K. Gokhale then spoke as follows].

Your Excellency — The Bill, as originally drafted, contained so many provisions of a distinctly retrograde character and bore on its face such evident impress of a desire on the part of the framers to recede from the position of 1884, that few of us, I confess, had any hopes that it would emerge from the Select Committee in the form which it has now taken. It is true that the Honourable Sir Evan James, who was then in charge of the Bill, introduced the measure in a speech which, for breadth of view and for a generous appreciation of the work and difficulties of municipal bodies, was a notable utterance, and which, if it had stood alone, would have been a source of sincere satisfaction to the people. Unfortunately, the speech was accompanied by a Bill so much at variance with the sentiments expressed by the mover, that the Honourable Mr. Justice Chandavarkar could not help exclaiming on that occasion how he wished that the Bill had been as good as its author. Those, however, were perhaps peculiar times. At any rate, on going through the proceedings on that occasion, I could not repress a smile of amusement at the boldness of some of the claims advanced.

Thus, the mover of the Bill, in replying to the debate on the first reading, said that he was not at all dissatisfied with the reception the Bill had met with, in spite of the fact that the measure had evoked a perfect storm of protest both in the Council and outside it. Why, Sir, even my honourable friend, Mr. Desai, whose mental eye appeared at that time to range over free fights among Municipal Councillors, their want of capacity and want of principle, was all the while imagining that he was speaking as an ardent advocate of local self-government.

All this, however, is now a matter of history, and if I recall the circumstance to Your Excellency's mind on this occasion, it is only to show what great reason the people of this Presidency have to feel grateful to the Honourable 'Sir Charles O'Hivant for the conciliatory manner in which he has led the Select Committee in its deliberations on this Bill and for striving to meet the public wishes at least half way. Every one of us who served on the Select Committee was impressed not only with his great knowledge of municipal affairs — that, of course, was well-known — but with the enormous industry which he bestowed upon the Bill, drafting, redrafting and drafting again so many of its provisions, and with the anxious solicitude which he throughout evinced to enter into the spirit of non-official criticisms and objections and remove, as far as he could, the causes for reasonable apprehensions.

Happily, his view of local self-government coincides largely with that held by many thoughtful persons in this country, both Natives and Europeans, as to the scope and purpose of municipal institutions. There are, as many here are no doubt aware, two ways of looking at this question of local self-government. One view is that, while the work of deliberation requires the assistance of many minds, all executive work must be entrusted to a single officer with large statutory powers. The other view is that not only the work of deliberation but also executive work ought to be entrusted to Municipal Councillors, who should do the latter by means of small subcommittees, thereby enabling the chosen representatives of the people to acquire direct experience of executive work and of a proper performance of civic responsibilities.

The first view is finding increased favour in the United States and has largely influenced the Municipal legislation of our Presidency towns. The second view is strongly held in England and on the continent of Europe, and it has supplied the lines on which municipal legislation in mofussil towns in India is based. Now, my Lord, I am willing to admit that the first scheme is perhaps better suited to the Presidency towns by reason of the largeness of their areas and the diversity of their populations, on the score of race, colour and creed, and the magnitude of the interests involved.

But there is no justification for extending such legislation to mofussil towns, which greatly appreciate the lines on which their present municipal Constitution is based. It seems to me, my Lord, that in this matter of local self-government, Government sometimes manage to do, by almost an irony of fate, just the thing which the people do not care for. Thus, in 1888, when the Bombay Municipal Act was revised, Government sought to assimilate the Constitution of the Bombay Corporation to that obtaining in the mofussil, when the citizens of Bombay did not require such a change; and it was only after a strong protest on the part of the Bombay Corporation, which was ably voiced by the Honourable Mr. Mehta and the late Mr. Justice Telang, that Government abandoned their proposals. Here, on the other hand, when people in the mofussil are satisfied with their existing Constitution, Government proposed to change that Constitution into something analogous to that of Bombay. Fortunately, under the direction of the Honourable Sir Charles Ollivant, that attempt has now been abandoned. Having made these few general observations, I will now, with Your Excellency's permission, proceed to say a few words on the Bill before us. I wish to state at the outset that, although the public feel deeply grateful to the honourable member in charge of the Bill for several important modifications which, under his guidance, the Select Committee has introduced, some of these modifications do not go far enough, and if we have proposed no amendments in regard to them, it is because those of us who represented the other side of the question in the Select Committee, accepted the modifications there in a spirit of compromise on the principle that half a loaf is better than no-bread. Moreover, there are even in this revised Bill some provisions which it is impossible for us to approve, and, of course, in regard to them we have given notice of the amendments which we intend to move. My Lord, the Bill before us may be considered under five heads: (1) Constitution; (2) Administrative procedure; (3) Duties and obligations; (4) Municipal powers; (5) Government control.

With reference to the first of these divisions, viz. Constitution, I beg leave to observe that, while the revised Bill is a great improvement on the original draft, there are one or two points under this head which are open to serious objection. I refer specially to the proposed provision for conferring the elective franchise on sections of inhabitants.

I think, my Lord, when the history of this question of the introduction of the elective franchise into the Constitution of Municipalities comes to be considered, it will be admitted that those among us who believe — and believe sincerely — that the right policy in such matters is that of a steady, though cautious advance, have behaved with great moderation in not moving amendments suggesting an extension of the present franchise. When the Act of 1884 was under consideration and when the Government of that day proposed to fix the minimum of elected members at one-half, it was contended by some of the non-official members that the minimum was low in the case of the more advanced municipalities at least and that in their case a more extended franchise was essential. Sir James Peile, who was in charge of that Bill, thereupon gave the assurance, and he repeated it again arid again in the course of the debates that, though the Bill prescribed a minimum of one-half, there was nothing to prevent Government from prescribing a higher proportion for individual

Municipalities in consideration of their fitness as determined by the level of intelligence and growth of civic spirit among them. Sir James Fergusson, who was then Governor, also stated that it was his hope that, if not during his time, at any rate during the time of his successor, it might be possible for Government to allow a higher proportion of elected to nominated members in the case of the leading Municipalities at least. Nothing, however, was done during the last fifteen years by Government to carry out this undertaking except in the case of Poona, where the proportion of two-thirds to one-third was granted during Lord Reay's time; but this special privilege has recently been, for all practical purposes, withdrawn. Though, therefore, it might have been justified in proposing that the Legislature should now prescribe a higher minimum in the case of the more advanced Municipalities at least, we have refrained from adopting this course with the object of minimising the points of difference between the official and the non-official members; and yet Government have thought it right to adhere to this retrograde provision for conferring the elective franchise on sections of inhabitants.

My Lord, in 1884, Sir James Peile, as representing the Bombay Government, stated in distinct terms that Government wanted to retain in their own hands the power of nominating members up to a maximum of one-half, because it might happen that sections of thc community, or certain minorities, might not be able to obtain adequate representation by means of the rate-payers' election, and in that case it would be desirable for Government to have this reserve of power in their hands to supply the deficiency. The representations of sections and minorities was thus provided for in 1884 by reserving to Government the right of nominating up to a maximum of one-half of members of Municipal Corporations.

In the present Bill, however, Government retain this power of nominating up to a maximum of one-half, and propose in addition that sections and minorities should have seats specially assigned to them out of the minimum of one-half, thrown open to election. I strongly feel, my Lord, it is most undesirable that Government should go back now upon what they distinctly guaranteed in 1884. My Lord, in this matter of the elective franchise our Presidency is already behind the other provinces of India. I have been looking up the Municipal Administration Reports of other Provinces, and I find that in Madras there are 19 Municipalities which are allowed to elect three-fourths of their members. In the North-West Provinces all the Municipalities to which the elective franchise is extended are allowed to elect three-fourths of the member. In the Central Provinces it is the same. In Bengal and the Punjab most of the Municipalities consist of two-thirds elected and one-third nominated members.

Here alone, in the Bombay Presidency, the proportion of elected members is rigidly kept down at half and even that, so far as the general ratepayers are concerned, the Legislature now proposes to reduce. The Bombay Government have often claimed that we in this Presidency are far ahead of other provinces in matters of Municipal administration. Such a boast, however justified on other grounds, is certainly not justified on the ground of the proportion of elected to nominated members on Municipal Boards. I quite admit that it is possible that some sections or minorities might like to be represented by elected instead of by nominated members. In their case, however, all that the Government has got to do is to set aside a certain number of seats which are at Government's own disposal for election by such sections or minorities.

Another provision coming under the head of Constitution is in connection with the creation of Notified areas. The original proposal to turn villages or groups of villages into 'Notified areas' has now been abandoned in favour of another adopted by the Select Committee, which restricts the provision on this subject to towns, which are the headquarters of talukas, and to hamlets that spring up in the vicinity of railway stations.

In assenting to this new proposal, I am not without apprehension that even in this new form it is capable of being worked in a manner which will cause hardship, and I earnestly trust that Government will be very sparing in the use of the powers which this provision confers upon them and as a result of which people in rural areas will have to bear municipal taxation without corresponding municipal privileges. The analogy of the Punjab has been quoted, but it should not be forgotten that in that province there are at present only 31 'Notified areas' in existence, whereas the Honourable Sir Evan James, in his detailed Statement of Objects and Reasons, has mentioned more than 150 places in this Presidency as fit to be turned into 'Notified areas.'

The third point under Constitution, about which I desire to say a word, is the position of the Chief Officer, whom City Municipalities will in certain cases have to appoint. I admit that under the revised provisions the Chief Officer will no longer be master of City Municipalities, as the original Bill practically proposed, and that the powers now conferred upon him by statute are such as may safely be entrusted to an Executive Officer acting under the full control and supervision of a City Municipality. The provisions about his appointment and removal are, however, in my opinion, not quite satisfactory, and if some of us have accepted them in Select Committee, it was done, as I have already observed, only in a spirit of reasonable compromise. Coming next to the question of 'Administrative Procedure' provided, I may state at once that I have nothing but praise to give to this portion of the Bill.

I am fully persuaded that the provisions on this subject are a great improvement on the Act of 1884, and I have no doubt that Municipal Corporations will feel grateful to the Legislature for this part of the Bill. Coming now to the question of 'Duties and Obligations' I think it necessary, my Lord, to enter my respectful but emphatic protest against the proposal to impose additional obligations under this Bill on Municipal Corporations.

The list of 'Obligatory Duties,' as set forth in Section M of this Bill, is already so long and covers such a vast variety of functions, that, if the obligations which that clause imposes upon Municipalities were to be literally construed, it would be impossible for the richest Municipality in the world to discharge those obligations satisfactorily, and yet the Legislature now proposes to make additions on very inconclusive grounds to that tearfully long list. It is now proposed, in addition to the obligatory duties already recognised, to call upon Municipalities to bear the cost of combating plague and famine, and to make contributions to the Provincial exchequer for Provincial roads passing through their limits, and for leper asylums and for lunatic asylums which Government may establish outside the Municipal limits. Now in regard to the first of these additions, viz. about plague and famine,

I submit to Your Excellency that the proposal in the original draft was much worse than the proposal now before us. In the original draft it was proposed to include this duty among the obligatory duties of a Municipality without any qualification whatsoever, but in the Select Committee the honourable member in charge of the Bill advanced so far in the direction of meeting popular objections as to provide that the obligatory duties mentioned in Clause 54 should take precedence of the duties in regard to plague and famine, and that the Municipalities should not provide for the later until after making reasonable provision for the former.

I confess I am not satisfied even with this modification made in the Select Committee, and if I assented to the modified proposal, it was only because I felt convinced that was the only way to get rid of the original proposal. I believe the Local Government are acting in this matter under instructions from the Government of India, and we had to make our choice between the proposal as originally drafted and the proposal now contained in this Bill. With reference to the provisions for levying contributions from Municipalities in connection with Provincial roads and leper and lunatic asylums, I respectfully submit, my Lord, that the proposal is inequitable and ought to be abandoned by Government. In the first place the contributions by themselves will be very small, and I ask if it is worth the while of Government to cause needless irritation for such small amounts? Secondly, as I have before observed, the list of obligatory duties is already so long, that any addition to them, however small, ought in my opinion to be deprecated unless Government are prepared to surrender to Municipal bodies corresponding revenues.

This was the spirit of the policy enunciated by the Government of India in 1882. But while the list of obligatory duties has grown enormously, I regret to say that there is not a single instance in which Government have transferred to Municipal bodies any of their receipts, and I submit that if new obligations continue to be imposed on the shoulders of Municipalities in this manner, such legislation will come to be regarded by the public not as a scheme of local self-government but as a scheme of local exactions. Next, with regard to the powers conferred on Municipal bodies, I cordially welcome the proposal to extend these powers in several important directions. I think this extension will make Municipal Administration more efficient and Municipal bodies will be able to deal with various difficulties, which crop up in the work of administration, in a simpler and more effective manner than at present. I am aware that there is some difference of opinion among non-official critics of the present Bill as to the Advisability of conferring drastic powers on Municipal bodies to deal with epidemics such as plague.

But I beg leave to point out that on this point we had to choose between conferring these powers or Municipalities and leaving these powers under the Epidemic Diseases Act in the hands of Plague Committees-appointed by Government and acting with no sense of responsibility to the public; and I believe that, when this question comes to be looked at from that standpoint, the proposal contained in the Bill to confer these powers on Municipal bodies will meet with general approval. Lastly, coming to the question of 'Government Control' I confess, my Lord, that my mind is not free from anxiety and apprehension, and that these powers of control might prove a source of unnecessary trouble in the hands of unsympathetic officers. I am free to admit that some such powers must be lodged in the hands of Government to make Municipal bodies feel that, if they do not realise their responsibilities properly, there is a speedy and effective method provided to call them to account.

At the same time, there is the obvious risk of Government officers - sometimes not understanding properly the difficulties of Municipalities or not making allowances in a generous spirit for small shortcomings and in such cases it would be open to them to suggest to Government the enforcement of the bludgeon-clauses to the humiliation of Municipal bodies and to the prejudice of the cause of local self-government; and this, my Lord, brings me to the concluding portion of my remarks. My Lord, what little practical experience of Municipal administration I possess has taught me one thing clearly, and it is that the District Officers have it in their power to make local self-government a greater success than it is at present, by taking steady and continuous interest in Municipal administration and regarding the work and difficulties of Municipal bodies with greater sympathy than so many of them do at present, I regret to say, my Lord that in some instances District Officers are found to regard the work of Municipalities with indifference till matters assume a serious aspect and then they suddenly come down upon them with the bludgeon-clauses in their hand. In other cases these officers interfere so constantly and in such a tone of authority that they appear more like dictators than like sympathetic guides, such as, in my humble opinion, they ought always to strive to be. I need hardly say that neither the one attitude nor the other on the part of District Officers is desirable in the interests of local self-government, and I earnestly appeal to them from this place to realise, in a spirit of, generosity and even forbearance, the difficulties and shortcomings of our Municipal Corporations, always remembering that, while it is easy to discredit work done by men who are new to their responsibilities, it is not equally easy to stimulate public-spirited citizens to greater exertions when once their ardour is damped by what they might regard as harsh and unsympathetic criticism or judgement.

Mr. John Stuart Mill has stated in his book on " Representative Government " that the object of Municipal institutions is not merely to get local work efficiently done, but also to develop civic spirit and raise the level of general intelligence among the people. I respectfully submit that; in judging the work of Municipal bodies, both these objects, and not only the first, should be stood kept in view. A higher public life has only just begun in the land, and it behooves those who represent the power that has introduced this life into this country to give whatever guidance might be needed with great tact and in a spirit of sympathy, encouraging those who need encouragement and steadying the footsteps of the weak. It is only by such cordial cooperation between District officers and Municipal Corporations that the success of local self-government would be ensured, and it is necessary to ensure this success, because in it are involved the best interests of both the rulers and the ruled.

[At the same meeting, when the Bill had been read a second time, and was being considered in detail, the Hon'ble Mr. Gokhale moved in clause 11, lines 19 and 20, to delete the words or by sections of the inhabitants].

Your Excellency — This question of sectional representation has been so fully dealt with by various honourable members in the debate on the second reading that I will not take up the time of the Council by making any lengthy remarks on this subject today. My first objection to the inclusion of these words is that they are an attempt to go back clearly on what was expressly guaranteed to the general ratepayers of the mofussil by Sir James Peile, speaking in the name of the Bombay Government.

As was pointed out yesterday, Sir James Peile in 1884 stated in distinct and unequivocal terms that a minimum of one-half of the total number of seats was to be filled by means of election by Municipal ratepayers without distinction of race, class or creed, and that the other half or any smaller proportion, whichever it might be, would be filled by Government by nomination in order to secure adequate representation of special interests, including those of sections or minorities. My second point is that, if it is thought that these sections or minorities may wish to be represented by elected, instead of by nominated members, there is nothing to prevent Government from setting aside a few of the seats which are at their free disposal for election by such sections.

The honourable member in charge of the Bill stated, in winding up the debate on the second reading, that the half retained by Government in their own hands was required for putting experts in certain matters on Municipal Corporations. From such experience of Mofussil Municipalities as I have, I am in a position to say that even in the largest Municipalities there are no more than two or three nominated members who may, in any way, be called experts in any branch, and that in some Municipalities there are no such persons appointed at all. Therefore, there would always be a large margin of reserve in the hands of Government even alter making adequate provision for the appointment of experts.

My next objection to this provision is that it tends to defeat the most important object of local self-government. We value local self-government not only for the fact that local work thereby is better done, but also for the fact it teaches men of different castes and creeds, who have long been kept more or less apart to work together for a common purpose. There are in all conscience causes for differences enough among the different sections in this land,

and I submit, my Lord, that the Legislature should not, in the best interests of the country, without the very strongest reasons, give any statutory recognition to these differences. There is nothing in the nature of local self government which implies any conflict between the interests of one section and another. If the Council will turn to the list of obligatory duties' and optional duties it will be seen that, except perhaps on the question of slaughterhouses, there is no chance of a conflict of interest arising between the different communities. And on that particular question, if the Hindu Councillors anywhere neglected to construct slaughterhouses for the benefit of Muhammadans and other inhabitants, Governments have it in their power, under the provisions of the 'Control Chapter,' to require recalcitrant Municipalities to perform that duty.

Then, my Lord, if different sections are to be represented, why talk of the Hindu community as a whole by itself? There are so many castes and sections of this community, and some of them stand so wide apart from one another, that it will be necessary to recognise their differences, and then where are the Government going to stop? The honourable member in charge of the Bill just asked what special merit there was in a road or water-course that it should supply a standard to divide a municipal district into wards, and why the inhabitants of a city would be better divided for municipal purposes into wards than into sections, I think the answer to that is somewhat simple.

You divide your presidency for administrative purposes into districts, your districts into talukas your talukas into towns and villages; for a similar reason municipal district has got to be divided into wards. If it was possible for all the electors to assemble and vote together and elect all their representatives, I for one would not attach any importance to election by wards. Then there is another reason why it is convenient to divide municipal districts into wards for election purposes. Men residing in the same ward have certain interests in common; those, for instance, connected with roads, lighting and the valuation of properties for the purpose of assessment and conservancy and so forth; and from this standpoint therefore, election by wards is perfectly intelligible. For these reasons, my Lord, I propose that the words pointed out in my amendment should be omitted from this clause.

Before sitting down, I may mention that I have no objection to Government providing for sectional representation by means of election, provided they guarantee to the general ratepayers a minimum of half the seats.

Female Education in India

[Paper read at the Educational Congress held in connection with the Women's Section (Education) of the Victorian Era Exhibition, 1897, by Professor G. K. *Gokhale].*

Standing here as I do, my mind cannot help being filled with thoughts in which regret and gratitude and hope are all strangely blended together. I stand before you as a representative of the only part of this great Empire which is far behind the rest in its enjoyment of the blessings of what may be called modern civilization. And yet we were the first to emerge from barbarism, and my nation was not only great, but was the greatest of all on the face of the earth, long before any one had heard anything of the oldest states of the West. Time, however, which brings ripeness to the raw fruit brings also decay to the ripe one, and the country which was once the cradle and long the home of a noble religion, a noble philosophy, and science and art of every kind, is at the present day steeped in ignorance and superstition and ail the moral helplessness which comes of such darkness.

But while this reflection fills me with what you will all admit to be a natural feeling of sadness, it is coupled with brighter thoughts, for they are the thoughts of gratitude and hope. Among the many achievements and triumphs of this Victorian Era, which you are celebrating with such legitimate satisfaction, there is, to my mind, nothing comparable to the work — the thrice blessed work — of regenerating ancient India which you have on numerous occasions pledged yourselves to achieve, and which has already been so worthily begun. The situation is, in many respects, perfectly unique in the history of the world. A great Eastern civilization, stationary for many centuries, is being once again galvanised into life by reason of its coming in contact with a younger and much more vigorous civilization of the West. The retention of all that is great and noble in our national life, as it has come down to us from the past, and the fullest absorption of what is great and noble in the life of the West, as revealed to us by our connection with England — this is now the work which has to be accomplished before we can once more hold our head high as a nation. How far such an ideal union of the different elements constituting the two civilizations is possible time alone will show. The task is one of extreme difficulty, but when it is achieved, if it can be achieved at all, the reward will be correspondingly great.

A wide diffusion of female education in all its branches is a factor of the highest value to the true well-being of every nation. In India it assumes additional importance by reason of the bondage of caste and custom which tries to keep us tied down to certain fixed ways of life and fixed modes of thought, and which so often cripples all efforts at the most elementary reforms. One peculiarity of the Indian life of the present day is the manner in which almost every single act of our daily life is regarded as regulated by some religious notion or another. We must eat, and sleep, and even stand, and sit, and walk only in accordance with certain religious beliefs, and the slightest departure from the accepted ideas in these matters is understood to increase the difficulties in the path of our salvation. And, naturally, these ideas have a far stronger hold on the minds of women than of men.

All who know anything of Indian women know that the turn of their mind is intensely religious — a result due in no small measure to their being shut out from all other intellectual pursuits. And this combination of enforced ignorance and overdone religion not only makes them willing victims of customs unjust and hurtful in the highest degree, but it also makes them the most formidable, because the most effective, opponents of all attempts at change or innovation. It is obvious that, under the circumstances, a wide diffusion of education, with all its solvent influences, among the women of India, is the only means of emancipating their minds from this degrading thralldom to ideas inherited through a long past and that such emancipation will not only restore our women to the honoured position which they at one time occupied in India, but will also facilitate, more than anything else, cur assimilation of those elements of Western civilization without which all thoughts of India's regeneration are mere idle dreams, and all attempts at it foredoomed to failure. The solution appears simple enough, and yet no problem in India is surrounded with greater difficulties or requires a more delicate and patient handling.

You, in this country, who are far more fortunately circumstanced, will find it hard to realise the exact nature or the full meaning of these difficulties. You have long left behind the period when it was necessary for any one to demonstrate to you the necessity of vindicating the dignity of female education. And practically, at the present day, the highest education which this great country of yours can provide in the different sciences and arts is freely available to your women, and is freely availed of by them. It is true that the lingering bigotry of men still tries here and there to throw small obstacles in your way, but they are, comparatively speaking, of little importance.

If, for instance, men will not allow you to be called Senior Wranglers, that only enables you to claim a higher distinction, — that of excelling Senior Wranglers. The freedom to acquire knowledge, and secure the culture of mind that knowledge brings, is enjoyed in this country by men and women in an equal degree, and if any individual fails to take due advantage of this freedom, the responsibility for such neglect belongs to that individual, or that individual's guardians, and to no one else. In India, however, the state of things is entirely different. The position there cannot be better described than in the words of Lord Ripon's Education Commission, which ran thus: The social customs of India, in regard to child-marriage and the seclusion in which women of the well-to-do classes spend their married life in most parts of the country, create difficulties which embarrass the promoters of female education at every step. The duration of the school-going age for girls is much shorter than that for boys.

It usually terminates at nine and seldom extends beyond the eleventh year. At so early an age girl's education is scarcely begun; and in very few cases- has the married child the opportunity of going on with her education after she leaves school. I must state here that this description does not apply to the Brahmins in Bengal, who, though Hindus by race, have broken from all Hindu traditions, and have cut themselves off from the Hindu community. It does not apply to the Parsees and the Native Christians. These three classes no longer suffer from the evils of early marriages, or, rather, early betrothals, and there is no enforced seclusion of married women among them; but, after all, numerically speaking, they are a mere drop in the ocean. The description is essentially true of the whole Muhammadan community, and of the vast bulk of the Hindu community.

And yet, so far as the Hindus are concerned, their women occupied a much more honoured and dignified position than this at one time. There is no doubt whatever, as stated by Dr. Bhandarkar, the foremost Sanskrit scholar in Western India at the present day, that in very old times Indian women were not debarred from the highest education. In the Vedic period — the remotest past of which we have any record — about five thousand years- ago they were among the inspired writers of sacred hymns, on which our religion is based. In the Upanishads — philosophical writings subsequent to the Vedas — they are mentioned as taking part in the discussions of the assemblages of learned Rishis, in which the highest problems about the world and the Supreme and the Individual Soul were discussed.

In our great epic poems — descriptive of a period subsequent to the Upanishads, but still considerably anterior to the Christian era — they are represented as going through a regular course of education, of which drawing, music, and even dancing (which is now considered degrading) formed part; they mixed freely with men and entered into learned discussions with them on spiritual and other difficult subjects. When Buddhism took its birth in India by way of protest against the sacrificial and ritual part of Hinduism, we find women actively assisting the reform which Buddha had inaugurated, and discussing with him abstruse points about duty, virtue and absolution. It is only when we come to the period of our dramatic literature that we perceive a tendency in women to fall behind men in learning. We then find them not as well versed as men in the classical language, but even then they could read and write and compose poetry in the popular languages. And even so late as the 11th century — the century which first attracted Muhammadan invaders to our land — we find instances of women possessing a high degree of education and engaged in intellectual pursuits. Then, almost suddenly, all light seemed to be extinguished, and for the last seven centuries our female world has been enveloped in a kind of intellectual gloom.

My friend, Mr. Ramesh Chunder Dutt, thus writes about the position of women in ancient India, in his admirable work on "Civilization in Ancient India": "We cherish the picture of the cultured lady, Viswavara, which has been handed down to us through thousands of years, a pious lady who composed sacred hymns, performed sacrifices, and with simple fervency invoked the God Agni to regulate rind keep within virtuous bounds the mutual relations of married couples. We meet with the names of other ladies, also, who were among the writers of the sacred hymns of the Rig Veda." In another place Mr. Dutt writes: "We have seen that the absolute seclusion of women was unknown in ancient India. Hindu women held an honoured place from the dawn of Hindu civilization four thousand years ago; they inherited and possessed property; they took a share in sacrifices and religious duties; they attended great assemblies on State occasions; they often distinguished themselves in science and the learning of their times.

And they even had their legitimate influence, on politics and administration. Considered as the intellectual companions of their husbands, as their friends and loving helpers in the journey of life, as the partners of their religious duties, and the centre of their domestic bliss, Hindu wives were honoured and respected in ancient times." And again: "We saw in our account of the Epic period that ladies sometimes devoted themselves to the pursuit of philosophy, that Gargi Vacaknavi distinguished herself among the learned men of the Court of Janaka....... Megasthenes is a witness to the fact that sacred learning and philosophy were not forbidden in the rationalistic period to such ladies as desired to devote themselves to such studies."

Education, enlightened freedom, and an honoured position in society, these — and not enforced seclusion and ignorance — are the rightful inheritance of Indian women. The last seven centuries of darkness have, however, so effectually done their work that any one who reminds the Indian people of this past state of things, and asks them to make an attempt to return to it, runs the risk of being set down as an innovator. And in this, as in several other matters, it is England that is awakening us to a true sense of our duty. Of course, even before the advent of the British into India, instruction of a most rudimentary character in reading and writing was sometimes imparted here and thereto girls of the upper classes, but this instruction was not -based on any system, and it possessed no organised character. Its nature is thus described by the Education Commission: "Apart from the Sanskrit traditions of women of learning and literary merit in pre-historic and medieval times, there can be no doubt that when the British obtained possession of the country, a section of the female population was educated up to the modest requirements of household life. In certain provinces little girls occasionally attended the indigenous village schools and learned the same lessons as their brothers. Many women of the upper class had their minds stored with the legends of the Puranas and Epic poems, which supply impressive lessons in morality and in India from the substitute for history. Among the lower orders the keeping of the daily accounts fell in some households to the mother or chief female of the family. The arithmetic of the homestead was often conducted by primitive methods, addition and subtraction being performed by means of flowers or any rude counters which came to hand. Among the more actively religious sects and races girls received education as a necessary part of their spiritual training. In the Punjab they may still be seen seated in groups around some venerable Sikh priest, learning to read and recite the national scriptures or *granth*, and the Brahmin tutor of wealthy Hindu families does not confine his instruction to the sons alone. In some parts of the country such education as girls obtained was confined ostensibly to reading and arithmetic, writing being an art not held suitable for women of respectable life..... As a matter of fact, there always have been women of great accomplishments and strong talents for business in India. At this moment one of the best administered Native States has been ruled during two generations by ladies — the successive Begums of Bhopal. Many of the most ably managed of the great landed properties or Zemindaris of Bengal are entirely in the hands of females; while in commercial life, women, conduct, through their agents, lucrative and complicated concerns. But the idea of giving girls a school education, as a necessary part of their training for life, did not originate in India until quite within our own days. The intellectual activity of Indian women is very keen, and it seems frequently to last longer in life than the mental energies of the men. The intelligence of Indian women is certainly far in advance of their opportunities of obtaining school instruction, and promises well for their education in the future."

It will thus be seen that, for systematic and organised efforts for the promotion of female education, as also for a correct appreciation of its importance as a factor of individual improvement and national progress, we are indebted almost exclusively to the influence introduced into the country by British rule, and these influences, moreover, have been brought to bear on us on a large scale only since the accession of the present sovereign to the throne. A brief account of the work achieved so far in this field in the different provinces of India will not be out of place in this paper.

Beginning with my own Presidency, Bombay, we find that the credit of making the first organised effort to educate Indian girls belongs to the American Missionary Society, who opened in 1824, the first native girls' school in Bombay. By the year 1829, no fewer than 400 female pupils were receiving instruction in their schools. The Scottish Missionary Society was not long in following the example of the American Society, and Dr. Wilson, one of the most respected names in India, established on its behalf six schools for native girls in Bombay in 1829. In 1840, this society opened five schools for high-class Hindu girls in the neighbourhood of Poona. It was not till 1851 that the Indians themselves came forward to work in this field. In that year the Students' Literary and Scientific Society was formed, which counted among its founders and earliest workers such men as Mr. Dadabhai Naoroji, the late Mr. Mandik, rind others, and which has, on the whole, done most excellent work. This Society began its operations with nine vernacular free schools, attended by more than 650 girls.

In 1854, the Court of Directors addressed to the Government of India the famous Dispatch on Education, which laid down the lines on which the work of educating the Indian people was to be undertaken by the Government. It is a wonderful document, and no wonder that it is so, seeing that it is reputed to have emanated from the pen of John Stuart Mill. This Dispatch laid great stress on the urgency and importance of female education in India, and led to Government joining in the good work, which till then had been left entirely to private enterprise. Later on, the visit of Miss Mary Carpenter, whose name will always be gratefully cherished by the Indian people, gave a great and much needed impetus to the movement, and Female Normal Schools for the supply of female teachers were established in Bombay, Poona and Ahmedabad. The progress in female education in the Bombay Presidency during the last half century has indeed been continuous and remarkable. In 1854, there were 65 girls' schools, attended by 3,500 pupils. In 1869, the number of schools had risen to 209, and that of pupils to over 9,000. In 1881 the number of schools stood at 343, with over 26,000 pupils. Last year there were 900 schools for girls with an attendance of over 84,000 pupils.

In the Madras Presidency, the first attempt at providing schools for native girls was made in 1841 by the Missionaries of the Scottish Church. In 1845, the first girls' school under partial native management was opened. When the Dispatch of 1854 arrived in India, there were in the Madras Presidency 256 girls' schools, attended by 3,000 girls. In 1881, the number of schools had risen to 557, and that of pupils to over 35,000. Last year there were in the Madras Presidency over 1,000 schools, attended by nearly 110,000 girls.

The Dispatch of 1854 found 288 girls' schools, with nearly 7,000 pupils, in Bengal. But included in this number as an institution which has since become famous in the history of female education in India — the Bethune Girls' School in Calcutta. The following account of this institution is given in the report of the Education Commission: This institution was established in 1849, and bears the name of its founder, Mr. Drinkwater Bethune, then Legal Member of Council, who took an active part in many movements for the advancement of native society. It was opened under the name of 'the Hindu Female School, with 23 pupils and was for some time maintained at the entire cost and under the direct management of Mr. Bethune, who also by his will left lands and other property in Calcutta for its endowment in perpetuity.

On his death, in 1851, it was taken up by Lord Dalhousie, who for nearly five years paid 8,000 rupees annually for its maintenance from his private purse. The charge was afterwards transferred to the State, although the direct management of the school continued and still continues in the hands of a Committee. Unlike the earlier Missionary efforts, the Bethune School rests on a secular basis; and the Committee aims at conducting it in accordance with national Indian feeling. It derives its pupils chiefly from the higher classes, exacts an adequate payment for boarding and other charges, and carries its instruction up-to University Standard." The number of girls' schools in 1881 stood at over 1,000, with an attendance of over 41,000 pupils. Last year these figures were 3,352 schools and 114,000 pupils.

The early efforts of the Missionary societies towards the spread of female education were not very successful in the North-West Provinces, and the Dispatch of 1854 found only 17 Missionary schools for girls, with an attendance of 386 pupils. After the receipt of the Dispatch, Government took up the work with great zeal, and by 1871 the number of girls' schools in these Provinces had reached 640, and the number of pupils nearly 14,000. Then the progress was suddenly arrested, and for ten years there was actually a retrograde movement, which is thus described by the Education Commission: Between 1871 and 1881 a great decrease took place in girls' schools.

Their abolition was mainly due to the financial position of the Government. It was felt that, if retrenchments were necessary, they could be carried out in the girls' schools with thc last prejudice to education. By 1881 the number of schools had dropped from 640 to 308 and the number of pupils from 14,000 to less than 9,000. The ground thus lost has not been recovered yet. Last year the numbers of girls' schools in these provinces stood at 425, and the number of pupils at about 12,500.

In the Punjab, the indigenous schools for religious instruction have always been careful in imparting the rudiments of reading and writing to females, and even at the present day we have over 900 of such schools attended by nearly 13,000 girls. In addition to such schools - the Dispatch of 1854 found 17 Missionary schools attended by 300 girls. Then the numbers began to decrease, as in the North-West Provinces, and by 1881 they had dropped to 311 schools and 9,000 pupils. Last year these figures stood at 362 and a little over 13,000, respectively.

Thus, in these five provinces, we had, in 1854, about 600 schools for girls, attended by about 19,000 pupils. Instead, we have now over 6,000 schools, attended by nearly 260,000 girls. The progress indicated by these figures is beyond all doubt most striking and so far very satisfactory. In one respect, however, there is room for dissatisfaction and even disappointment. Nearly all the progress, remarkable as it is, is confined to primary education. Taking the Bombay Presidency, for instance, we find that among the 900 and odd schools for girls, there are only 60 for secondary education, and even these are for the most part European, Eurasian or Parsee schools. The number of secondary schools for Hindu girls is only 4, with an attendance of less than 200 pupils — the most notable of these being the female high school in Poona, which owes so much to the inspiration, sympathy, and support of our good friend Sir William Wedderburn.

As for higher education there is not a single female college — arts or professional — in the whole Presidency. The main difficulty in the way of the higher or secondary education of Hindu girls is, of course, the fact that these girls must be married, or rather betrothed, before a certain age — the present limit being about 11 or 12 years — and that they are, as a rule, withdrawn from school immediately after such marriage or betrothal. The question is thus intimately connected with another necessary reform, namely, raising the marriageable age of Hindu girls. And the position may be correctly described in the following; words of the late Mr. Justice Telang: In discussing this matter, we seem sometimes to move in a vicious circle.

We cannot successfully raise the age of marriage for girls among any large portions of our community without a wide spread of female education. And, on the other hand, any considerable spread of real female education is hardly possible until the age of marriage is raised. There is a real difficulty here, but the way to meet it is at one and the same time to push on female education to the extent that is possible, under present conditions, and to extend the limits of marriageable age in the same way. And as every advance is secured along either of these lines, the further advance will become more and more easy. Our progress in the later stages will be accelerated, if I may say so, in geometrical progression.

Even the progress in primary education, which appears so striking, marks, after all, only the commencement of the great work that in reality lies before us. The following figures will make my meaning clear. In the Madras Presidency, according to the last census, out of a total female population of 20,000,000, only 250,000, females can read and write, or are under instruction, which gives a ratio of 1 in 80. In the Bombay Presidency, the figures are 100,000, out of a total female population of about 13,000,000, thus giving a ratio of 1 in 130. In Bengal, out of 37,000,000 females, only 150,000 can read and write or are under instruction which means a ratio of 1 in 259. In the Punjab, the figures are 35,000, out of a total of 110 millions — a ratio of 1 in 330. In the North- West Provinces we have 50,000 females who can read and write, or are under instruction out of a total of 23,000,000 which gives a ratio of 1 in 410. The .Central Provinces have a female population of 6.5 millions, and of these only 12,000 — i.e. 1 in 548 — are attending schools or can read and write. Comments on these figures are really superfluous.

The difficulties, apart even from social customs, are many and serious. The supply of good female teachers is certainly far short of the needs of the country. The female training colleges are doing useful work in this connection, but there is a general feeling that they do not attract a sufficiently large number from those classes of women whose employment as teachers would inspire general confidence. Then the question of determining the proper curriculum for girls' schools is surrounded with difficulties.

As the appreciation of female education becomes more widespread, men will come to recognise that there ought to be no more impediments in the path of girls then in that of boys in selecting the subjects they are to study or choosing the books they are to read. In our present circumstances, however, when it is necessary for us to work along the line of least resistance, it is necessary to take note of the different surroundings of boys and girls in Indian Society in determining the course of instruction, and to make some concession even to popular prejudices on the subject. I fear this has not been done in the past to the extent that is desirable. The worst defect in the present system of female education in India is the utterly dry, mechanical and uninteresting character of the methods of instruction. Women naturally possess more refined sensibilities than men, and have a finer, more delicate aesthetic perception; and a course of instruction which merely overloads the memory and fails to appeal to the imagination is not calculated to leave on the minds of small girls very agreeable impressions of their brief school career. But, as I have observed above, the good work of female education is only just begun in India, and what has been already accomplished is as nothing compared with what yet remains to be achieved. And I have firm faith that in course of time all the deficiencies which at present constitute so many obstacles in our path will one by one disappear. Here, if anywhere, we feel that the flowing tide is with us.

The opposition of my countrymen to the education of their girls, at one time so general and so pronounced has already softened into indifference, into toleration. And from this to active appreciation is but a single step, though I must admit it is not a short step. Happily there is no trace of hesitation or misgiving in the minds of our rulers on the subject, and philanthropic ladies and gentlemen in this country, to whose sympathy and assistance we are already so much indebted, may well be trusted to continue their good work in the future. What has been said of charity is also true of education. It blessed those that give as also those that receive. And if any words of mine, addressed to you today, lead any to join in the emancipating work of female education in India, I shall, feel that my humble labours have been amply rewarded.

Home Charges

[A very largely attended public meeting of the inhabitants of Bombay was held on Saturday, July 15th, 1893, in the hall of the Framjee Cowasjee Institute, under the auspices of the Bombay Presidency Association, to adopt a Memorial to the House of Commons on the subject of the Home Military Charges in India. The Hon. Sir (then Mr.) P. M. Mehta was in the chair, and Mr. Gokhale moved the adoption of the Memorial in the following speech].

Mr. Chairman and Gentlemen,—Under ordinary circumstances, I should have hesitated to take upon myself the responsibility of proposing a resolution on so difficult and so complicated a question as the Home Military charges of India. But my task has become materially lightened by the very interesting debate which took place on this subject in the House of Lords about two months ago on a motion brought forward by the Earl of Northbrook. I think, gentlemen, and I am sure you all think with me, that Lord Northbrook has rendered a high and valuable service to the people of this country by raising his voice in the way he has done — I mean by raising his voice in so firm and emphatic a manner — against the injustice to which India has, for years past, been subjected in this matter of the Home Military charges.

It is clear that His Lordship means business, for he has followed up the debate of 15th May by moving for papers that passed between the Government of India and the Home Government between 1874 and 1876, i.e. at a time when he himself was Viceroy of India. Gentlemen, it is an undoubted advantage to our country that so cautious and so hard-headed a man as Lord Northbrook has, on the present occasion, stood up for justice to her. For if it means anything, it means that there is something really rotten and really intolerable in the existing arrangements.

Remember, gentlemen, Lord Northbrook speaks with uncommon authority and unrivalled knowledge on this subject. He was at one time Viceroy of India, and it was while he was Viceroy that a Select Committee of the House of Commons — I mean the East India Finance Committee of 1874 — made an exhaustive enquiry into this matter and reported that India was unjustly burdened with many charges which ought in fairness to be borne by the British Exchequer. Naturally Lord Northbrook had then to pay great attention to this subject, and he pleaded the cause of India with great earnestness and force. Then, since his return to England, he presided, with some short intervals up to last year, over a Commission which was appointed by the British Treasury in connection with this matter.

His Lordship has thus had this question before him, as he himself stated in the House of Lords the other day for full twenty years. And his utterances in regard to it are therefore entitled to the greatest weight. Then, gentlemen, remember it is not Lord Northbrook alone who has raised this question. Indian public opinion — as represented by Mr. Martin Wood, the late Robert

Knight, the late Kristodas Paul, the late Mr. Naoroji Furdunji, and Mr. Dadabhai Naoroji — has in the past often protested against the iniquity of the treatment accorded to India.

And before the first National Congress, my friend Mr. Wacha made a remarkable speech on this subject. I call that speech remarkable because, as you will find if you read it, in that speech our friend anticipates Lord Northbrook in many of his complaints. And when you think of that, when you think of the earnest and patient study which our friend has given to this and other equally difficult subjects, I am sure you will say to yourselves — as I said to myself.

How much better it will be if some of those who are disposed to find fault with our friend, because sometimes he speaks out his mind too directly and disdains to act on the principle that language is more for the concealment of thought than for its expression, would take a leaf out of his book and devote some portion of their time to a study of these important questions!

Then, gentlemen — and this is a matter of far greater importance — successive Viceroys and Secretaries of State for India have, one after another, protested against these charges as excessive and unjust. Lord Mayo did this; Lord Northbrook, as I have already said, did in the past and is yet doing it. Lord Lytton wrote against these charges and wrote strongly arid with his usual candour. The Marquis of Ripon addressed to the Home Government a very earnest remonstrance on the subject.

Lord Dufferin followed his example and, judging from Lord Northbrook's speech of 15th May last, it would appear that Lord Lansdowne has also recently raised his voice against these charges. Then, as regards - Secretaries of State, Sir Charles Wood, Sir Stafford Northcote, the Duke of Argyll, Lord Salisbury, Lord Hartington, Lord Kimberley, Lord Cross — all in their time have remonstrated with the British Treasury and the War Office that the Home Military charges of India were exorbitant and unfair. But, as Lord Kimberley himself said the other day, the Secretary of State for India possesses less influence than any other Minister in the English Cabinet, and thus the remonstrances of all these men have hitherto been of no avail. It is, therefore, a matter for congratulation that Lord Northbrook has made up his mind to invoke the authority of Parliament to set matters right. And it is also a matter for congratulation that our friends in the House of Commons.

Mr. Caine, Mr. Macfarlane and others, have taken prompt steps to strengthen Lord Northbrook's hands. Gentlemen, the controversy which Lord Northbrook has raised, and to which alone we confine ourselves on this occasion, refers to that portion of the Home charges which is shown as Military. The total Home charges of India are exceedingly heavy and so is the total Military expenditure. But on this occasion we speak neither of the Home charges as a whole nor of the Military as a whole. We confine ourselves only to the Military portion of the Home charges. This charge for the year that has closed has been nearly 5 millions sterling, i.e. over 1 crores of rupees.

It is, as many of you may be aware, made up of two parts, effective and non-effective, each being about half of the whole. The effective charges chiefly include a large sum annually paid to the War Office, because the British troops serving in India are recruited and sent out here by that office, an equally large sum for the stores supplied to these troops, a considerable sum for the expenses of the Indian Troop Service of the transport ships which bring out British troops here and take them back to England, and the furlough allowances of the officers and men in the British Army in India. The non-effective charges consist principally of payment to the War Office for retired pay and pensions of British troops for service in India and pay and pension of non-effective officers and retired officers of the Indian Service.

Gentlemen, it is most unfortunate that since the amalgamation of the armies in England and India, i.e. during the last thirty years and more, these Home Military charges have been, owing to one thing or another, increasing almost from year to year and this has gone on in spite of strong remonstrances from the Government of India and the Secretary of State for India, only because English Ministers try to relieve English budgets at the expense of India, and the people of this country have no voice in the English Parliament I must invite your attention to a few figures to make my meaning clear to you. Thirty years ago, i.e. is 1862, the total Home Military charges of India were only a little over two millions sterling. Today they are close upon 5 millions. I will not, gentlemen, weary you with figures for all these thirty years, but I will divide these years into six periods of 5 years each and give you the average figures for the quinquennial periods. From 1862 to 1867, the average Home Military expenditure was nearly 2 millions a year. In the next period, i.e. from 867 to 1872, it was a little less than 3 millions sterling.

From 1872 to 1877, it was a little over 3 millions, 6 hundred thousand pounds. From 1877 to 1882, it was a little over 4 millions. This average was maintained during the next period, i.e. from 1882 to 1887. The tendency of the charges to increase was for a time checked by a new scheme of making payment for pensions, which was introduced in 1884, and which for the time considerably reduced the annual charge for pensions. From 1887 to 1892, the average was a little less than 4 millions, and for the years 1892-93, these charges were close upon five millions. Gentlemen, I hope you now see how these charges have been constantly increasing and how in thirty years have more than doubled themselves. The burden thrown on the Indian revenues by the charges has again, during recent years, been rendered more heavy by the fall in exchange and if you take this fall in exchange into account, you will find that India pays today for these charges more than three times of what she paid thirty years ago.

Further, this increase appears still more serious when it is remembered that the part of this expenditure, which is under the control of the Government of India, has been steadily reduced and also that Government now purchases a part of the stores in India itself. I now briefly refer to the principal details of these charges. The first item among the effective charges is the payment annually made to the War Office for the recruitment expenses of the British forces in India. Last year this charge was nearly a million sterling, though generally it is about three-fourths of a million.

Owing to the amalgamation of the English and Indian Armies in 1859, the Government of India is forced to depend for her British troops on the English War Office, and has, therefore, to pay for their recruitment practically whatever price the War Office demands. There are various interesting points connected with this question of recruitment, but I will not trouble you with them. I will mention to you only one fact, that high military authorities have repeatedly expressed the opinion that the sum demanded by the War Office for recruitment is a most exorbitant one and that if the Indian Government were allowed liberty of action in the matter, it could get the required recruits for a small fraction of the sum. Sir Charles Dilke, who is one of the highest authorities on these subjects, says, in his Imperial Defence, that the sum charged at present to India is monstrously large and that nearly the whole of it could be saved to India, if the Government of India were allowed to take its own measures for the recruitment of its troops. The next effective charge to which I would call your attention is the charge for stores.

The charge naturally varies from year to year, but it is never less than half a million and last year it was nearly nine hundred thousand pounds. Now, here also the discretion of the Government of India is, for the most part, fettered and it has to purchase its stores from the War Office. And the complaint has been repeatedly made that the War Office demands excessive prices for these stores, and practically tries to make a large profit out of the arrangement. The next item is that of the Indian Troop Service. Gentlemen, I have already explained to you that this charge means the expenses of the transport ships that are built and kept at India's expense for the purpose of bringing out here and taking back again to England the British troops that serve in this country.

Last year this charge came to about two hundred and forty thousand pounds. Now it has often been urged, and rightly urged, that there is no necessity in these days to maintain three ships at such enormous cost, because British troops could very well be brought out and sent back like other passengers. The maintaining of these ships by Government for the sole use of British troops involves a large waste of our money, as may be seen from the fact that for five months in the year these vessels do absolutely nothing and yet their establishments have to be paid for all the same during this time. Then there is the question of the furlough allowances. But it is a comparatively small question and I will not go into that on this occasion. So far I have dealt with the effective charges.

As regards the non-effective charges, there are only two principal items and these are payments to the War Office for retired pay and pensions of British forces for service in India and the pay and'« pensions of non-effective and retired officers of the Indian Service. The first of these two items is not now as heavy as it was before 1884. For the last year it was a little over one-third of a million. But, as was anticipated in 1884, and as was pointed out by Lord Northbrook and Lord Kimberley in their speeches of 15th May, this charge will now rapidly grow, and in a short time, under existing arrangements, it may become heavier than it ever was. It is in regard to this charge that Lord Northbrook stated the other day that, during the last fourteen years, the War Office had taken from India four millions sterling more than was fair or just.

We cannot, therefore, do better than ask the protection of the House of Commons in regard to this charge. As regards the other non-effective item, it is, gentlemen, really a very serious matter. For the last year this charge stood at the huge figure of about one million nine hundred thousand pounds, i.e. about two crores and seventy-five lakhs of rupees. During the last thirty years, this expenditure has more than doubled itself. I am aware, gentlemen, that this part of the question is one which is beset with great difficulties. On the one hand, there are liabilities incurred by the Government in expectations legitimately formed by men in the service. But, on the other hand, there are the claims of the poor tax-payer of India to be considered, and if things are allowed to drift on as at present, there is no knowing to what figure this charge may grow.

Our prayer, therefore, is that Government should now look on this item carefully and take whatever measures may be necessary to stop its alarming growth. But, gentlemen, even if it were to be put aside, this large figure of pensions to officers of the Indian Service, a large saving in respect of the other item — effective and non-effective — is what we are clearly entitled to. And, in my humble opinion, the sum so saved will come to from a million to a million and a half sterling, from a crore and a half to two crores of rupees every year, and this I consider to be a moderate estimate. There is another point raised by Lord Northbrook in his speech which finds a place in your memorial of today. England has in the past borrowed troops from India for expeditions undertaken from considerations of Imperial policy, such as the expeditions to China and Persia, the Abyssinian Expedition and others, and on all these occasions, all the ordinary expenses of these troops have been taken from India, England defraying their extraordinary expenses alone.

On the other hand, when India had to borrow troops from England, as on the occasion of the Sindh Campaign of 1845, the Punjab Campaign of 1849, and the Mutiny of 1357, every farthing of the expenses of these ordinary and extraordinary, including even the expenditure on their recruitment, was extorted from India. I think, gentlemen, I have now made it sufficiently clear to you that for years past India has been most unjustly treated by England in the matter of Home Military charges. Our prayer, therefore, now to the House of Commons is that the House be pleased (1st) to direct rich England to refund to poor India whatever has been unjustly extorted from her in the past; (2nd) to order tha no charges, which, in fairness, - ought to be borne by the Britisl Exchequer, should hereafter be thrown on India; and lastly, to Jay down by Act of Parliament the amount or proportion of the non-effective charges of the British forces for service in India, that should hereafter annually be borne by this country.

Gentlemen, do not suppose that when we ask for a refund of the money overdrawn by England in the past, we are making an unreasonable request. For the War Office itself has often in the past acted on this principle by compelling India to pay large sums as arrears and this selfish and despotic office has at times gonc to such a length that even when, owing to its own dilatoriness in presenting bills to the India Office, its claims remained for a time unpaid, it extorted from India afterwards not only the full payment of those claims, but charged interest and, in some cases, even compound interest.

Then, as regards our second request, I think the House of Commons is, in common justice, bound to grant it, and when that is done a substantial relief will come to the finances of India, for a crore and a half of rupees every year means a good deal to the people of this country. Then, in preferring the third request, viz., for Parliamentary legislation to fix the amount or proportion which we should annually pay to the War Office for non-effective charges, we are only reiterating a proposal made by Lord Ripon's Government in 1883. The advantages of such an arrangement are many and obvious. But the most important of these advantages is, in my opinion, this, that whenever these charges are increased they will come to be carefully examined by the House of Commons, because the English charges also will be proportionately increased and thus a sort of Parliamentary supervision will be ensured to our own charges.

But, gentlemen, before the House of Commons can do all this, it is necessary that it should order a thorough enquiry into the subject and we, therefore, pray in the Memorial that a Select Committee be appointed for the purpose. Gentlemen, I hope I have made all the points in the Memorial clear to you. I have already taken up too much of your time, but there is one aspect of the question, about which I will say just a word before I conclude. You may be aware how critical the condition of Indian finance at present is.

Government has exhausted every available resource and no further taxation is now possible without inflicting intolerable hardship on the poor and miserable millions of this country. The Herschell Committee has practically admitted this fact in its recent report. On one hand, there is - ever-deepening gulf of the Home charges and the military expenditure necessitating a grasping and relentless-revenue policy and an intolerably burdensome duty on the poor man's salt; on the other hand, there are millions upon millions of people, sunk in the lowest depths of poverty and misery, paying taxes far beyond their means, and therefore panting for relief. I think, gentlemen, that, in such circumstances, it is the bounden duty of the Government of this country and of the British Parliament to effect all possible economies in the expenditure of the country and thereby give these millions groaning under their burden the relief they seek.

I think a Government which lends a willing ear to the complaints of the well-paid European cannot, in common humanity, shut its eyes to the misery of the poor peasant, who toils and moils from dawn to dark only to find himself badly clothed and worse fed. I think, if Government effects the economies in the Home Military charges which have been repeatedly pointed out to it, the poor man's salt can, at any rate, be made cheaper to him, even if no other relief be possible. Gentlemen, England is strong, but let her not abuse her strength by extorting from poor India more than she has a right to receive.

England professes to be anxious to do justice to India. We have had nearly a century of these professions and it is now time we had a little of the practice of the thing. I, therefore, trust that the House of Commons will grant our prayer. It is in this hope that I propose this Resolution and it is in this hope that I earnestly call upon you to adopt it.

8

Golden Words of Gokhale

- "One has only to look around to realise where a movement for independence is bound to land us. Meanwhile it means the sure destruction, or at any rate, the indefinite postponement of all those opportunities for slow but peaceful progress, which arc at present within our reach."
- "The whole life of a people, which is broader and deeper than what is touched by purely political institutions, is enriched even by failure, provided the effort has been all that it should be."
- "The greatest work of Western education in the present state of India is . . . the liberation of the Indian mind from the thralldom of old-world ideas."

9

Gokhale's Life at a Glance

May 9, 1866: Gopal Krishna Gokhale was born in the Ratnagiri.

1884: The DES was established by the stalwarts of India's freedom struggle, laid by Agarkar and Tilak and later built by great personalities of the era like Gopal Krishna Gokhale and Dhondo Keshav Karve (honoured with Bharat Ratna). These visionaries aimed to channelise the devotion and energy of the youth that could drive ordinary men to do extra ordinary things. The DES was established to streamline the spiralling unrest among the youth in the pre-independence era. Being one of the first generations of Indians to receive a university education, Gokhale graduated from Elphinstone College.

1885: Gopal Krishna Gokhale moved on to Pune and became one of the founding members of Fergusson College, along with his colleagues in Deccan Education Society. Gopal Krishna Gokhale gave nearly two decades of his life to Fergusson College and rose to become principal of the college. During this time, Gokhale came in contact with Mahadev Govind Ranade. Ranade was a judge, scholar, and social reformer, whom Gokhale called his guru.

1887: He regularly voiced views on social and economic reform at the annual sessions of the Indian National Social Conference, which he founded in 1887. Ranade inspired many other Indian social reformers, most notably the educator and legislator Gopal Krishna Gokhale.

1888: Gopal Krishna Gokhale completed his secondary education from Rajaram High School in Kolhapur. After completion of highs school he moved to Bombay for further studies at the Elphinstone College. He completed his graduation. He was a hardworking and talented student in the last year of his college he was awarded a scholarship of Rs. 20.

1889: Gokhale became a member of the Indian National Congress, as a protege of social reformer Mahadev Govind Ranade.

1891-92: Gokhale's first major confrontation with Tilak centred around one of his pet projects, the Age of Consent Bill introduced by the British Imperial Government.

1892: Indian National Congress became a highly select, exclusive club, drawing in such notables as Gopal Krishna Gokhale, a Bombay leader and close associate of Gandhi, Dadabhai Naoroji, a Parsee intellectual and cotton trader who became a Liberal MP for Finsbury Central, and Romesh Chandra Dutt, an economic historian and writer from Calcutta. It also included Motilal Nehru, the father of India's first Prime Minister, Jawaharlal Nehru, and, initially, Muhammad Ali Jinnah also.

1893: They promoted solidarity among Hindus by organising a ten day Ganpati festival. While the reformists such as Dadabhai Naoroji, Madhava Govinda Ranade and Gopal Krishna Gokhale promoted reforms in Hindu culture, the revivalists like the followers of Arya Samaj and Bal Gangadhar Tilak and his Congress faction opposed any kind of reform.

1894: Gokhale visited Ireland and had arranged for an Irish nationalist, Alfred Webb, to serve as President of the Indian National Congress.

1896: Jinnah was called to London's Bar from Lincoln's Inn, and returned home to launch his singularly successful legal career in Bombay. At 34, he was elected to serve as the Bombay Presidency's Muslim representative on the Viceroy's Central Legislative, whose members then included ex-Congress president Gopal Krishna Gokhale, hailed by Mahatma Gandhi as "my political guru".

1899: Gokhale was elected to the Bombay Legislative Council.

22 May, 1903: Gokhale was elected to the Council of India of Governor General of India as non-officiating member representing Bombay Province.

1904: Gokhale developed so great a reputation among the British that he was invited to London to meet with secretary of state Lord John Morley, with whom he established a rapport. Gokhale would help during visit to shape the Morley-Minto Reforms introduced in 1909. Gokhale was appointed a CIE (Companion of the Order of the Indian Empire) in the New Year's Honours List, a formal recognition by the Empire of his service.

December 1904: Jinnah met Gopal Krishna Gokhale, first at the twentieth session of the Indian National Congress. At the very first meeting, Jinnah was so captivated by the wisdom, fairness and moderation of him, that Jinnah became his ardent admirer and later stated that his fond ambition is to become the "Muslim Gokhale."

1905: The Servants of India Society established by Gopal Krishna Gokhale, political mentor of Mahatma Gandhi. Gokhale became president of the Indian National Congress.

July 1906: National leaders like Bal Gangadhar Tilak, Bipin Chandra Pal and Gopal Krishna Gokhale visited Allahabad and sought Vidyarthi's support for national struggle.

July 1909: This "India House" soon became notorious as a centre of a secret conspiracy; and its activities, tolerated for years, culminated in the murders of Sir William Gurzon Wyllie and Dr. Lalkaka at the Imperial Institute. The congress supported the boycott in Bengal. The president was Gopal Krishna Gokhale, who had acquired considerable reputation as a politician, an educationist and a member of the imperial legislative council.

1911: The masses of labourers with one meal a day, and the huts in which they live, they would find cause for thought. And if the educated men talked freely with them they would be surprised at their bitterness. Gopal Krishna Gokhale put the whole matter very plainly. One of the fundamental conditions of the peculiar position of the British Government in this country is that it should be a continuously progressive Government.

1912: The leader of the Indian Congress Party at that time was Gopal Krishna Gokhale, who had visited and toured South Africa. Gokhale had known Gandhi for years and was very impressed both by him as an individual and his work in South Africa. He had a marvellous spiritual power to turn ordinary men into heroes and martyrs.

1913: Gopal Krishna Gokhale (Leader of the Indian Nationalists in Bombay) cabled to the Indians in South Africa, advising them to boycott the Royal Commissioners' enquiries.

1915: Excessive exertion and the resulting exhaustion only aggravated his diabetes and cardiac asthma. The end came peacefully, however, pointing his finger towards heaven and then folding his hands respectfully. The years of hard work and devotion of Gopal Krishna Gokhale did much for the country, but sadly also took their toll on the health of this great leader. Gopal Krishna Gokhale had made his final statement to an audience, a fond farewell.

Appendix

Servants of India Society

[The following is the Constitution of the Servants of India Society founded by G. K. Gokhale, at Poona, on the 12th June 1905].

For some time past, the conviction has been forcing itself on many earnest and thoughtful minds that a stage has been reached in the work of nation-building in India, when, for further progress, the devoted labour of a specially trained agency, applying itself to the task in a true missionary spirit, are required. The work that has been accomplished so far has indeed been of the highest value. The growth during the last fifty years of a feeling of common nationality, based upon common traditions and ties, common hopes and aspirations, and even common disabilities, has been most striking. The fact that we are Indians first and Hindus, Mahomdcans, Parsees or Christians afterwards, is being realised in a steadily increasing measure, and the idea of a united and renovated India, matching onwards to a place among the nations of the world, worthy of her great past, is no longer a mere idle dream of a few imaginative minds, but is the definitely accepted creed of those who form the brain of the community — the educated classes of the country.

A creditable beginning has already been made in matters of education and of local self-government; and all classes of the people are slowly but steadily coming under the influence of liberal ideas. The claims of public life are every day receiving wider recognition, and attachment to the land of our birth is growing into a strong and deeply cherished passion of the heart. The annual meetings of Congresses and Conferences, the work of public bodies and associations, the writings in the columns of the Indian Press — all bear witness to the new life that is coursing in the veins of the people. The results achieved so far are undoubtedly most gratifying, but they only mean that the jungle has been cleared and the foundations laid. The great work of rearing the superstructure has yet to be taken in hand and the situation demands on the part of workers devotion and sacrifices proportionate to the magnitude of the task.

The Servants of India Society has been established to meet in some measure these requirements of the situation. Its members frankly accept the British connection as ordained, in the inscrutable dispensation of Providence, for India's good. Self-Government within the Empire for their country and a higher life generally for their countrymen is their goal. This goal, they recognise, cannot be attained without years of earnest and patient effort and sacrifices worthy of the cause.

Much of the work must be directed towards building up in the country a higher type of character and capacity than is generally available at present and the advance can only be slow. Moreover, the path is beset with great difficulties; there will be constant temptations to turn back; bitter disappointments will repeatedly try the faith of those who have put their hand to the work. But the weary toil can have but one end, if only the workers grow not faint-hearted on the way. One essential condition of success in this work is that a sufficient number of our countrymen must now come forward to devote themselves to the cause in the spirit in which religious work is undertaken.

Public life must be spiritualised. Love of country must so fill the heart that all else shall appear as of little moment by its side. A fervent patriotism which rejoices at every opportunity of sacrifice for the motherland, a dauntless heart which refuses to be turned back from its object by difficulty or danger, a deep faith in the purpose of Providence which nothing can shake — equipped with these, the worker must start on his mission and reverently seek the joy which comes of spending oneself in the service of one's country.

The Servants of India Society will train men prepared to devote their lives to the cause of the country in a religious spirit, and will seek to promote, by all -constitutional means, the national interests of the Indian people. Its members will direct their efforts principally.

Towards: (1) creating among the people, by example and by precept, a deep and passionate love of the motherland, seeking its highest fulfilment in service and sacrifice; (2) organising the work of political education and agitation, basing it on a careful study of public questions, and strengthening generally the public life of the country; (3) promoting relations of cordial goodwill and cooperation among the different communities; (4) assisting educational movements, especially those for the education of women, the education of backward classes and industrial and scientific education; (5) helping forward the industrial development of the country; and (6) the elevation of the depressed classes. The headquarters of the Society will be at Poona, where it will maintain a Home for its members, and, attached to it, a Library for the study of subjects bearing on its work. The following Constitution has been adopted for the Society:

1. The Society shall be called "The Servants of India Society."
2. The objects of the Society are to train national missionaries for the service of Indians to promote by all constitutional means, the true interests of the Indian people.
3. The Society will consist of, *(a)* a First Member or President, *(b)* Ordinary Members, and *(c)* Members under training.
4. The First Member or President will be the Head of the Society.
5. Every member, on admission, shall undergo a special training for a period of five years. During this period, he will be known as a 'Member under training.' When a member has completed his five years' discipline, he will be styled an Ordinary Member of the Society.
6. Subject to rules 12 and 13, every member of the Society shall be a member for life.
7. The affairs of the Society will be managed, ID-accordance with bye-laws framed for the purpose, by the First Member

or President assisted by a council of three Ordinary Members, who shall be elected by the Ordinary Members of the Society. Every year one member of the Council, whose name shall be drawn by lot, shall retire; but he will be eligible for re-election.

8. No person will be admitted as a member of the Society, unless his admission is recommended by the Council and the recommendation accepted by the First Member or President.

9. Every member at the time of admission shall take the following seven vows:

   (i) That the country will always be the first in his thoughts and he will give to her service the best that is in him.

   (ii) That in serving the country he will seek no personal advantage for himself.

   (iii) That he will regard all Indians as brothers and will work for the advancement of all, without distinction of caste or creed.

   (iv) That he will be content with such provision for himself and his family, if he has any, as the Society may be able to make. He will devote no part of his energies to earning money for himself.

   (v) That he will lead a pure personal life.

   (vi) That he will engage in no personal quarrel with any one.

   (vii) That he will always keep in view the aims of the Society and watch over its interests with the utmost zeal, doing all he can to advance its work. He will never do anything which is inconsistent with the objects of the Society.

10. Every member under training shall, during the time that he is under training, place himself under the entire guidance and control of the First Member or President and shall do such work and devote himself to such studies as the First Member or President may direct.

11. An Ordinary Member may be sent by the First Member or President and Council to any part of India on special duty or for general work in connection with the Society. He will be bound to do the work assigned to him under the general direction of the First Member or President and Council, and will obey all orders and instructions that may be received from them.

12. The Society may release a member and permit him to resign his membership on the ground of continued ill health or for other sufficient cause on a recommendation to that effect being made by the Council, with the concurrence of not less than three-fourths of the members of the Society, and the recommendation being accepted by the First Member or President.

13. The Society may remove the name of any member from its roll of members on a recommendation to that effect being made by the Council, with the concurrence of not less than three-fourths of the members of the Society, and the recommendation being accepted by the First Member or President.

14. The First Member will hold office for life. It will be the duty of the First Member to recommend in writing to the Council the names of three Ordinary Members, out of whom the members of the Society shall elect a successor to him as First Member on a vacancy occurring. If no such recommendation has been received by the Council when the vacancy occurs, the members of the Society may elect any Ordinary Member, or, in the absence of a suitable Ordinary Member, any member to succeed as First Member. In case, however, it appears undesirable to elect any member as First Member, the members may elect one of their number to be President of the Society for a period of three years.

15. When a vacancy occurs in the First Membership or Presidentship of the Society, the Council for the time being shall exercise all the powers vested by the rules in the First Member or President singly or the First Member or President and Council until such time as a new First

Member or President is duly elected; and any act done by the Council, during such time shall be deemed valid, provided that the Council takes steps with all reasonable dispatch to arrange for the election of a new First Member or President under rule 14.

16. In special circumstances, the First Member or President and Council may exempt, for reasons to be Accorded in writing, any member of the Society from the operation of any rule, save rule No. 9.

17. An applicant for membership may be required to pass through a period of probation before admission as a member and may, in that case, be enrolled as a Probationer on such terms and for such period as the First Member or president and Council may determine.

18. The First Member or President and Council may remove the name of any Probationer from the list of Probationers before the expiry of the period of probation. The Society will not be bound to disclose the reasons for such removal.

19. The First Member or President and Council may admit any person, who in their opinion is capable of being trained to assist efficiently members of the Society in their work and who is prepared to devote his life to such work, as a Permanent Assistant of the Society, on such terms as the First Member or President and Council may determine. Permanent Assistants will be divided into two classes — Senior and Junior — according to their educational and other qualifications.

20. A Permanent Assistant may, on grounds of special fitness and after a period of approved service of not less than three years, be admitted as a member of the Society.

21. The First Member or President and Council may remove the name of any Permanent Assistant from the list of Permanent Assistants of the Society. The Society will not be bound to disclose the reasons for such removal.

22. The First Member or President and Council may admit any person, who is in full sympathy with the objects of the Society and is prepared to devote his life to such work

as may be assigned to him for the benefit of the Society, as an Attache of the Society on such terms and under such control as the First Member or President and Council may determine.

23. The First Member or President and Council may remove the name of any Attache from the list of Attaches- of the Society. The Society will not be bound to disclose the reasons for such removal.

24. The First Member or President and Council may enrol any person, who is in full sympathy with its objects and who is prepared to devote a portion of his time and resources to the furtherance of its work, as an Associate of the Society.

25. Probationers, Permanent Assistants, Attaches and Associates will have no voice in the management of the affairs of the Society and no interest in the Society's property or funds.

26. All property of the Society shall belong to the Society in its corporate character, and no member, in his individual capacity, nor the heirs, executors or assignees of any member shall have any right to any portion of it.

27. The property of the Society shall be held by three trustees, one of whom shall be the First Member or President for the time being and the other two, such Members as may be elected by the Members of the Society for the purpose.

28. All contracts, entered into for and on behalf of the Society, shall be in the name of the First Member or President. In all suits brought by or against the Society, the Society shall be represented by the First Member or President.

29. The Society shall not be dissolved by the death, secession or removal of any member.

30. The First Member or President may, with the concurrence of a majority of the Ordinary Members of the Society, make, alter or rescind, any bye-laws for:

    (1) the management of the affairs of the Society and the conduct of its business;

(2) the custody, disposal and control of the funds of the Society;

(3) the provision to be made for members of the Society and their families and the grant of special allowances to them in special circumstances;

(4) the grant of leave to members of the Society;

(5) the grant of allowances to Permanent Assistants and Attaches of the Society; and

(6) the carrying out in other ways of the objects of the Society.

31. The first Member or President and Council shall have the power to take whatever steps may be deemed necessary in the interest of the Society, provided that they are not inconsistent with the objects of the Society or with the provisions or spirit of any of the rules or bye-laws at the time in force.

32. No alteration shall be made in this Constitution, unless it is recommended by the Council with the concurrence of not less than three-fourths of the members of the Society, and the recommendation accepted by the First Member or President.

The following Bye-Laws have been made under rule 30:

(1) The Society shall, as circumstances permit, establish Branches for work in different parts of the country. At the head of each Branch there shall be a Senior Member whose appointment and removal shall vest in the First Member or President and Council. The affairs of each Branch shall be managed by a Board consisting of the Senior Member and the Ordinary Members belonging to it.

(2) *(a)* Every Member under training will be granted an allowance of Rs. 30 a month for the first two years of his training and Rs. 35 for the next three. *(b)* Every Ordinary Member will be granted an allowance of Rs. 55 a month for the first five years, Rs. 60 for the next five years and Rs. 65 afterwards. *(c)* All Members, whether under training

or Ordinary will be granted a personal allowance of Rs. 10 per month in addition to the allowances mentioned above. *(d)* The Senior Member of a Branch will be granted a special allowance of Rs. 10 a month. *(e)* A rent allowance, not exceeding Rs. 15 a month in Bombay and Rs. 10 elsewhere, or the actual rent paid if less, will be granted to Ordinary Members, in case there are no quarters available on the premises of the Society. *(f)* The allowance of Junior Permanent Assistants will be Rs. 15 to Rs. 20 and that of Senior Permanent Assistants Rs. *20* to Rs. 30 per month.

(3) (a) A Member under training is entitled to two- months' leave every year, which can be granted by the First Member or President, and, if the applicant is attached to a Branch the Senior Member of that Branch. *(b)* Ordinary Members are entitled to a month's leave every year, which can be granted by the First Member or President, and, if the applicant is attached to a Branch, the Senior Member of that Branch. *(c)* Ordinary Members of the Central Provinces and Berar are entitled to one month and ten days' privilege leave if they go on leave on the 1st of May. *(d)* All members are entitled to twenty days' casual leave in a year. *(e)* Both casual and privilege leave mentioned above will only be sanctioned if the work of the Society permits.

(4) *(a)* The life of every member will, on admission, be assured by the Society, in favour of the First Member or the President for the time being, for a sum of Rs. 3,000 payable at death. If no Insurance Company accepts the life of any member for assurance, the First Member or President and Council may make such other arrangement as they deem fit to secure, in the case of such member, the object of this Bye-Law. *(b)* On the death of a member, whose life has been assured, the First Member or the President shall pay the amount recovered on the life-policy of the deceased to such member or members of his family as the deceased member may, by will or otherwise in writing, have directed. In the absence of such direction, the First Member or the President and Council shall have the power to

determine whether the amount recovered may be paid to any member or members of the deceased's family, and if so, to whom.

(5) The First Member or President and Council may grant, in special circumstances, a special allowance to a member, suited to the requirements of his case.

(6) If a member secedes from the Society he and his family shall forfeit all claim to the benefit secured to him or them under these Bye-Laws.

Bibliography

Anil Kumar Jana: *Quit India Movement in Bengal: A Study of Contai Subdivision*, Indian Publication, 2004.

B. R. Nanda: *Gokhale: The Indian Moderates and the British Raj*, Oxford, Princeton, 1998.

————: *Three Statesmen Gokhale, Gandhi, and Nehru*, Oxford University Press, 2004.

Balkrishna Govind Gokhale: *Ancient India: History and Culture*, Popular, 1995.

Bhattacharya, B. K.: *India's Freedom Movement: Legacy of Bipin Chandra Pal*, Deep and Deep, New Delhi, 2007.

C. P. Sharma: *Encyclopaedia on Gokhale (Vols 1 and 2 Set)*, Anmol Publication, New Delhi, 2009.

Chandra, Bipan: *India's Struggle For Independence*, Penguin Books India (P) Ltd., New Delhi, 1989.

D. B. Mathur: *Gokhale: A Political Biography: A Study of His Services and Political Ideas*, Manaktalas, Bombay, 1966.

D. Mackenzie Brown: *Indian Political Thought from Ranade to Bhave*, University of California Press, Los Angeles, 1961.

Ganjoo, S.: *Muslim Freedom Fighters of India*, Anmol Publication, New Delhi, 2002.

Govind Talwalkar: *Gopal Krishna Gokhale: His Life and Times*, Rupa Publication, New Delhi, 2006.

Goyal, P. K.: *Battle of India's Freedom Movement*, Vista International, 2005.

Iyengar, A. S.: *Role of Press and Indian Freedom Struggle: All through the Gandhian Era*, APH, 2001.

Jim Masselos: *Indian Nationalism: An History*, Sterling Publishers, Bangalore, 1991.

John S. Hoyland: *Gopal Krishna Gokhale: His Life and Speeches*, Rupa Publication, Calcutta, 2003.

Kailash Khanna: *History of Indian Freedom Struggle*, Commonwealth Publication, 2004.

Kamat, Jyostna: *The Pioneers: Kamaladevi Chattopadhyaya*, Kamat's, 2003.

Kaushik, A. S.: *Great Freedom Fighters of India*, Indian Publication, 2007.

Khairul Anam, Md.: *Indian Freedom Movement and Murshidabad District 1905-1947*, Bagchi, K. P., 2008.

Krishan Mohan: *Encyclopaedic History of Indian Freedom Movement (4 Vols-Set)*, Book Enclave, 1999.

Lion Agrawal, M. G.: *Freedom Fighters of India (4 Vols-Set)*, Isha Books, 2008.

M. K. Singh: *Gopal Krishna Gokhale*, Anmol Publication, New Delhi, 2008.

Majumdar, R. C.: *History of the Freedom Movement in India (3 Vols-Set)*, Firma KLM, 1997.

Manju Verma: *The Role of Women in the Freedom Movement in Punjab (1919-1947)*, Abhijeet, 2003.

Maulana Syed Mohammad Mian: *The Prisoners of Malta (Asira'n-E-Malta): The Heart-Rending Tale of Muslim Freedom Fighters in British Period*, Manak, 2005.

Mazhar Kibriya: *Gandhi and Indian Freedom Struggle*, APH, 1999.

Muthaiah, S.: *Women Freedom Fighters*, The Hindu, 2004.

N. Jayapalan: *Makers of Modern India: Gokhale, Gandhi and Tagore*, Book Enclave, 2006.

Nanda, S. P.: *Freedom Movement and Constitutional Development in India*, Dominant, 2004.

Om Prakash: *Encyclopaedic History of Indian Freedom Movement (12 to 21 Vols)*, Anmol, 2003.

Omesh Saigal: *Shaheed Bhagat Singh: Unique Martyr in Freedom Movement*, Gyan Publication, 2002.

Parmanand Parashar: *Kashmir and the Freedom Movement*, Sarup, 2004.

Pradhan, K. B.: *Freedom Movement in India*, Arise Pub, 2007.

Prafulla Kumar Pattanaik: *The First Indian War of Independence: Freedom Movement in Orissa, 1804-1825*, APH, 2005.

Rafiya Nisar: *Shaikh-Ul-Hind Maulana Mahmud Hasan and Indian Freedom Movement*, Manak Pub, 2008.

Raj Kumar: *Essays on Indian Freedom Movement*, History and Culture Series, Discovery, 2003.

Ram Sharma, S.: *Education of Women and Freedom Movement*, Discovery, 1996.

Ram, S. and Kumar, R.: *Encyclopaedia of Indian Freedom Struggle (10 Vols-Set)*, Commonwealth Pub, 2008.

————: *Quit India Movement: 1942-1945*, Commonwealth Pub, 2008.

Ramanathan, K. V.: *The Satyamurti Letters, Vol. II: The Indian Freedom Struggle Through the Eyes of a Parliamentarian*, Dorling Kindersley for Pearson Longman an Imprint of Pearson Education, 2008.

Ramu, P. S.: *Azad Hind Fauj (I.N.A.) and The Freedom Movement*, Freedom Movement Memorial Comm, 1998.

Ratna Ghosh: *Netaji Subhas Chandra Bose and Indian Freedom Struggle (2 Vols-Set)*, Deep and Deep, 2006.

Ravindra Kumar: *Champaran to Quit India Movement*, Mittal, 2002.

S. R. Sharma: *Life and Works of Gopal Krishan Gokhale*, Book Enclave, 2006.

Shachi Chakravarty: *Quit India Movement: A Study*, New Century Publication, 2002.

Shailesh Chandra: *90 Years of India's Struggle for Independence: 1857-1947,* Alfa Pub, 2008.

Shantinath Gupta: *Great Freedom Fighters of India,* Anmol, 2006.

Sharma, S. K.: *Eminent Indian Freedom Fighters (2 Vols-Set),* Anmol Publication, New Delhi, 2004.

Sirisa Kumar Shadangi: *The Prisons of South Orissa and the Freedom Fighters in Incarceration, 1900 - 1947,* Punthi Pustak, 2005.

Stanley Wolpert: *Tilak and Gokhale: Revolution and Reform in the Making of Modem India,* U. California, Berkeley, 1962.

Sumiti Malhotra: *Thoughts of Great Personalities in 20 Century,* Raj Publishing, 2003.

Sundaram, V.: *Great Crusader for Women's Emancipation,* News Today, 2005.

Taneja, Anup: *Gandhi, Women and the National Movement, 1920-47,* Har-Anand Publications, Delhi, 2005.

Thapar-Bjorkert, Suruchi: *Women in the Indian Nationalist Movement,* Sage Publication India (P) Ltd., New Delhi, 2006.

Verma B. R. and Unnikrishnan K.: *Encyclopaedic Biography of Indian Freedom Fighters,* Commonwealth, 2004.

Vishnoo Bhagwan: *Indian Freedom Movement and Constitutional Acts,* Atma Ram, 1999.

W. R. Mujawar: *Speeches and Writings of Gopal Krishna Gokhale, Vol. I - IV,* Manglam Publication, 2009.

Wolpert, Stanley: *Tilak and Gokhale: Revolution and Reform in the Making of Modern India,* Cambridge University, Cambridge, 1962.

Zimmer, Heinrich: *The Art of Indian Asia,* Pantheon, New York, 1955.

Index

❑❑❑